ESSENTIAL SAILING DESTINATIONS

THE WORLD'S MOST SPECTACULAR CRUISING AREAS

ESSENTIAL SAILING DESTINATIONS

THE WORLD'S MOST SPECTACULAR CRUISING AREAS

SHERIDAN HOUSE

This edition published 2009 by

Sheridan House Inc.
145 Palisade Street
Dobbs Ferry, NY 10522
www.sheridanhouse.com

First edition copyright © 2008 by Automobile
Association Developments Limited

Cartography provided by the Mapping Services
Department of AA Publishing

Map Images supplied by Mountain High Maps®
Copyright© 1993 Digital Wisdom, Inc.

A CIP catalog record for this book is available
from the Library of Congress, Washington, DC.

ISBN 978-1-57409-281-3

Produced by Studio Cactus
Editor-in-chief: Adrian Morgan
Editorial Staff: Rona Johnson, Jennifer Close
Design: Sharon Rudd
Indexer: Penelope Kent

Color separation by Mullis Morgan

Printed in Dubai

A04011

SHERIDAN HOUSE

Contents

Foreword

Sailing as a sport has exploded in the last 40 years, but whilst the media attention has been on racing there has been far greater growth in the number of people who buy or charter a boat to go cruising.

The oceans and seas are free. Of course you have to go through formalities when you reach your chosen destination, but there are no other borders in between. This is a rare freedom in our increasingly bureaucratic era. And once you reach that destination your boat allows you to access coastlines that cannot be visited except by boat.

But where to go? The choice is vast! The world has been opening up and places that were politically unapproachable only 15 years ago now welcome maritime tourists. It is said that planning a cruise is almost as much fun as actually making the voyage; I am not sure I totally agree with this, but the long winter evenings do make for a good time to dream a little of warm climates, interesting places and blue seas. This is where information on the choices can be so invaluable. The Duke of Wellington famously said that time spent on reconnaissance was seldom time wasted. This beautifully illustrated book is an ideal companion for the sofa-bound planner on those long winter evenings.

SIR ROBIN KNOX-JOHNSTON

THE WEST COAST and islands of Italy offer the supreme blend of art, architecture, history, culture, regional cuisine, world-class scenery and superb summer weather.

Author's Introduction

When the world was younger and many of its reefs, and even some islands, were either uncharted, marked "position uncertain" or still bore the legend "surveyed by Captain Cook", sailing could be an adventurous, if hazardous, pastime. Great voyagers such as Joshua Slocum, Captain Muhlhauser, Conor Cruise O'Brien and Erling Tambs relied on their wits, and innate seamanship. And, nevertheless, even they occasionally came a cropper.

Today, few sea areas remain uncharted and most have been opened up by intrepid cruising yachtsmen. In many of these waters, charter bases have sprung up. You can now hire a boat from Thailand to the Tuamotus, the Arctic to Alaska. The choice is vast, so a little "local knowledge" is welcome.

"Where in the world shall we go?" you ask.

Andrew Bray might say "the Morbihan", with its seafood and sluicing tides, Chris Caswell would be hard pressed to choose between the balmy Florida Keys and wild Pacific North-west. Paul Gelder was struck by the San Blas islands off the coast of Panama, while Colin Jarman would not swap England's east coast for any Caribbean island.

Tom Cunliffe is equally certain: "I've been astounded by the impossible islands of Thailand, I've swum from tropic beaches of dazzling coral sand and I've watched Pico rise from the Atlantic after weeks at sea, but, if it's scenery you want, for my money you can forget the lot. Save yourself trouble and go straight to Norway."

Let them be your guides to the world's best charter destinations. Lynda Childress will tempt you with wine-dark seas and Greek islands, while Captain Pat Rains swears by Mexico's Gold Coast. Tim Jeffery would have you cruise the Guinness bars of southern Ireland, but James Clarke would rather explore the inlets of Chile. Pete Nielsen says "look no further than Massachusetts Bay", almost literally on his Boston doorstep, and Roger Lean-Vercoe was intrigued by the Aeolians. Sarah Norbury, however, couldn't get enough of Tobago Cays and Mike Owen would go anywhere, so long as he could take his young family.

To every man and woman his island, each one different. Ask me and I would direct you to Bequia, where I first landed many years ago salt-encrusted and broke in a small wooden sloop, 21 days out from the Canaries.

Between them the authors, experienced sailors, editors and travel writers all, have covered many hundreds of thousands of sea miles. Jimmy Cornell alone has circumnavigated three times, over 200,000 miles. His first choice is to sail back down to Antarctica and complete unfinished business.

Each recommended sailing destination has a panel with a locator map and useful at-a-glance information, including best cruising months and a selection of relevant Admiralty charts. Symbols (representing a score out of five) relate to navigational difficulty, family friendliness, facilities for diving, shoreside eating and sightseeing. Of course, you are strongly advised to look into each area in more detail and always sail well within your own limitations.

Finally, a word of caution: many innocent families who booked a flotilla holiday in the Ionian have found themselves a few years later homeless, and living aboard a well-found sloop, bound for the South Seas. For as Masefield said "...the call of the running tide/Is a wild call and a clear call that may not be denied".

Contributors

Jimmy Cornell
Author, circumnavigator

An accomplished yachtsman and best-selling author, Jimmy has sailed 200,000 miles, including three circumnavigations as well as voyages to Antarctica, Alaska and Spitsbergen. His *World Cruising Routes* is regarded as the bible for offshore sailors. Founder of the ARC transatlantic rally, Jimmy is credited with having devised the offshore cruising rally concept.

Tom Cunliffe
Author

Sailing writer, RYA/MCA Yachtmaster Instructor examiner. Tom is one of Britain's leading writers on sailing and the sea and has worked on vessels from dinghies to large gaff schooners. Author of 25 books, including two "Best Book of the Sea" award winners, he edits *The Shell Channel Pilot* and is a columnist for *Yachting Monthly*, *Yachting World* and *SAIL* magazine.

Paul Gelder
Yachting Monthly Editor

Paul has crewed for Robin Knox-Johnston, cruised the Arctic, the South Pacific and Mexico's Sea of Cortez. He has sailed the Caribbean, from Belize to the Bahamas, and the Mediterranean. Author of three books on round-the-world sailing, he took part in the first British Steel Challenge, and edits *Total Loss*, an anthology of stories of yachts lost at sea.

Colin Jarman
Sailing author, East Coast Pilot

Colin was born and bred on the East Coast, and has sailed small cruising boats there for 50 years. A freelance sailing writer and photographer, he works regularly for the British magazines *Sailing Today* and *Anglia Afloat*. He and his wife cruise a small gaffer with a centreplate, which enables them to seek out the remotest anchorages.

Tim Jeffery
Daily Telegraph Yachting Correspondent

Tim has worked at *Yachting World* and *The Daily Telegraph*. He started sailing in Strangford Lough and keeps a 32ft Dufour there today. He has sailed and raced in Scotland, Scandinavia and Maine, the Red Sea, Caribbean and Thailand, and also the Southern Ocean. Frustratingly he rounded Cape Horn in 30 knots, driving rain and saw nothing but greybeard seas.

Roger Lean-Vercoe
Sailing writer and photographer

Born in Weymouth on England's south coast, Roger grew up with dinghies, yachts and the sea. He has been the editor of *The Superyachts* book since it was first published 21 years ago, and is Superyachts Editor of *Boat International*. Currently, he is the Chairman of the World Superyacht Awards. Cruising far-flung waters is his relaxation and passion.

Andrew Bray
Yachting World Editor

Andrew has been Editor of *Yachting World* for 15 years and *Yachting Monthly* for seven. He has cruised in many parts of the world, and raced in short-handed events including the AZAB, OSTAR, TWOSTAR, Round Britain and Ireland two-handed and the ARC, most recently in his 43ft fast cruiser, *Firefly*.

Chris Caswell
Author and US sailing writer

Nautical journalist for 40 years, currently Senior Editor of *Yachting Magazine* (USA), Chris is author of nine books on boating and has cruised the length and breadth of both east and west coastlines. A dedicated boater who says he's owned more boats than he wants either his banker or his wife to know about, he also has the largest moustache of any boating writer.

Sarah Norbury
Practical Boat Owner Editor

Sarah edits the UK's largest circulation yachting magazine, *Practical Boat Owner*. She previously edited *Yachting Monthly* and has written for *The Times*, *The Daily Telegraph* and many magazines. She is a passionate advocate of chartering as a way for people to discover sailing and extend their experience. In her spare time she races dinghies and keelboats, and cruises on the South Coast.

Captain Pat Miller Rains
Pilot book author and sailing writer

Pat, who holds a US Coast Guard 100-Ton Masters License, delivers yachts worldwide with her husband, Captain John E. Rains. She started cruising her 26ft trimaran around the Sea of Cortez for five years, alone and with friends. Recently, the Rains are looking for their own next boat – this time to circumnavigate slowly.

Lynda Childress
Cruising editor and charter yacht owner

Lynda grew up sailing in Newport, Rhode Island. A cruising guide co-author, she is the former managing editor of *Cruising World*. She now operates crewed charters in the Greek islands with her husband, Kostas Ghiokas, aboard their Atlantic 70 cutter, *Stressbuster*.

Adrian Morgan
Sailing writer and editor

Adrian was for 15 years the *Daily Mail*'s sailing correspondent and has written for the *Times*, *Telegraph* and *Independent* on sailing and travel. Formerly Assistant Editor on *Yachting Monthly*, he writes a column for *Classic Boat*. He has sailed the Atlantic twice, and cruised in the Caribbean, Europe and Scotland, where he builds traditional wooden boats.

Peter Nielsen
US SAIL Editor

A New Zealander by birth, and highly experienced yachtsman, Peter is the Editor of America's foremost cruising and racing magazine. A prolific sailing writer, he left *Yachting Monthly* to edit *SAIL*, and is now based in Boston where he is refitting a 1973 Norlin 34 from the keel up. He now sails mainly on the US East Coast.

Mike Owen
Yachting journalist

Mike is a freelance yachting writer, and former editor of *Boat International*. An accomplished sailor, he has competed in the two-handed Round Britain and Ireland Race, charters whenever he can and now sails on the south coast of England with his wife and two daughters.

James Clarke
Sailing author, RYA Chief Instructor

James circumnavigated in his own boat via Capes Horn and Good Hope in the early 80s, and is an authority on ocean navigation. An RYA Chief Instructor and Ocean Yachtmaster, he is based on the Hamble.

Rona Johnson
Editor

Rona was a front-line editor at the *Daily Mail* for ten years. She is a freelance book editor and sails a classic wooden boat based in Ullapool, Scotland with her partner Adrian and their short-haired pointer Bran.

A World of Sailing

Some like it hot, others prefer their water on the cooler side: the Pacific North-west or the Sea of Cortez; Antarctica or the Florida Keys, the choice is so vast that to pick a favourite cruising ground is like selecting a dish from the menu at the Ritz.

DIVIDING THE WORLD into seven areas makes geographical sense, but within these areas lie huge differences of climate and culture, transcending national boundaries, encompassing physical features as diverse as glacier and desert, coral reef and rocky coastline. And a yacht is the key to this world; a world denied to the land-bound, open only to those arriving from the sea. Purist navigators revel in the intricacies of simply getting there; most prefer to treat their yacht as a magic carpet, a transport to their personal paradise. Whatever your inclination, there is a whole world of sailing to explore.

THE MEDITERRANEAN *"Croatia is the hottest cruising destination in the Mediterranean. Its main attraction is an almost bewildering choice of scores of picturesque harbours and medieval ports…"* Jimmy Cornell

NORTH AMERICA, EAST COAST *"One of my fondest memories is sailing aboard a perfectly restored Concordia yawl into Hadley's Harbor, as a dense New England fog descended…"* Chris Caswell

THE AMERICAS, WEST COAST *"So few people live in the Baja California desert that yachts usually have all the anchorages to themselves, for free, for days on end…"* Pat Rains

WESTERN EUROPE AND NORTH ATLANTIC ISLANDS *"The first time I anchored in the Scilly Isles, the perfume of a thousand flowers wafted down the breeze…"*
Tom Cunliffe

THE CARIBBEAN *"Bequia felt to us like the real Caribbean; islands of pirates and rum, slaves and wild mulatto women, spices and the pulsating rhythms of the steel band…"*
Adrian Morgan

THE PACIFIC *"No printer's ink could ever capture the iridescent shades of indigo and emerald that greet sailors in the palm-fringed lagoons of the South Pacific islands…"*
Paul Gelder

AUSTRALASIA AND THE FAR EAST *"The most memorable feature of the Whitsundays is the quality and clarity of the air, as unpolluted as you'll find anywhere on the planet…"*
Andrew Bray

Living the Dream

"There's the island, ahead," called the navigator as I steered our boat down the Caribbean waves. We were browner than we'd ever been in our lives, and living on freshly caught fish, tropical fruits and whatever secret recipe each bartender uses to make his island's signature rum punch.

A WEEK LATER WE'D BE BACK AT OUR OFFICE DESKS, but for now we were adventurers on the high seas, discovering exotic destinations we'd only ever read about in sailing magazines.

Not many people know that for the same price as a decent package holiday you can be captain and crew of your own luxury yacht, exploring places that other holidaymakers can't reach.

I've rowed a yacht's tender into the Blue Cave of Bisevo where, just before noon, for just a few moments, the cavern is filled with an electric blue light, so otherworldly it's like being in a sci-fi film. Bisevo is a tiny island off a slightly larger island off the coast of Croatia, and my backpacking friends are envious that I've been there.

In a bareboat, I've anchored off desert islands with only pelicans and palm trees for company; I've dined on Mustique, where Mick Jagger's house is marked on the map and Princess Margaret held her famous house parties, and drunk Red Stripe to the sounds of reggae in a makeshift beach bar.

To visit the beautiful Tobago Cays in the Grenadines is impossible for the "ordinary" tourist as you can only get there by boat. I'll never forget steering among reefs and rocks to emerge into the amazing turquoise lagoon dotted with desert islands. We dropped anchor onto perfect white sand, protected from the crashing Atlantic rollers by a semi-circle of coral. You know those fabulous pink cartoon sea-shells that you hold to your ear to hear the sea? In the Grenadines conch are as common as cockles in Cornwall. We picked up so many we couldn't fit them into our luggage, and now just one pearly pink shell on a shelf reminds us of our Caribbean dream-holiday.

Navigation is easy – boats had satnav years before the Tom Tom was invented but you need to know basic navigation just in case the satnav goes on the blink. How much sailing experience do you have? If you know how to sail a yacht and can show the charter company a Day Skipper or ICC certificate issued by the

JAMESBY ISLAND is a classic island paradise in the Tobago Cays, complete with white sand beaches, crystal waters and swaying palms.

Royal Yachting Association you can charter a "bareboat", just you and your crew on your own. If you don't have much experience, why not splash out on a skippered charter, which most sailing holiday companies will arrange for you? Your own private skipper will know the best places to go and give you as much or as little coaching as you like.

But by far the most popular option for beginners – cheaper than a skippered charter and more sociable than bareboating – is a flotilla holiday. This is where ten or so boats make up a group under the gentle supervision of a "lead boat" crewed by a flotilla leader, a hostess and an engineer who are on hand day and night to advise on everything from where to anchor for lunch to where to find the nearest bank, bakery or bar, and if you break down, the engineer will fix your boat for you.

For first-time sailors the classic way to start chartering is a flotilla in the Greek Ionian islands. Gorgeous clear blue water, white sand

SAILING is about exploring secluded coves that other tourists can't reach, and a whole new world beneath the waves.

SAILORS enjoy some truly magical encounters with wildlife; whales and dolphins are particularly spectacular.

Navigating Coral

In good light conditions coral reefs show up clearly and are relatively easy to avoid. In bad light reefs are difficult to distinguish.

THE LIGHTER THE BLUE, the shallower the water should be the coral pilot's mantra, and green/brown usually means a coral head lying close beneath the surface. In bad light it's best to have the sun high in the sky and, if possible, limit your sailing among coral to within two or three hours either side of local noon. Better, too, to have the sun at your back, especially if it is lower in the sky.

Post a good lookout, preferably up the mast. The height will ensure that reefs can be easily seen in time for avoiding action. Lookout and helmsman should be wearing polaroid sunglasses, which cut out glare and dramatically improve visibility.

Arrange some simple hand signals between lookout and helm. The vigorous continental arm waving approach can be highly entertaining, but is rather hit and miss, and generally more hit than miss. It is often enough to simply differentiate between pointing at a danger (perhaps with a single finger) and indicating a required turn (with a flat hand). Both signals can be accentuated with movement, but the danger of confusing them is obvious.

One last tip on entering lagoons. Passages through barrier reefs are notoriously difficult to spot. Try to confirm your line with a visual bearing onto the island, as chart datums are often uncertain in far-flung locations. It will help to keep you on track too – there is often a swell running, as well as a current.

LOCAL KNOWLEDGE can be cheaply bought in the form of aerial views on postcards. It would be foolish to rely on them for primary navigation, but they can usefully complement a chart.

beaches, light winds and no tide give easy sailing in beautiful surroundings. In the late afternoon the flotilla boats come together in the next charming little fishing harbour on the itinerary, the lead crew stand ready to catch your mooring ropes, then you step ashore and try and decide which of the welcoming tavernas to choose for dinner.

You meet all kinds of people on flotilla holidays. If it's the school holidays, children and teenagers quickly make new friends at the beach barbecues and lunch-time stops. Out of school holidays you meet adults of every generation, from twenties to retireds. Evenings are invariably fun: how could they not be with all the stories of the day's sailing adventures to share?

Some charter companies don't require you to have a sailing certificate to hire a flotilla boat, others do; some companies will "show you the ropes" for free, while others steer you towards their paid-for courses. If you fancy getting yourself some tuition, there are lots of options, including holidays starting with a week's learning then a week with a flotilla, or a course run by a charter company or sailing school somewhere hot, or at a sailing school in the UK.

With a little more experience, try a bareboat in the "easy Caribbean" playground – the British Virgin Islands. This place is cruising heaven, sheltered from the trade winds, easy anchoring and mooring, and no open-sea passages. I particularly recommend the Soggy Dollar Bar on White Bay on the island of Jost Van Dyke, so called because when you swim ashore your dollars get wet. Drink "painkiller" rum cocktails then snooze the afternoon away in a hammock under the palm trees.

Your choice of boat, too, is important. Most people start with monohulls but catamarans are increasingly popular – they are fast, they don't heel over and spill your drinks, and the sleeping cabins are well separated for better privacy. Perhaps most importantly, because catamarans have a shallow draft you can cruise and anchor in areas that monohulls can't get into. At the Sunsail base in St Martin I commented on the sheer number of huge catamarans. The manager replied that "lots of people use them as floating apartments, they motor straight for St Barts (the latest holiday spot for models and film stars) and park there for a week, they don't even use the sails." Chartering is whatever you want it to be – big-sea adventure or floating hotel holiday.

Thanks to yacht charter holidays I've swum with dolphins, watched hummingbirds sipping from tropical flowers, tried to count the stars in the Southern Cross. I've also seen things I wish I hadn't, namely a boat full of naked sailors who anchored just a little too close to us in Croatia (a country that caters wholeheartedly to the German and Austrian penchant for unclothed boating).

You could holiday every year in the Mediterranean and Caribbean and not sail into every harbour, but there's the whole world to choose from. How about New Zealand, the Pacific North-west, Tahiti, Thailand, Australia or Baja Mexico?

Let this book inspire you, and then, get ordering those brochures!

IN THE END sailing is really all about…well, sailing; and for most sailors the key ingredient for a sailing paradise is wind.

Sailing with Children

Postponing your sailing dreams until the kids are grown up? Don't! Kids and sailing go together like *Swallows and Amazons*, but a difference in ages means a difference in needs.

RULE NUMBER ONE is to make and keep both yacht and child safe, and that extends beyond physical to psychological…make it fun. Involve the kids, without overstretching. Older sailors love talking technical; don't, keep it simple, certainly until the child moves beyond basics. Demonstrate, don't pontificate…and avoid negative criticism, stay positive (whatever the crisis!).

Sailing together is a great opportunity to bond. The boat provides a focus away from the familiar, an adventure. But it's still a home inside, and younger children, though generally quicker to adapt than parents, will seek a routine. Wrap these elements together and you'll find success afloat.

Whenever on deck and no matter how hot the weather, life jackets – available for all from 6.5lb (3kg) upwards – are a must. They should be put on before boarding or, if coming up from the cabin, then before leaving the companionway. Make it the habit: think seatbelts. Take the analogy further: for pre-toddlers, bring the car seat. Secure that in the corner of the cockpit and junior can gurgle, watching parents work the boat. Pad out the forepeak, cushioning corners, closing off with an expandable kiddies' gate, and you'll have a safe playzone.

Safety nets can be rigged around lifelines. If chartering, these are often available on request. Before younger children leave the cockpit, safety harnesses should be worn and clipped on to secure points.

Until familiar, keep passages short, 30 miles (50km) maximum per day. Children love sleeping underway; lee cloths will provide comfort and security. If winds are light or on the nose, fire the engine. Motivation is in movement…getting ashore fast to let off steam.

Invest in fishing and snorkelling gear. For the youngest, plastic cups and a bucket of water in the cockpit provide hours of fun.

From talking books to talking to dolphins, there's hardly a better way to broaden horizons – together. Oh, and remember the paper, crayons and glue, of the washable variety, please… and, of course, batteries for the teenager's iPod!

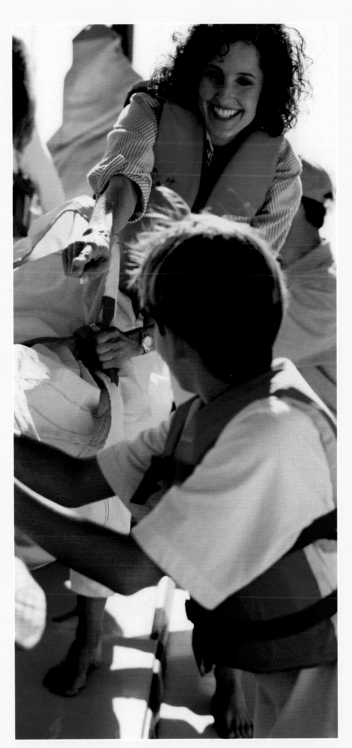

DEMONSTRATE, don't pontificate. Avoid negative criticism and stay positive at all times.

DUBROVNIK in Croatia is known as "The Jewel of the Mediterranean". Croatia has more than a thousand islands to explore.

The Mediterranean

Enclosed by three continents – Europe to the north, Africa to the south and Asia to the east – the Mediterranean is a treasure trove whose cultural and historical riches are unparalleled anywhere else on Earth. Being enclosed, its tidal ranges rank among the lowest in the world, averaging a mere 28cm (11in), which is good news for less experienced sailors. Long, hot summers and mild winters mean sunshine is more or less guaranteed all year round. Wind is less predictable; surrounding mountains and deserts create strong local winds, such as the hot, dry sirocco from the south. Not surprisingly, it is one of the world's most popular sailing areas.

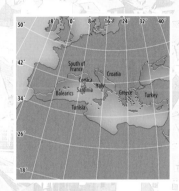

THE MEDITERRANEAN SEA spans 2,000 miles (3,380km) from the Israeli shores in the east to Gibraltar in the west.

FRENCH RIVIERA

BALEARICS

THE CRADLE OF CIVILIZATION

The reputation of the Mediterranean Sea as the cradle of western civilization is undisputed and its deep blue waters have been plied by sailing vessels since time immemorial. From the pyramids of Egypt to the Minoan remains on Crete, from the treasures of Asia Minor to the wonders of Ancient Rome, from the elegance of the French Riviera to the biblical heritage of Israel, the shores and islands abound in history and many ancient sites are close to the sea. The people of the Mediterranean have always looked to the sea for inspiration and one never has far to go to get a taste of the fascinating world that has existed for centuries along these shores.

Spread over 2,000 miles (3,380km), from the Israeli shores in the east to the Rock of Gibraltar in the west, the Mediterranean can take years to explore. The most attractive cruising areas are the Balearics, the Dalmatian coast of Croatia and, of course, Greek waters in general and the Aegean islands in particular, but there are many other hidden gems to be discovered and enjoyed. Charter fleets, both sail and power, are based in all

Generally, the southern and eastern shores are warmer and have a better winter climate.

popular spots and are backed up by a comprehensive network of airlines that provide flights to all major cities in Europe with good onward connections to the rest of the world.

In most of the Mediterranean, the sailing season extends from early April until November, but is best enjoyed in the spring and autumn when the ports are not crowded and the weather is more pleasant. The benign winters attract many cruising yachts that spend the off season in one of the many marinas, the most popular wintering spots being the Balearics, Spain's Costa del Sol, the French Riviera, Corsica, the Portuguese Algarve, Cyprus, Turkey, Malta and Tunisia. Generally, the southern and eastern shores are warmer and have a better winter climate.

The imposition by the European Union of a maximum six-month stay in any 18 months for non-EU (European Union) boats means that such boats must occasionally leave EU waters to spend time in non-EU countries such as Tunisia, Croatia or Turkey. Yachting facilities are well developed in most parts of the Mediterranean and even countries with no yachting tradition have developed excellent facilities in recent years.

GREEK ISLANDS

CROATIA

THE FRENCH Mediterranean coast borders Spain and Italy.

France
The French Riviera

CHART 1705, 1974, 1998	**CURRENCY** Euro (€)
BEST FOR CRUISING May – September	**NAVIGATIONAL DIFFICULTY**
AVERAGE TEMPERATURE 21ºC 70ºF (27ºC 80ºF July/August)	**FAMILY FRIENDLY**
	DIVING/SNORKELLING
PREVAILING WIND Variable	**SHORE-SIDE EATING**
TIME ZONE GMT +1	**SIGHTSEEING**
LANGUAGE French	

The French Mediterranean coastline from the Spanish border in the west to the Italian border offers warm water, superb weather and a complete range of cruising and sightseeing opportunities – in short, it is a magnet for any cruising yachtsman.

THE DIFFERENCE between east and west of here is chalk and cheese. To the east of Marseilles lies France's "high-rent" coastline – sophisticated, expensively built up and scenically rugged, whose water's edge is dotted with a good selection of marinas and provided with every facility that the wealthy residents, boat owners and tourists would wish for. To the west, once north of the pretty little port of Collioure just 10 miles (16km) from the Spanish border, the low-lying Languedoc-Roussillon coastline is unspectacular. Devoted, in general, to low-cost mass tourism, its few gems are well hidden from the casual visitor.

Faced with this somewhat bleak prospect, most cruising yachts entering the Mediterranean bypass this region and sail directly to the Côte d'Azur from mainland Spain, pausing awhile among the Balearic Islands. Smaller yachts, with a draft of less than 5.2ft (1.6m), a beam of less than 18ft (5.5m), a centreline air draft of below 9.8ft (3m) and an overall length of less than 98.4ft (30m), have the option of taking the short cut from the Bay of Biscay through the Canal du Midi to the Mediterranean, emerging in Sète or Agde on the Languedoc-Roussillon coast, both small islands of Gallic charm.

Sète, the largest French Mediterranean fishing port, is a pretty town with good seafood restaurants; Agde's narrow streets, originally laid out by the Ancient Greeks for whom it was a trading port, are well worth a look, but today the town's

PORT-FREJUS marina is equidistant to the famed resorts of Cannes and Saint-Tropez.

ROMAN ARCHITECTURE

THE SOUTH OF FRANCE is a treasure trove of Ancient Roman architecture. This amphitheatre in Nimes, built around 1AD, is still used today – for bullfighting.

*A chalk and cheese coast where
Marseilles divides the west's low-lying
marshlands from cobbled streets, cafés
and glamorous Riviera chic.*

SAINT-TROPEZ has been a favourite glitterati
getaway destination for four decades, and is
synonymous with Gallic glitz and glamour.

commercial life seems more centred on the nudist resorts at nearby Cap d'Agde.

Further east on the Golfe du Lion, the other exit point from Europe's canals is at Port Saint-Louis on the Grand Rhône. Sandwiched between bleak salt flats on one side and the monster oil terminal at Fos on the other, it should not be considered anything but a place to restep one's mast, unless its marina is used as a base from which to venture inland to the glorious Roman settlements of Nîmes, Arles or Avignon, or the landmark aqueduct of the Pont du Gard.

East again, Marseilles is the gateway to what is perhaps the most glamorous cruising ground in the world and is worth a stop if only to see the sights around its Vieux Port, the ancient heart of the city. This is the place to enjoy excellent cosmopolitan food, including the signature fish stew – bouillabaisse – but do avoid the tourist traps and dine only where the locals eat. Once past the city, the beauty of the rugged coastline shines through; steep

HYÈRES is the oldest of the Côte d'Azur's winter resorts. This walled town, with its traffic-free streets, is well worth a visit.

PORT VIEUX at Marseilles is overlooked by the famed cathedral crowned with a golden statue of the Virgin and Child.

hills, often with exposed limestone caps, are set against a backdrop of mountains. Explore the calanques – miniature fjords cut into the limestone hills – and the charming seaside resorts of Cassis, Bandol and Sanary-sur-Mer, all with large marinas.

Passing by Toulon, whose waterfront is largely taken up by commercial and naval interests, the next stop simply has to be Hyères and its off-lying islands. This is the prime "unspoilt" cruising area of the Côte d'Azur, away from the urbanized glitz of the eastern part of the region. The bay of Hyères, protected from the west by the Giens peninsula and from the south and south-east by the Îles d'Hyères, is a great cruising ground in itself, especially if one takes in Saint-Tropez, just a little to the north-east, to add a touch of style, nightlife and jet-set glamour. The town of Hyères – the oldest of the Côte d'Azure's winter resorts – lies a few miles inland and the old walled town, with steep, narrow, traffic-free streets, is certainly worth a visit. For sailors, however, Hyères means Port Saint-Pierre, the huge marina with its attendant boatyards a few miles to the south of the town that form the centre of the area's maritime life. Visitor berths are usually available, as are all kinds of chandlery, spare parts and fuel, while the modern yet attractive quays are lined with excellent restaurants.

PORQUEROLLES MARINA is usually crammed to capacity but visiting yachts can anchor off one of the many beaches.

But this is just the base. Six miles (9.6km) away, the little island of Porquerolles – just five miles by two (8 x 3km) – is a jewel from another world. The largest of the three main Îles d'Hyères, Porquerolles boasts a marina, but as this is usually crammed to capacity one should anchor off one of the many beaches. The island's heart is the charmingly dusty village square, where outdoor dining, drinking coffee and playing petanque seem to be the main pastimes. Refreshingly, the island is practically car-free, so transport is by bicycle (available from many rental shops), an ideal means of exploring the scenic tracks that meander through vineyards and pine woods to link the many sheltered coves and beaches.

The two further islands, Port-Cros and Île du Levant, are equally delightful, perhaps more so if your taste is for remoteness or snorkelling.

On the mainland shore, once past the salt-pans to the east of Hyères, there are many pretty villages and delightfully isolated sandy coves towards Cap Benat, after which much of the shoreline below the Maures mountain range is built up until one approaches Cap Lardier. Here, Cap Taillat is a great anchorage and beach while, past Cap Camaret, the famous sandy stretch of Pampelonne beach will delight children of all ages.

You either love or hate Saint-Tropez. Once a little fishing village with an attractive facade of houses and a quay lined with fishing boats, it is today the playground of squillionaires, whose gleaming white motor yachts moor fender-to-fender, blocking

PORT-CROS is a nature reserve. No cars are allowed on the island and scuba-diving and anchoring are prohibited.

CROISETTE BEACH is synonymous with the Cannes Film Festival, which takes place for 10 days each May.

PORT GRIMAUD is renowned for its charming pastel-coloured architecture and tranquil, car-free streets.

the view and filling the air with the reek of diesel exhausts. Others will see Saint-Tropez' great charm and atmosphere: a wealth of fashion and tourist shopping, superb dining – from quayside tourist bistros to a plethora of Michelin-starred establishments – and, on top of all that, plenty of celebrities to spot. Take it or leave it – your choice – but don't even think of asking for a berth in the harbour unless you are a close relative of the mayor or harbourmaster.

East again, to call at Port Grimaud and admire the architecture and style of its marina housing project. Thereafter, until one arrives at the super-resort of Cannes, the main attraction of this coastline are the dramatic red hills of the Esterel mountains and their rocky shoreline where, in calm conditions, one can moor, swim, dive and laze in the sun.

After that, nature stops and bright city lights beckon. Everyone should experience Cannes, Antibes, Nice and (momentarily leaving France) Monaco at least once in their lives – the epitome of Mediterranean cities, where chic and squalor rub shoulders. For a perfect day out in Cannes, anchor in the shelter of the Lerins Islands, land near the Palm Beach Casino and walk the Croisette beachfront towards the old harbour, lunch at any of the small café-bistros, then stroll back

EZE is a truly magical village perched on top of a towering cliff with sensational views as far as Corsica.

along the Rue d'Antibes to take in exclusive boutique (window?) shopping and movie theatres.

A few miles to the north-east, past the fashionable resort of Juan-les-Pins and the enviable villas of the Cap d'Antibes peninsula, is the town of Antibes with great markets, smart shops and, moored along its "Quai des Milliardes" in Port Vauban, the world's largest and most expensive yachts. Ten miles (16km) further on is Nice – today, more working town than resort – where walking (or roller-blading) its Promenade des Anglais is another of life's should-have experiences, along with an alfresco dinner in its old city or port.

Ten more miles (16km) along the coast will pass the sheltered anchorages of Villefranche and Saint Jean Cap Ferrat – where, again, you'll always find a good selection of superyachts – but any stops along this stretch should include the magical village of Eze, perched like a crow's nest on the top of the high cliffs with truly magnificent views, sometimes as far as Corsica.

While renowned for glamour and its Formula 1 event, Monaco is, in reality, a principality of extremely highly priced apartments owned (but not always inhabited) by those who can afford not to pay tax. Here, the "must-sees" are fewer than one might imagine: a climb up the hill to La Condamine and the Palace, a stroll

around the harbour and the sumptuous superyachts, a walk along the elevated terraces on the Monte Carlo side.

Beyond Monaco, the few miles of coastline that stretch to the Italian border belong to France and include Roquebrune and Menton, the picturesque resort towns that mark the end of the Côte d'Azur.

MONACO is famously a tax haven for the super rich with their spectacular superyachts.

CANNES is enormously popular with the jet-set, and tourists flock to the harbours to admire the superb sailing boats.

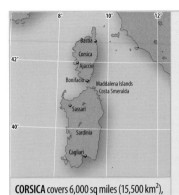

CORSICA covers 6,000 sq miles (15,500 km²), about a third the surface area of Sardinia.

France/Spain
Corsica and Sardinia

CHART Corsica 1424, 1425; Sardinia 1202, 1210, 1212
BEST FOR CRUISING May – September
AVERAGE TEMPERATURE Corsica 25ºC 77ºF (28ºC 82ºF July/August); Sardinia 20ºC 68ºF (26ºC 79ºF July/August)
PREVAILING WIND W/seabreeze in summer
TIME ZONE GMT + 1
LANGUAGE Corsica: Corsican & French; Sardinia: Italian

CURRENCY Euro (€)
NAVIGATIONAL DIFFICULTY ⚙ ⚙ ⚙
FAMILY FRIENDLY ♟ ♟ ♟ ♟
DIVING/SNORKELLING 🐟 🐟 🐟
SHORE-SIDE EATING 🍽 🍽 🍽 🍽 🍽
SIGHTSEEING ♜ ♜ ♜ ♜

They are the fourth (Corsica) and second (Sardinia) largest islands in the Mediterranean, mountains in the Middle Sea, each one distinct and diverse despite their proximity.

THE COASTLINE is spectacular anywhere, but sailing along the southern side of Corsica the land rises until the towering cliffs at Bonifacio, which must rank as one of the most unforgettable harbour entrances to be found anywhere.

Corsica is famous as Napoleon's birthplace but these islands have a depth of history and culture that is breathtaking. A human bone found in Sardinia was dated to 250,000BC, putting the comings and goings of the last 2,500 years firmly in perspective. If the Med is the "crossroads of civilization" then these islands have borne much of the traffic.

Yet it is their natural beauty that draws sailors. Each island has tough, mountainous interiors, low-lying rocky bays and sublime sandy beaches. The summer sea breezes are good – strong even

COSTA SMERALDA is expensive and fashionable for the short summer season but year-round beautiful with ink-blue seas.

in the afternoon – and there can be days of calms as well as really robust winds. Nowadays, both islands are well served by airlines and offer a well-developed yacht charter business.

Corsica's main towns of Ajaccio and Bastia are bustling, more Marseilles or Toulon in flavour than Nice, but everywhere you can enjoy the taste of islands. Head into Corsica's mountains if big-flavoured game is your thing. Or do as we did, and put on the snorkel, fins, tough gloves and a mask and free dive in a secluded anchorage and collect sea urchins for a cockpit lunch – washed down with a salmon-pink rosé wine.

Across the Strait are two Sardinias, divided by the fantastic sounds and passages of the Maddalena Islands. Both Sardinias have fabulously sculpted white/pink granite rocks slashing through fragrant scrub, and beaches of sintered white coral, but one is touristy with modest villas, trattoria and campsites, albeit low density by Med standards, the other is Palm Springs by the sea. This is Costa Smeralda, a 34-mile (55km) stretch of coast that is a playground for yachts, be they racing at the exclusive Yacht Club Costa Smeralda or cruising, with Cala di Volpe routinely populated by fabulous superyachts.

ST FLORENT is a magnet for the Provençal jet-set but retains an ageless charm with its old houses, shops and wine bars.

AJACCIO is a bustling Corsican town with a busy marketplace lined with palm trees. It is famous as the birthplace of Napoleon.

THE WESTERN COAST of Italy is a prime cruising area.

Italy
Portofino to Amalfi

CHART 1998, 1999, 1911, 1908, 908
BEST FOR CRUISING May – October
AVERAGE TEMPERATURE 25°C 77°F
PREVAILING WIND Variable/NW
TIME ZONE GMT + 1
LANGUAGE Italian
CURRENCY Euro (€)

NAVIGATIONAL DIFFICULTY
FAMILY FRIENDLY
DIVING/SNORKELLING
SHORE-SIDE EATING
SIGHTSEEING

The western coastline and magical islands of Italy certainly rank among the Mediterranean's more interesting cruising grounds, offering a supreme blend of art, architecture, history, culture, regional cuisine, world-class scenery and superb summer weather. One could happily cruise these shores for a lifetime.

TAKE A SHELTERED COVE, line it with a tall facade of fishermen's houses painted in the earthy pastels of Italy, throw in a charming quayside, top it off with a couple of prominent churches, and that is Portofino, one of the region's true gems. The downside, of course, is that every guidebook says so and, in consequence, this Genoese village is now one huge, noisy restaurant – its tiny streets and beautiful square are lined with stylish boutiques and the traffic jam on the narrow approach road is legendary. Arriving by boat is the best way but, as at Saint-Tropez, obtaining a berth is difficult. The real mission, however, is to take a picture of your yacht against this famous backdrop, so take the tender ashore, order a coffee and tarry awhile soaking in the atmosphere, then climb to the church above the harbour, snap and go.

To the south of Portofino, in eastern Liguria, the Cinque Terra (literally translated as "Five Lands") is home to five villages – Monterosso al Mare, Vernazza, Corniglia, Manarola and Riomaggiore – dotted along the shoreline at the foot of steep, spectacularly beautiful terraced hills and vineyards. Historically, the main access to the villages was by sea but in bad weather a donkey path cut into the cliffs, the Strada dei Santuari, provided a

PORTOFINO

VERNAZZA

MANAROLA

CORNIGLIA is one of the spectacular "Cinque Terra" villages that dot the shoreline in the eastern Liguria, south of Portofino.

vital lifeline and today this makes a scenic coastal walk. If time is short, just visit Vernazza, the only one of the five to boast a little harbour, where there is a charming, café-lined square enclosed by tall, shabby-chic houses and overlooked by a striking church. Beyond the Cinque Terra to the south-east, the little mainland fishing settlement of Portovenere, tucked behind the island of Palmaria at the entrance to the naval port of La Spezia, is also worthy of a visit.

For sailors, the real gems of Tuscany are Capraia and Elba. These two islands, part of the Tuscan archipelago, lie within startlingly clear turquoise waters between Piombino on the mainland and Cap Corse on the northern tip of Corsica.

The jewel of the chain is Elba, whose rocky coastline is heavily indented by coves and larger sandy bays. Just seven miles (11km) off the Italian mainland, Elba is a pleasantly popular summer holiday destination but at weekends it becomes a focus for every cabin cruiser and sailing yacht within reach, so try to plan your visit accordingly. The harbour of Portoferraio (the island's capital) in the north provides the best shelter and shopping alongside relics of Napoleon's "Little Empire". The island's real attraction,

ELBA is just a few miles from the Italian mainland and attracts boats of all shapes and sizes every weekend in summer.

FETOVAIA BEACH is a popular destination on the island of Elba, situated within a narrow inlet.

however, lies in its natural beauty with wooded mountains rising to more than 3,000ft (1,000m), isolated sandy coves – such as Zuccale and Fetovaia on the south coast – and the beaches of Marino di Campo.

Unspoilt Capraia offers fewer beaches but plenty of coves and superb walking through the aromatic Mediterranean scrub of the interior. For something special, anchor beneath the red rocks of the little Cala Rossa in the south.

PONZA overlooks a vast harbour and anchorage that is usually so crowded that finding a spot to anchor is difficult.

The islands of Giglio and Giannutri lie offshore of the Monte Argentario peninsula. Rich in flora and fauna, their interiors are a mix of barren rock and forest, while rocky coves and sandy beaches make them heaven for sailors of all ages. Of the other islands in the Tuscan archipelago, Gorgona houses a high security prison and it is forbidden to close the shore or land except in dire emergency; landing without permission is also forbidden on Pianosa and Montecristo.

Further south along the Italian coast, close to Naples, are the less well-known Pontine Islands – which include Ponza flanked by its smaller neighbours, Ponziane, Zannone and Ventotene – and the more famous islands of Ischia and Capri.

Ponza is particularly beautiful at sunset when its vertiginous, sharp-crested cliffs turn a multitude of pastel hues – the most spectacular are on the island's southern tip, topped by the Punta della Guardia lighthouse. While places to anchor, swim and dive can be found all round the island, the town of Ponza – a charming place to shop for souvenirs or enjoy an alfresco meal – overlooks a vast harbour and anchorage that is usually so crowded that finding a spot to anchor is invariably difficult. Even more peaceful and equally pretty are Ventotene and the little green island, a nature reserve, of Zannone.

In sharp contrast are the islands of Ischia and Capri positioned, north and south respectively, off the horns of the Bay of Naples. Sophisticated, cosmopolitan and with anchorages, beaches, gourmet restaurants and shopping in abundance, both islands are popular holiday destinations and are especially busy during July and August.

Ischia is arguably the more beautiful. Don't be tempted by the busy commercial harbour at Ischia Porto: the best anchorage is at Ischia Ponte under the shadow of a superb Aragonese fortress. And do head up above the encircling belt of expensive villas and into the island's volcanic centre where the views are magnificent. Capri is much smaller than Ischia, but it has been dosed with steroids – and money. Book ahead to secure a place in the marina, then take the funicular railway from the port up to Capri town's Plaza Umberto – a magical place to sit with a coffee and watch the wealthy world go by. The town's twisting main street boasts more top-name stores than London's Bond Street – a measure of the clientele attracted to this island. Inland there is much to look out upon but don't miss the wonderful view from Villa Jovis, the palace of Emperor Augustus and, on the coast, the iridescent light of the Blue Grotto and the jagged, wave-pierced Faraglioni Islands are impressive, to say the least.

POSITANO is known as the town 'of stairways' with enchanting sights, shops and architecture at every turn.

Italy
Aeolian Islands and Sicily

CHART Aeolian 172; Sicily 1976, 1941	**CURRENCY** Euro (€)
BEST FOR CRUISING May – October	**NAVIGATIONAL DIFFICULTY** ✱ ✱ ✱
AVERAGE TEMPERATURE 26ºC 79ºF (33ºC 91ºF July/August)	**FAMILY FRIENDLY** 🍸 🍸 🍸
PREVAILING WIND Variable/NW	**DIVING/SNORKELLING** 🤿 🤿 🤿
TIME ZONE GMT + 1	**SHORE-SIDE EATING** 🍽 🍽 🍽 🍽
LANGUAGE Italian	**SIGHTSEEING** ♟ ♟ ♟ ♟

The Aeolian archipelago on the north-eastern tip of Sicily comprises Lipari, Stromboli, Salina, Filicudi, Panarea, Basiluzzo, Alicudi and Vulcano, whose names and conical outlines define the islands' volcanic origins. Appealingly remote, they are less touristed than Italy's more northern islands, possibly because of their black sands and sulphurous aromas; especially strong on Vulcano.

TAORMINA, in Sicily, has a spectacular Greek amphitheatre that hosts a world-class arts programme in the summer.

CHIC PANAREA is the prettiest of the islands, while the quietest are rocky Filicudi with its great cliffs and grottos and Alicudi. On historic Lipari you'll find spa baths, a Roman sauna cave, plenty of shops, restaurants and lively bars as well as a pumice quarry where some of the produce simply floats away. Outlying Stromboli is famous for its active crater in a near-perpetual state of eruption – spectacular by night.

Just to the south lies Sicily. Everyone should see Palermo, the capital, with its dramatic blend of architecture from the many cultures that have ruled here. Baroque splendour flourishes, as do dusty museums and boisterous markets, but one should be aware of the darker side of this polluted, edgy, chaotic and sometimes dangerous city, so stop awhile in its marina, see the sights and move on.

Elsewhere, Sicily offers relatively few examples of delightful, sheltered coves that make memorable anchorages. If these are what you seek the best area is perhaps the rugged coast to the west of Palermo, and in the Egadi archipelago a few miles off Trapani on the island's north-west corner. Among these islands – Favignana, Levanza and Marettimo – you will find rugged beauty and water with crystal clarity, together with sheltered bays and grottos that equal any in Italy.

Other Sicilian attractions include the town of Taormina on the island's east coast, which is renowned for its beauty, while, sailing southwards, a visit to the ancient city of Syracusa (ancient Syracuse) and an ascent of the volcanic summit of Mount Etna also provide rewarding excursions.

ALICUDI is a island sanctuary for sailors; all but one of its beaches can be reached only by boat.

AEOLIAN ISLANDS in the Tyrrhenian Sea –
home to Aeolus, Greek god of the winds, and
to the Roman Vulcan, god of volcanoes.

VENICE is situated in Italy's north-east corner known as the Veneto region.

Italy
Venice

CHART 1483, 1442
BEST FOR CRUISING May – October
AVERAGE TEMPERATURE 24ºC 75ºF
PREVAILING WIND N/A
TIME ZONE GMT + 1
LANGUAGE Italian
CURRENCY Euro (€)

NAVIGATIONAL DIFFICULTY
FAMILY FRIENDLY
DIVING/SNORKELLING
SHORE-SIDE EATING
SIGHTSEEING

At the height of its power during the Middle Ages the "Serene Republic" spread its trading tentacles far and wide; throughout the Mediterranean – and all along the Adriatic coast – we come across ancient Venetian ports, massive forts and elegant civic buildings. And Venice, whether as the starting point for a charter or as part of an Adriatic cruise, is guaranteed to provide a unique highlight.

IT DID NOT take long to make the 50-mile (80km) trip from Croatia to Italy. It was late in the day and therefore, rather than make for the city itself, we took a side canal and anchored off the old fishing island of Burano. As the sun was setting on the far side of the lagoon, we took our dinghy through the narrow canals that crisscross the small town. We tied up to some steps in the main square and were amazed to find it deserted. The day tourists had all returned to their city-centre hotels and we had the place to ourselves. The following morning we docked Aventura right by the 6th-century cathedral on Torcello, a tiny island where the Venetian settlement had actually begun while the Roman Empire was disintegrating elsewhere.

Saint Mark's distinctive campanile acted as a beacon as we followed the main canal, dodging all kinds of craft, from huge cruise ships to one-man gondolas, not to mention the countless vaporetti – the battered waterbuses that ply the canal, day and night, between Venice's various suburbs. We somehow managed to shoehorn Aventura into a tight mooring at San Giorgio Maggiore marina that occupies a fabulous location in the very heart of the city.

To top it all, one afternoon we took our inflatable dinghy on a grand tour of the canals. Motoring slowly past elegant palaces, massive churches, once opulent but now crumbling residences we revelled in a truly unforgettable view of *Venezia, "La Serenissima"*, undoubtedly the most beautiful city in Europe, if not the entire world.

THE ISLES OF VENICE are linked by more than 400 bridges.

BURANO is an island of bridges and brightly coloured houses.

VENICE is built on 117 islands, linked by 150 canals. The ubiquitous gondolas are the traditional form of transport.

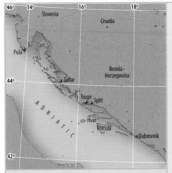

THE DALMATIAN COAST is peppered with over a thousand islands.

Croatia
The Dalmatian Coast

CHART 1440, 683, 2712	**CURRENCY** Kuna (HRK)
BEST FOR CRUISING May – June & September	**NAVIGATIONAL DIFFICULTY**
AVERAGE TEMPERATURE 22°C 71°F (25°C 77°F July/August)	**FAMILY FRIENDLY**
	DIVING/SNORKELLING
PREVAILING WIND NW	**SHORE-SIDE EATING**
TIME ZONE GMT + 1	**SIGHTSEEING**
LANGUAGE Croatian	

For boats arriving from the south, Dubrovnik – on the Adriatic Sea – is the ideal gateway into Croatia. Declared a world heritage site, it is considered one of the most beautiful and well-preserved medieval cities in the world.

CROATIA IS CURRENTLY the hottest cruising destination in the Mediterranean. It has a most attractive coastline with hundreds of islands and unlimited cruising opportunities, small ports and well-appointed marinas. More than any other country in the Mediterranean, the Croatian authorities have encouraged a wide-ranging programme of infrastructure development. There are now scores of marinas – most with their own repair yards – and every port has an area set aside for visiting boats. As a result, there is a profusion of charter companies offering a wide range of boats, from bare monohulls and catamarans to large motor yachts, as well as the ubiquitous flotilla holidays.

Due to its convenient location, the Dalmatian coast can be reached easily from several central European countries and during

DUBROVNIK'S market on Gunduliceva poljana sells a wide range of local fruit, vegetables and first-rate cheeses.

the peak summer months of July and August ports, marinas and popular bays can get crowded. The situation is much better earlier or later in the season, which lasts from April to October.

Fortunately there is such a choice of marinas and anchorages that however busy they may be, it is always possible to find a sheltered place within reasonable distance. Croatia's main attraction is this rich variety that offers the visitor an almost bewildering choice between scores of picturesque harbours on its offshore islands or perfectly preserved medieval ports, such as Split, Trogir, Hvar, Zadar, Pula and countless others.

History is a permanent presence when sailing these waters and nowhere more so than in Korcula, which had been high on my list of priorities for a long time, not least because its attractive capital is reputed to be the place where Marco Polo was born in 1254. The old port, which shares its name with that of the island, played an important role when the Venetians ruled this part of the world, and the house where that greatest of medieval travellers first saw the light of day still stands in a narrow side street.

HVAR is just one of many perfectly preserved medieval ports along the Dalmatian coast.

KORCULA town is a mini-fortress enclosed with honey-coloured stone walls, and was the birthplace of the great explorer Marco Polo.

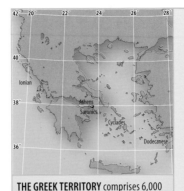

THE GREEK TERRITORY comprises 6,000 islands and islets; 227 are inhabited.

Greece
Greek Islands

CHART 5771-6 (Folio charts), 180; Imray-Tetra Chart No. G-3

BEST FOR CRUISING May – September

AVERAGE TEMPERATURE 28ºC 83ºF

PREVAILING WIND N (meltémi)

TIME ZONE GMT +2

LANGUAGE Greek, English widely spoken

CURRENCY Euro (€)

NAVIGATIONAL DIFFICULTY ✹ ✹ ✹

FAMILY FRIENDLY 👶 👶 👶 👶 👶

DIVING/SNORKELLING 🤿 🤿 🤿

SHORE-SIDE EATING 🍽 🍽 🍽 🍽 🍽

SIGHTSEEING 🏰 🏰 🏰 🏰 🏰

The Cyclades Islands – of which Santorini is one – are the most popular vacation destination of all the Greek island groups, but there are other archipelagos and coastal destinations, less actively promoted and therefore often overlooked, that offer a diverse and equally enchanting travel experience. Here, we'll take a thumbnail look at the Cyclades, plus three other top island groups for yacht charter, and what each has to offer.

THE CYCLADES ISLANDS are the hands-down first choice among charterers. Situated in the centre of the Aegean Sea, the islands get their collective name from the Greek word *kíiklos*, meaning "ring" or "circle" – because they form a circle around Delos island, the now-abandoned ancient, sacred city that was the region's ancient centre of commerce and religion. In summer, the Cyclades are arid and somewhat barren against the deep-blue sea. Quintessentially Greek, bright-white stucco buildings perch on hillsides like scattered sugar cubes beneath cerulean skies, and the landscape is sprinkled with windmills.

The options for the charterer who chooses the Cyclades are diverse: from the bustling waterfront towns and nightlife on Mykonos, Paros, and Ios, to the vistas of and from Santorini's cliff-top villages, to the tranquillity and peace of smaller islands such as Folegandros and Amorgos. The islands are renowned for their multitude of excellent beaches, though the water here tends to be cooler – 24ºC (75ºF) in July – than in other island groups. History buffs won't be disappointed either: Delos, for example, is one of the most wondrous archaeological sites in the world – this

DELOS

SANTORINI

GREEK CHURCHES

THE ISLAND of Mykonos alone has more than 250 churches, the most famous being the Panagia Paraportiani. Churches are a characteristic and inextricable element of the Greek landscape.

THERA CHURCH, SANTORINI, with its deep-blue church dome framed against the backdrop of a sapphire sea, is picture perfect.

deserted city, sometimes compared to Pompeii, has a magic about it that is palpable. On the island of Paros, the 5th-century church of Panagia Ekatontapiliani (Our Lady of the Hundred Gates) and the archaeology museum are star attractions, and on neighbouring Antiparos the "Stalactite Cave" is a natural wonder that looks like a Disney creation and is said to have Lord Byron's mark carved at the bottom.

For those arriving by yacht, there are several considerations. First is time frame. The first of the Cyclades Islands, Kea, is 45 miles (72km) from Athens, the port from which most chartered yachts depart. The distances between the islands in this group should be considered: The Cyclades are farther apart than those in other island groups, leaving less time for sightseeing ashore and requiring more time underway, with less time for lunch-and-swimming stops. The second consideration – for both sail and power yachts – is wind. Because the islands are in the Aegean's centre, they lie unprotected by the mountainous mainland, and when the meltémi – a strong, seasonal north wind of Force 5 to 6, sometimes as high as Force 8 or 9 – kicks up, it can mean rough weather at best, or lost sailing days due to Port Authority-

THE DORIC TEMPLE of Aphaia is a 2.5-mile (4km) walk from Agia Marina on the island of Aegina in the Saronics.

imposed sailing bans at worst. The meltémi is at its peak in July and August, though it can blow sporadically in late June and early September.

That said, the Cyclades are everyone's dream of the Greek islands, and with their number – some thirty-nine – and diversity, there's something here to realize anyone's dream.

HORSES and donkeys are the only form of transportation permitted on the island of Hydra, making it a haven of tranquility.

POROS is a picturesque town on the island of Poros in the Saronics, with plenty of bars, shops and tavernas. Stop by to stock up on supplies or enjoy the vibrant nightlife.

THE SARONIC GROUP was one of Greece's first island vacation spots due to the proximity to Athens, and today the Saronics remain popular among locals and visitors alike. More lush and green than the Cyclades, these islands also have the advantage of being protected by the mainland; sailing conditions even in strong winds are generally calmer because seas don't build to the extent that they do in the unprotected Cyclades.

Sea temperatures are generally warmer – around 28°C (82°F) in July – than in the Cyclades, and though the beaches don't rival those in the Cyclades, there are plenty of excellent places to swim.

With a short (four- to seven-day) time frame, these islands are an excellent choice. Highlights of a Saronics cruise generally include bustling Poros, the closest of all the Greek islands to the mainland, separated from it only by a picturesque, narrow channel offering views of the island on one side and the craggy,

MONEMVASSIA is a restored Byzantine town in the Saronics known as the "Gibraltar of the Aegean".

green mountains of the Peloponnese on the other, Hydra, the "Saint-Tropez of Greece", Spetses and Aegina.

A Saronics cruise often also includes stops on the Peloponnese east coast and mainland: the tiny villages of Ermioni and Leonidion; perhaps the beautiful city of Nafplion, the second capital of Greece and one of its most picturesque sites, crowned by the towering Palamidi Fort. With more time, it's possible to include on this itinerary the hamlet of Yerakas – a village nestled between mountains and entered via Greece's only fjord – and Monemvassia, the restored Byzantine town perched on a peak that's often called the "Gibraltar of the Aegean", little known to foreign tourists but possibly rivalling Santorini for its vistas and romance.

THE IONIAN ISLANDS, stretching along the west-northwest coast of the Peloponnese and the Greek mainland, lie 200 miles (320km) from Athens in the Ionian (also known as the Adriatic) Sea. They are known as the "Caribbean of Greece" – and with good reason: lush, green islands rise out of an aquamarine sea, good beaches (sandy and pebble) abound, water and air temperatures are milder than in other islands and winds are generally lighter. Corfu, Paxi, Lefkada, Ithaka, Kefalonia, Zakynthos and Kythira are the seven main islands among a scatter of others which comprise this group – although isolated Kythira, with its landscape more reminiscent of the Cyclades, lies between the Aegean and the Ionian Sea and is considered by some to belong to the Saronic group.

Snorkelling in the Ionian is some of the best in Greece. Marine life includes masses of colourful tropical fish, octopus, moray, sea turtles and, off Zakynthos, the rare seal, *Monachus monachus*.

Invasion and occupation over many centuries have resulted in the islands' rich and wide-ranging cultural and architectural influences – the Romans, Venetians, Turks and French have each held sway over the Ionians. Architecturally the Venetian influence predominates, with red-tile-roofed homes and buildings painted in a colourful array of pastel hues. Throughout these islands the bustle and grandeur of their larger towns and harbours contrasts happily with sleepier, traditional villages clustered along tree-lined sand or pebble bays.

The Ionian also boasts literary connections: the famous island of Ithaka, allegedly the realm of real-or-mythical Greek king Odysseus – though you are likely to suspend any disbelief on a cruise around this magical, mountainous little island; Corfu, which has been described as a "luxuriant Garden of Eden" and has inspired writers such as Shakespeare (it's said to be the magical island in *The Tempest*) and brothers Lawrence and Gerald Durrell, in *Prospero's Cell* and *My Family and Other Animals* respectively; Kefalonia, the island on which Louis de Bernières set his book *Captain Corelli's Mandolin*.

For charterers leaving from Athens, reaching these islands requires a transit of the Corinth Canal (3.9 miles/6.3km) – itself worth seeing. From Athens, 10 days' minimum in the Ionian is a must; alternatively, fly in to the islands, most probably to Lefkada, and join the yacht there for a more relaxed exploration of these lovely islands.

SNORKELLING in the Ionian is some of the best in Greece, with magnificent coral reefs, cave systems and underwater arcs, and abundant marine life.

KIPOURIA MONASTRY on the west coast of the Pali peninsula, Kefalonia, was built on the edge of a rocky cliff 295ft (90m) above the sea.

CORFU (above) has been described as a "luxuriant Garden of Eden" and inspired the work of Lawrence and Gerald Durrell, who grew up on the island during the 1930s.

CORFU (right) is one of the largest and most verdant Ionian islands. It is a landscape of vibrant wild flowers and slender cypress spires that shimmer among olive groves.

AGHIOFILI BEACH (far right) on the island of Lefkada is a wonderful beach that is accessible only by boat. It lies to the east of the village of Vasiliki with a wide range of bars and restaurants.

THE DODECANESE, so named because there are 12 of them – dódeka in Greek – are an island chain stretching along the east coast of Turkey in the eastern Aegean, and lying 250 miles (400km) from Athens. Sailing from Patmos in the north to Rhodes in the south, charterers will find not only distinctive scenery and architecture, but also plenty of other attractions, including the

SYMI is a friendly island with a population of around 2,500, which still retains the traditional Greek island way of life.

site on Patmos where Saint John is said to have written the *Apocalypse*. Then, to name but a few, there's the slumbering volcano on little island of Nissiros; the Castle of the Knights of the

Order of Saint John within the old town walls on Rhodes, and also the fortified artists' colony of Lindos – itself an archaeological site – and, on Kos, the ancient shrine to the healing god Asklepeios and Hippocrates' plane tree.

From piney forests in the north to palm trees in the south, the atmosphere is as varied as the terrain. Classic white stucco on some islands contrasts with Venetian and Turkish influenced architecture on others; and there are bustling hubs with plenty of shopping and nightlife as well as secluded anchorages with beautiful beaches – such as those on Symi or Kalymnos, for example.

Charterers wishing to cruise here should consider meeting the boat in one of the northernmost Dodecanese islands, such as Patmos, and working south, perhaps ending the cruise at Rhodes. The islands, like the Saronics, are protected, in this case by the Turkish mainland; winds are generally steady but not overpowering, and the climate is mild.

Whatever island group charterers elect to cruise, the best approach to a Greek Islands charter is to set a loose itinerary and keep an open mind. Good yacht crews know the islands inside-out, and likely will be able to suggest spectacular places not found or featured in any island's guidebook. While charterers may not have ten years to roam the seas as did Odysseus, the credo "let the winds take us where they may" is an excellent one to follow when sailing these very beautiful and richly varied islands.

GROTTO OF ST JOHN, PATMOS, the site at which the exiled apostle wrote the *Apocalyse*.

THE CASTLE of the Knights of the Order of Saint John is situated near to the harbour entrance on the island of Rhodes.

RHODES is a particularly interesting island, blending ancient ruins, up-tempo resorts and enchanting villages.

POTAMI BEACH is just one of several wonderful beaches on the island of Samos.

PAROS is 13 miles (21km) long, and just five miles (8km) away from the island of Naxos.

Greece
Paros

CHART 1539
BEST FOR CRUISING May – September
AVERAGE TEMPERATURE 28°C 83°F
PREVAILING WIND N (meltémi)
TIME ZONE GMT + 2
LANGUAGE Greek, English widely spoken
CURRENCY Euro (€)

NAVIGATIONAL DIFFICULTY
FAMILY FRIENDLY
DIVING/SNORKELLING
SHORE-SIDE EATING
SIGHTSEEING

The island of Paros, in the Cyclades Islands, is an often-overlooked destination, but in my mind, it's one of the best in Greece. Apart from the fun of sailing in these waters, you will discover so many reasons to drop anchor and head inland – surely half the point of sailing.

THE ISLAND IS CHARACTERIZED by classic, white, Greek sugar-cube houses, pastoral landscapes, churches with blue domes and some of the best and most plentiful white-sand beaches in the country. As with many of the islands, it takes getting out of the main yacht harbour, Paroikia, to really appreciate what the island has to offer. However, with charter companies operating throughout the islands, for those arriving on yachts the harbour is convenient, with a supermarket and internet café right across from the docks and rental cars and motorbikes available all along the waterfront.

For those who don't want to rent cars or bikes, there's plenty to do in Paroikia: a walk through the old town, marked by a windmill on the waterfront; sunset at the Meltemi café on the harbour's extreme western end; dinner in the old town at the Happy Green Cows or Apollon. But if you do rent transport, I'd recommend a trip north to visit Naoussa, the island's second largest town. Naoussa is a classic fishing village where you can dine in tavernas on the quay and eat fresh seafood within metres of the harbour. Octopus dry on clotheslines in the sun; the food is home-cooked and fresh; Venetian fort ruins are within a stone's throw from it all.

A short distance west of Naoussa, Kolimbithres beach rivals the Caribbean's Baths at Virgin Gorda for swimming through rock formations while, nearer Paroikia, is the equally fine Marcello beach – most easily reached by water taxi (adjacent to the ferry docks). Or, for a natural attraction that evokes the set of a Walt Disney movie, take the short ferry ride to the neighboring island of Antiparos to see the fabulous stalactites in the famous cave.

NAOUSSA is a picturesque fishing village located in a large bay in the northern part of Paros.

PAROS, like most of the islands of the Cyclades, is decorated with innumerable churches, chapels and monasteries.

ROOMS

CLASSIC GREEK "sugar-cube" houses with wooden shutters painted in pastel shades make a stroll through Paros a total delight.

Greece
Hydra

CHART 1683
BEST FOR CRUISING May – September
AVERAGE TEMPERATURE 28°C 83°F
PREVAILING WIND N (meltémi)
TIME ZONE GMT + 2
LANGUAGE Greek, English widely spoken
CURRENCY Euro (€)

NAVIGATIONAL DIFFICULTY
FAMILY FRIENDLY
DIVING/SNORKELLING
SHORE-SIDE EATING
SIGHTSEEING

HYDRA is a small, elongated island with a coastline of 35 miles (56km).

Hydra town harbour is one of the most picturesque in the Greek islands. Lined by the stately old homes of sea captains, its streets are cobblestone and almost every structure is a well-maintained work of art.

ONE OF THE SARONIC ISLANDS, Hydra attracts the glitterati and its port is busy. Ferries and day boats laden with day-trippers discharge their passengers, and yachts vie for space. To ensure a berth along one of the two quays designated for yachts it is imperative you arrive by 2pm, at the latest. Thereafter, yachts raft up to one other, stern-to-bow, and anchoring fire-drills ensue – superb cocktail-hour entertainment for early arrivals.

That said, peace is still to be found in Hydra. There are no cars except for a garbage truck and a couple of construction vehicles. Here, the donkeys do it all. Water taxis run a regular service and the donkeys cluster next to them on the quay as if vying for business. Once your yacht is securely tied up, roam the cobbled

HYDRA is a peaceful island where donkeys, rather than cars, are the main form of transport.

streets to shop (provisions are available at several markets in town), visit one of the museums, go for a swim or stop for lunch. Or simply sip a cool drink at a waterfront café and people-watch: one of the best pastimes on this island. Hikers can head along a beautiful, flat, shoreside path that begins just above the west side of the harbour and ends at the small village of Kamini.

For swimming, there are several options: take a water taxi to Mandraki Beach or to Vlychos, a rocky beach with the added benefit of the excellent Enalion restaurant, which serves superb lunches, including the best paella this side of Spain (available on request). Many opt to do what the islanders do, and simply swim off the rocks at one of the several cement platforms with ladders a short walk from the harbour.

Don't miss out on an evening at Hydronetta Bar, also a short walk up the hill from the harbour, where you can combine swimming with the sunset. In this west-facing café complete with tiki huts, sunset is a ritual: special music plays, and a moment of silence inevitably ensues when the sun dips over the horizon. The drinks are expensive; the view is worth it.

FLOWERS are everywhere in Hydra, hanging from walls and window boxes or in classic Mediterranean-blue pots.

HYDRA HARBOUR is very popular! There are yachts moored all around the port and as more come in, they have to raft up to one another.

Greece
Kefalonia

CHART 203, 2402		**CURRENCY** Euro (€)	
BEST FOR CRUISING May – September		**NAVIGATIONAL DIFFICULTY**	
AVERAGE TEMPERATURE 28ºC 83ºF		**FAMILY FRIENDLY**	
PREVAILING WIND S in morning; prevailing NW from noon		**DIVING/SNORKELLING**	
		SHORE-SIDE EATING	
TIME ZONE GMT + 2		**SIGHTSEEING**	
LANGUAGE Greek, English widely spoken			

KEFALONIA is the largest of the Ionian islands at 266 sq miles (688km²).

Captain Corelli may have put Kefalonia on the map, but cruising sailors had this Ionian island on their charts long before Louis de Bernières put pen to paper. Why? Above all, Lixouri, across the bay from Argostili the capital, is an ideal base from which to learn to sail. Much better to gain a qualification here than on a wind-swept chunk of sea off Ouessant.

DRYING KALAMARI

THE IONIAN IS UNCHALLENGING, apart from a few well–marked hazards, and the weather predictable: morning winds light and from the south, with prevailing north-westerlies from midday reaching Force 5, and dropping at dusk.

Kefalonia is the largest of the Ionian islands and close neighbour to Ulysses' reputed birthplace, Ithaca, although the Kefalonians would dispute that. While Kefalonia is laid back, Ithaca is steeped in Ulyssean myth.

And the cruising ground? Think quintessential Greece and there you have it – tavernas, little harbours, rocky coves, women in black, donkeys, wind in the afternoon, none in the morning, and sun – guaranteed. With one noticeable difference: Kefalonia was flattened by an earthquake that struck without warning on a Sunday morning in 1953, demolishing 85 per cent of the houses. Today's Kefalonia is no more than three storeys high. No high-rise hotels; no hideous apartment blocks. In a word, delightful, and getting more so by the year as the patina of age softens the walls of the towns and bright colours begin to fade to pastel.

I first came here to gain a little experience in Mediterranean sailing from an outfit called Sea Trek. How many of us have a

TAVERNA – STOUPA TABLES

WILD DONKEYS

FISCARDO is a truly picturesque harbour with fishing boats around the bay and bougainvillea hanging from the Venetian-style houses.

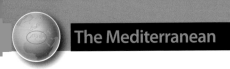
sneaking fear of making fools of ourselves in a crowded harbour? Who can honestly say their heart doesn't beat a little faster when they identify that tiny gap, commit to the final approach, hit reverse gear, prop racing, stern wave building, stone quay approaching, and a hundred pairs of eyes waiting (let's face it, hoping) for the crunch of glassfibre against granite?

Having mastered stern-to mooring, over the next four days we skirted the southern coast of Kefalonia, popped into Ag Efimia, headed over to Ithaca, dropped anchor in Pera Pigadi for lunch (where the returning Ulysses met his pig man) before settling

MIRTOS BEACH is a major tourist attraction, and has been ranked fifth worldwide for its beauty.

down for the night at Vathi on Meganisi, together with about 100 other charter yachts.

At Kioni we moored stern-to in front of an azure-blue house not far from a taverna, rented bikes and sped all over the island, trying to track down Ulysses' palace. In Anogi, up in the hills in the middle of the island, we met an old man by a café with stuffed birds on the walls who told us what was like to be occupied by Italians during the war, and what an earthquake feels like at 9am on a Sunday.

Polyphemus at Stavros on Ithaca was another favourite, lunching in the cool, open-air under olive trees, while back at Lixouri, the Metropolis Café seemed to be where the young crowd hang out to see and be seen in the main square.

KEFALONIA'S profile was raised in the late 1990s thanks to the novel *Captain Corelli's Mandolin*, by Louis de Bernières.

Lixouri is an excellent base, 50 minutes from the airport facing Argostili, across the gulf of the same name. Big enough to have all the shops and nightlife, but a far cry from the pulsating hell of the package holiday Greek town.

Apart from the food, a highlight of that trip was the walk we took in the hills, something few yachtsmen do. Seeing the islands from the sea, the only point of contact being the harbours, is to miss much. We left at crack of dawn to avoid the heat, walking swiftly through villages and olive groves, seeing the island wake and stretch itself, catching glimpses of island life we'd have missed.

THE ISLAND is relatively verdant with numerous attractive beaches, many of them inaccessible from land.

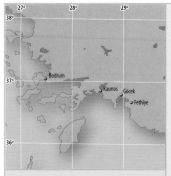

TURKEY has a wonderful, largely unspoilt coastline ideal for yachting.

Turkey
Bodrum to Fethiye

CHART 1055, 1054, 1644
BEST FOR CRUISING May – October
AVERAGE TEMPERATURE 25ºC 77ºF
PREVAILING WIND S to SW in the Liman, NW on coast (Meltem)
TIME ZONE GMT + 2

LANGUAGE Turkish, English widely spoken in resorts
CURRENCY New Turkish Lira (YTL)
NAVIGATIONAL DIFFICULTY 🧭 🧭
FAMILY FRIENDLY 🍸 🍸 🍸
DIVING/SNORKELLING 🤿 🤿 🤿
SHORE-SIDE EATING 🍽 🍽 🍽 🍽
SIGHTSEEING 🏰 🏰 🏰 🏰

From Bodrum down to Fethiye, the Turkish coast is rich in anchorages, bays and the ruins of ancient civilizations. Bodrum, the starting place for many of the boats which charter these waters, was a crusader stronghold; its castle dominates the harbour. Alexander the Great destroyed it, Heredotus, father of history was born here. Today carpet sellers haggle, and the smells and sights of a vibrant city assail the eyes and ears – the smells and sights of the real Turkey.

A FEW HOURS' sail away southwards, facing the Greek island of Kos, its two sheltered harbours separated by a narrow isthmus, is Cnidus where Praxiteles' statue of Venus once stood (a priest would charge tourists extra for a view of her perfectly formed rear). The outer bay once sheltered triremes, the southern bay is a landing place for sea-borne tourists, but you are likely to find the place deserted out of hours.

For the yachtsmen for whom dusty ruins hold no allure, it is the coastline further south that holds the greater attraction. These are arguably better cruising waters than Greece's, but outside the few marinas you are on your own. And there is an art to anchoring in these waters. The anchor is dropped 130 or 165 feet (40–50m) out, the boat reversed back towards the shore, a stern line taken to a convenient tree or rock and the boat, secure in theory, centred between the two.

Gocek is a charming town with excellent facilities for the yachtsman, including three marinas, the largest of which is the well-equipped Port Gocek. There is excellent shopping here, including a fascinating street market on Sundays with everything

BODRUM CASTLE

GOCEK

RUINS IN THE SEA

Gemiler and its vicinity are a significant centre for Christianity. It is a rocky terrain, and the foundations of ancient buildings are carved into the rocks. The ruins continue within the sea along the shore.

Explore magnificent ancient city ruins, hidden coves and islands, lunch somewhere different – afloat or ashore – every day, and shop for saffron and carpets at the bazaar.

GEMILER, or Father Christmas, Island is just around the headland from Fethiye. There are two restaurants in the bay.

from counterfeit designer goods to mouth-watering food and restaurants offering good dining at reasonable prices. Yacht tourism drives Gocek so you'll see no high-rise hotels and crowded beaches, just hundreds of yachts.

Skopea Liman is virtually a land-locked sea, a bay some eight miles long with a chain of islands two miles out that provide shelter from any seas, so flat water cruising can be enjoyed here. With some 20 bays and anchorages, some with small restaurants both ashore and afloat, there's plenty of scope for some gentle cruising, just a few miles a day with a different lunch stop each day – more than a week's worth for the less ambitious.

Favourites here are Tomb Bay, Ruin Bay and Boynuz Buku, where so-called 'free anchoring' is possible. And all the time Gocek is just an hour or so away for re-provisioning or for a wider choice of restaurant.

Nearby, just a couple of hours' sail away is the large town of Fethiye where you can anchor off and dinghy ashore. Fethiye has a much larger weekly market (on Tuesdays) than Gocek, but on other days there is the intriguing bazaar to explore where high-

THE FETHIYE SHORELINE offers dozens of fabulous bays and coves sheltered by the surrounding Toros mountain range.

GOCEK MARKET offers mouthwatering food and good dining at reasonable prices.

priced designer name shops rub shoulders with Turkish carpet sellers and stalls selling a huge selection of brightly coloured herbs and spices – stock up with saffron and cumin, garlic and rosemary. Here you can have a Turkish bath and massage or a trim at the Turkish barber's shop.

Just around the headland from Fethiye is Gemiler – or Father Christmas – Island where, again, you anchor stern to the island, bows pointing out across the wide and deep channel between you and the mainland. If you're lucky, in the early evening a small local boat will pull alongside and offer to cook you tasty cheese boreks. If it's sandy beaches you're after, the popular resort of Olu Deniz is nearby; if it's adventure you crave, you can always book a tandem paraglide from the local Mount Babadag landing, hopefully, on the nearby beach.

Half a day's sail to the north-west of Skopea Liman is the anchorage at Ekincik, which you can use as a base for an excursion up the Dalyan River nearby to visit the ancient city of Caunos. Hire a local boat for the day – there is not enough depth of water here for yachts – and follow the river winding between reed-covered banks. You may be lucky and spy a local fishing boat catching little blue crabs which you can buy for a few lira.

OLU DENIS resort is nestled behind a curved strip of beach that encircles a natural blue lagoon.

CAUNOS is a historic harbour city renowned for its Lycian tombs carved into the cliff face.

When you get to Caunos you can climb the ancient amphitheatre, admire the Lycian rock tombs set into the cliffs and, should the mood take you, go and wallow in mud at the baths a little further upstream. Make sure to have a good swim before going back on board.

North Africa
Tunisia

CHART 1712
BEST FOR CRUISING May – June & September – October
AVERAGE TEMPERATURE 24ºC 75ºF
PREVAILING WIND Variable
TIME ZONE GMT + 1
LANGUAGE Arabic & French (some English, Italian & German)

CURRENCY Tunisian Dinar (TND)
NAVIGATIONAL DIFFICULTY ⬤
FAMILY FRIENDLY ⛟ ⛟ ⛟ ⛟ ⛟
DIVING/SNORKELLING 🐟
SHORE-SIDE EATING 🍴 🍴 🍴 🍴
SIGHTSEEING ⛩ ⛩ ⛩ ⛩ ⛩

TUNISIA is situated approximately 100 miles (60km) south of Sicily.

Considered one of the most stable Muslim countries, Tunisia has seen a massive tourist boom. In parallel with the development of holiday resorts, a number of marinas have been built, usually as part of a large tourist complex.

THE BEST-KNOWN MARINA, Sidi Bou Said, lies in the Bay of Tunis, on the country's northern tip and close to the capital Tunis and its international airport. Tucked under tree-lined bluffs, this attractive marina is practically inside the ancient port of Carthage and close by are the remains of that once grand city. All other marinas are on Tunisia's east coast, including Yasmine Hammamet, close to a large tourist resort and within easy reach of the capital. Fine sandy beaches stretch along the gulf here, and there is much to see and do in bustling Hammamet – its old town, or medina, surrounded by ramparts. Further south are the attractive marinas El Kantaoui and Cap Monastir, both set in the midst of tourist developments. Monastir's marina lies in the shade of the fortified

PORT EL KANTAOUI is a purpose-built resort, with a marina and a mini market selling reasonably priced souvenirs.

city's 9th-century walls and a well-preserved Ribat tower stands tall above the much more recent hotels, coffee houses and boutiques. Besides these purpose-built marinas, docking facilities for visiting boats exist in a number of ports and fishing harbours. As Tunisia is not part of the European Union and the number of non-EU countries in the Mediterranean has shrunk, Tunisia is now a preferred winter destination for non-EU flagged boats.

Several civilizations have left their permanent mark on the Tunisian landscape: Phoenician, Roman, Byzantine, Ottoman, Arab, French. It is this rich diversity that makes this country, whose historic heritage is not widely known, such an interesting place to visit.

No less attractive are the medieval quarters of the ancient walled Arab towns with their vibrant markets and narrow alleyways. Shopping in the souks within the cities' medinas provides a taste of the exotic – spices, silver Berber jewellery, intricately decorated brass and copperware, leatherwork, carpets and embroidered wall-hangings can be bargained for – and, in addition, most towns and villages also hold a weekly morning market where anything and everything may be put up for sale.

THE GULF OF HAMMAMET harbours miles of fine sandy beaches, and is known as the "Tunisian Saint-Tropez".

MONASTIR typifies the country's dramatic and very practical juxtaposition of ancient and modern architecture.

THE AZORES: conifer forests and waterfalls in the mountains give way to sweet, green lowland pasture and pretty villages by sheltered bays.

Western Europe and the North Atlantic Islands

Stepping stones to the New World, the islands in the North Atlantic have for centuries tempted Europeans to voyage westward. Europe's shores from the southern tip of Spain to Spitsbergen face the setting sun, irresistible temptation for seafarers of all nations in every century: Vikings, Portuguese explorers, English pirates. Now yachtsmen in their hundreds seek each year to prove themselves on the high Atlantic seas, in search of paradise. Yet they leave behind rich cruising grounds, as varied and exotic as any. Nowhere will the yachtsman find greater cultural or culinary diversity. From the sluicing tides of the Faroes to the rock-strewn coasts of Brittany, Western Europe's waters also offer the sternest test in seamanship. Sail here and you can sail anywhere.

EUROPEANS are never far from the sea, whether it be the wild North Sea, the magical Baltic or the mighty Atlantic.

CHANNEL COAST

STRANGFORD LOUGH

WEST COAST

FAROE ISLANDS

MARITIME NATIONS

The countries on the western fringe of the European continent have been closely linked with the ocean from time immemorial. From the daring Vikings to the intrepid navigators of the Age of Exploration, sailors from these shores have reached the furthest points of the globe, a proud maritime tradition that continues even today. The North Atlantic islands have served throughout history as stepping stones for new discoveries and the routes of former explorers have been taken up by modern sailors.

A popular voyage undertaken by many European sailors is a circumnavigation of the North Atlantic that follows closely the route pioneered by Christopher Columbus, who was the first to realize that there was a definite pattern to Atlantic weather and took full advantage of this during his four transatlantic voyages. With good planning, the prevailing weather conditions make such an Atlantic circuit relatively easy to accomplish. Yachts setting off from Northern Europe normally sail south to Madeira and the Canaries with the Portuguese trades of summer, west to the Caribbean with the north-east trade winds and back east to

The southern islands of Bermuda, the Canaries, the Azores and Madeira are visited every year by hundreds of yachts on their way across the Atlantic.

the Azores with the westerlies of higher latitudes. These weather patterns are due to a permanent feature of the North Atlantic, an area of high atmospheric pressure situated near the Azores, whose name it bears. Because of its influence on sailing conditions over such a large area, the position of the Azores High must be watched carefully when planning an Atlantic crossing in either direction.

The sailing season in the North Atlantic extends from early spring to late summer, and while most European sailors planning a longer voyage continue to prefer the benign sailing conditions of lower latitudes, high-latitude voyages are gaining in popularity with Iceland and Spitsbergen attracting increasing numbers of yachts.

The southern islands benefit from a longer season and, being on the transatlantic circuit, have certain peak periods. Madeira and the Canaries are busiest between September and November when yachts prepare to cross to the Caribbean, while Bermuda and the Azores are busiest in May and June, when the movement is in the opposite direction.

NORWAY

SWEDEN

BRITTANY

MADEIRA

THE AREA includes the "Jurassic Coast": 95 miles (153km) of stunning coastline recording 185 million years of history.

England/Wales
The Channel Coast to the Menai Straits

CHART 2675, 2565, 2669, 1464
BEST FOR CRUISING April – October
AVERAGE TEMPERATURE 18.3°C 65°F
PREVAILING WIND W
TIME ZONE GMT + 0
LANGUAGE English/Welsh

CURRENCY Sterling (£)
NAVIGATIONAL DIFFICULTY
FAMILY FRIENDLY
DIVING/SNORKELLING
SHORE-SIDE EATING
SIGHTSEEING

The tide-swept English Channel has been Britain's bulwark in perpetuity. Since William of Normandy's successful challenge in 1066, it has seen off many military adventurers, including King Philip of Spain, Napoleon Bonaparte and, more recently, Adolf Hitler. You don't need much imagination to discern the ghostly galleons of the invincible Armada running ponderously to their doom past moonlit Plymouth.

ST IVES

I FIRST CROSSED this living stretch of water as master of my own 22-footer (6.7m) in 1971, little realizing that 30 years later I would become the third editor since 1935 of its most comprehensive pilot book.

The Channel winds are as important as they are anywhere else, but the tide is king. Ignore the direction of the stream and you may as well stay at home. Tidal ranges vary widely and in some areas rank among the highest in the world, rendering many lovely harbours inaccessibly dry at low water – no problem for the indigenous fishing craft designed for them, but a serious issue for a deep-keeled yacht. Prediction is the secret, and any of today's chart plotters worthy of the name can deliver a graph of tidal heights from now until the crack of doom, while streams can be read off from the almanacs all charter boats are obliged to carry.

The upside of tides is that with a favourable stream, a 5-knot yacht can run off 40 or even 50 miles (64–80.5km) in the right six hours of the cycle. You just have go with the flow, that's all. Follow me; I'll take you on a quick tour, starting with Scilly, a tiny archipelago forming a loose, seven-mile (11.2km) ring around a

TRESCO

TIDES

RANGES IN HEIGHT of tide run up to 40 feet (12m), rendering many lovely harbours, such as this one in Cornwall, dry at low water – a serious issue for deep-keeled yachts.

Befriend the wind and sail with the tide on a magnificent magic carpet ride in the wake of legendary sea battles. A heady mix of ancient myth and historic culture clashes in perfect pastoral paradise found. Even in the rain.

PORT ISAAC in Cornwall is an Area of Outstanding Natural Beauty with endless lovely walks along the coast, enjoying sensational scenery.

CLEAR WATER among the Scilly Isles where the colour, if not the temperature, of the sea is comparable to the Bahamas.

sound that varies in depth between readily navigable and dry for much of the time. Three thousand years ago, the region was virtually one big island, but the melt water from the death of the last Ice Age coupled with a local sinking of the land raised sea level sufficiently to drown the central area. Villages lie down there: some show their bones at low water, others are forever the kingdom of fish and mermaid. Today, the islands represent a halfway house between the Atlantic and the solid ground of Cornwall, 25 miles (40km) to the eastward. Their people take the sea for granted. Salt water is everything, and the life of the community is swayed by its ebb and flow.

The first time I anchored in New Grimsby Sound between the isles of Tresco and Bryher, I realized that this place was like no other. The water seemed miraculously calm after the ocean surging outside. The heather blazed bright purple on the sunlit hillside, the rapidly exposing sands were nearly white, and the perfume of a thousand flowers wafted down the breeze. The only person in evidence was a lobsterman who waved as though pleased to see me, and the colour of the sea was more like the Bahamas than anything else.

Working across from Tresco to the main island of St Mary's you cross half-tide shallows as they cover on the rising flood. The bottom will be in disturbingly clear view all the way, but as depths begin to increase you might get lucky and fall in with a gig. They are 30ft (9.1m) clinker-built boats, pulled by six people, each handling a 15ft (4.6m) oar. Their shapely lines and narrow beam belie their seaworthiness, and to see one ranting through a wind-whipped Atlantic swell under the combined muscle power of six stalwart Scillonians is an unsettlingly primitive thrill. Once,

GIGS were the lifeblood of the Scilly islands, pilot boats to the transatlantic trade.

A STONE MAZE at Bryher – a peaceful little island with the smallest of all the communities found on the Isles of Scilly.

ST MARY'S is the most populated of the Scilly Isles and the main administrative centre of the islands.

gigs carried pilots, contraband and mothers coming to St Mary's to give birth. They did duty saving life and carting salvage from wrecks on the outer rocks. Today, they race.

The Isles of Scilly feel so remote that they seem out of place in the English Channel. Magic and nature rule and, if you get lucky late on in the Mermaid Tavern, you might meet a girl who'll tell how her grandmother encouraged her to lean over the side of their boat to listen for the church bells chiming below the waves.

"Combe and Tor, green meadow and lane" – and a coastline that will stir your heart just as it did Sir Francis Drake's. South Devon and Cornwall specialize in deep-water harbours flanked by steep hillsides studded with quaint towns and villages. Passage making between the ports is a leisurely affair with short

distances and stunning cliff scenery. When you arrive, life ashore can dish up some of Britain's best pubs and restaurants. One word of advice: avoid July and August. When school's out, finding a berth can be a bit of a bunfight, the eateries are crowded and you'll be involved in more than your share of rafting up.

Like the West Country, the Solent is best visited when everyone else has gone home. Sheltered by 20 miles (32km) of the Isle of Wight, it enjoys some of the best yachting in southern Britain. It encompasses several delightful harbours and one or two anchorages that, but for the summer crowds, would have everything the nature-lover desires. Only 80 miles (129km) or so from London, it's a popular choice for keeping a boat or running a sailing school.

The answer is to come in early spring or late autumn. I prefer winter, because the cover of the Island keeps the waters free of swell and the temperature rarely falls far below freezing, so with

DARTMOUTH is a famous yachting centre with a long maritime history. The harbour is deep, sheltered and easy to enter.

a decent cabin heater, you can enjoy some of the best short-range cruising in the world. Whenever you come, you'll have a whale of a time working the mighty tides as they rip to and fro at up to five knots, helping the wise while confounding the efforts of the foolish.

When William of Normandy took over the management of England in 1066, relinquishing his hold over his properties in Normandy wasn't part of his game plan. The jewels of these, some might say, are what the French still call Les Îles Anglo-Normandes. Nestling in the bight between the Cotentin Peninsula and the north coast of Brittany, the Channel Islands are geographically a part of France, yet as the old Norman dependencies slowly leached back to their origins in the Middle Ages, somehow the islands never did.

THE CORNISH COAST (above) can be treacherous in the winter and innumerable ships have come to grief on the rocks.

PRAWLE POINT (right) is the southernmost point of Devon. The cottages were built in c.1900 to service the look-out station.

Today, a feast of interest awaits the passing sailor. There will be some very fast passages to look forward to as you career down the Race of Alderney at 14 knots over the ground in a six-knot sailing boat. Now there's a thrilling day out!

Arriving in Jersey or Guernsey, you might have to wait three hours for the 30ft (9m) tide to rise over the marina sill, but the islands are well worth hanging around for. On a summer afternoon, the wide, flat islands swim on a blue ocean with France glimmering just above the horizon and crusty old Britain nowhere to be seen! Ashore, French names abound, and cuisine. The cheap duty-free booze of yesterday has lost its lustre now that French prices are available via the EU, but the fact remains that if you pop into The Divers pub in Alderney and wait there long enough with a pint in your hand, every sailor you ever knew

GUERNSEY, where sailing is very much a way of life. And there is no better way to take in the island's landscape.

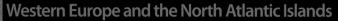
will sooner or later heave in through the doors and join you, each with a taller tale to tell.

Finally, dipping a toe, as it were, into Welsh waters, look no further than the Menai Straits (although a week would be insufficient to explore Milford Haven's many nooks and crannies.) In *Under Milk Wood*, Dylan Thomas put words into the mouth of the Reverend Eli Jenkins concerning the mountains of North Wales. He calls them, "mountains where King Arthur Dreams", and glories in the names. "Cader Idrys, tempest-torn, Penmaenmawr defiant", Carnedd Llewelyn, Moel yr Wyddfa and Plinlimmon also have their "mention". When you sail past the outpost lighthouse of Trwyn Du and swing southwest with Anglesey to starboard and Snowdonia rising like a great celtic wall to port, you'd be dead of soul if the back of your neck didn't tingle.

If you want to understand Wales and what it means to be Welsh, come here, run the ripping tides among the rocks of the "Swellies", moor awhile under the walls of Conwy Castle, built by the English to suppress the Welsh. Eight centuries later it's a noble monument to failure as the old language gains in strength with every passing year. Take a walk into the hills and see the worked-out slate mines whose produce was carried away to roof the world by tiny Welsh schooners, and know that this is a place you'd have been the poorer to miss.

CONWY CASTLE (above) was a key part of King Edward I's plan to surround Wales in "an iron ring of castles" to subdue the rebellious population.

SOUTH STACK, Anglesey (above right), is great for birdwatching. There are puffins in summer, plus razorbills, guillemots and other cliff-dwelling seabirds.

SNOWDONIA NATIONAL PARK in Anglesey (left) covers 823 square miles (1,325 km²) of the most beautiful and unspoilt countryside in North Wales.

PORTMEIRION (right) includes 70 acres (30ha) of sub-tropical woodlands as well as the village itself on the southern side of its own private peninsula in Snowdonia.

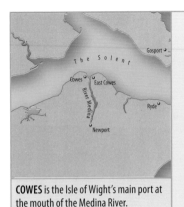

COWES is the Isle of Wight's main port at the mouth of the Medina River.

England
Cowes

CHART 2793
BEST FOR CRUISING Year-round
AVERAGE TEMPERATURE 17°C 63°F (summer)
14°C 57°F (winter)
PREVAILING WIND SW
TIME ZONE GMT + 0
LANGUAGE English

CURRENCY Sterling (£)
NAVIGATIONAL DIFFICULTY ✪ ✪ ✪ ✪
FAMILY FRIENDLY ♟ ♟ ♟
DIVING/SNORKELLING
SHORE-SIDE EATING 🍴 🍴 🍴
SIGHTSEEING 🏰 🏰 🏰

Cowes is unarguably Britain's principal sailing centre, a town whose waterfront yards have launched and serviced countless craft from men o' war to the finest ocean racers. This historic haven, sheltered from the prevailing westerlies, lines both sides of the Medina, a yacht-packed river almost bisecting the Isle of Wight

FROM THE HUGE naval base of Portsmouth to the east as far as unspoilt little Keyhaven in the west, the Solent is akin to an inland sea, the Needles Channel a gateway to the adventurous waters of the West Country, the Isles of Scilly and departure point for Channel crossings to France and the Channel Islands.

The Solent lies between the Hampshire coast to the north and Wight, its sheltered waters, intriguing harbours and safe marinas perfect for most types of sailing: top-level racing, cruising, chartering – capital waters on which to learn and practise the skills of seamanship and navigation.

For the less experienced the combination of speeding ferries, hot racing fleets, vast container ships and throbbing motor yachts can be unnerving, albeit highly instructive. Add complex tidal streams, significant tidal ranges – at Cowes the mean spring range is 12ft (3.6m) – myriad buoys, marks and lights, and the picture becomes more daunting still. Sail here, they say, and you can sail anywhere.

The peak season is definitely not for the faint hearted, but for racing yachtsmen, Cowes Week in the first week of August is unmissable, one of the largest, longest-running and most prestigious sailing regattas in the world. Around 8,500 sailors race every day, thousands more – afloat and ashore – flock to Cowes to watch and enjoy the racing and social scenes.

Throughout the year, Cowes offers first-rate facilities for the sailor and non-sailor alike, with plenty of pubs, bars, restaurants and cafés as well as chandleries, sailmakers and every kind of yacht repair service. During "The Week", Cowes Yacht Haven, East Cowes Marina and Shepards Wharf also lay on entertainment as well as berthing (but book early as competition is fierce). The week, carnival-like and cosmopolitan ashore, and cut-throat afloat, culminates in a magnificent fireworks display on the last Friday.

KEELBOAT RACING ON THE SOLENT

THE NEEDLES are a group of extraordinary white rock formations on the west coast of the Isle of Wight.

OSBORNE HOUSE, EAST COWES

THE BIRTHPLACE of yachting and home to the Royal Yacht Squadron, Cowes is the epicentre of the sailing playground they call the Solent.

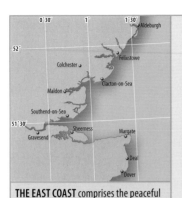

THE EAST COAST comprises the peaceful counties of Norfolk, Suffolk and Essex.

England
East Coast

CHART SC5606-7 (Folio charts); Imray 2000 & 2100 chart packs

BEST FOR CRUISING June – September

AVERAGE TEMPERATURE 18°C 64°F

PREVAILING WIND SW (can also be quite brisk easterlies from the North Sea)

TIME ZONE GMT + 0

LANGUAGE English

CURRENCY Sterling (£)

NAVIGATIONAL DIFFICULTY

FAMILY FRIENDLY

DIVING/SNORKELLING

SHORE-SIDE EATING

SIGHTSEEING

Mention sailing on the east coast of England and most people will warn of mud, shallow water and hidden sandbanks, but these, together with all sorts of waders, ducks, geese, low-lying shores and vast skies are the very things that get under the skin of East Coast sailors.

A SNUG ANCHORAGE between growing banks of gleaming mud with oysters squirting water to startle and scare off predatory oystercatchers, while terns drop from the sky to grab their supper from the creek and grey herons stalk and white little egrets step daintily along the tide line, stabbing occasionally with their sharp beaks to catch theirs; the sun lowering and turning the mud to gold, silhouetting a bushy-topped withy against the darkening sky; the gurgling chuckle of the running tide past the hull; these are the rewards for a day's sailing and careful navigation amid those off-lying, hidden sandbanks. Yes, they are cruel if you run onto them and the weather turns foul before you can get off again, but with modern navaids, a good

pilot and a careful eye on the buoys, these lurking snares can be avoided. They can also help by providing a wonderful lee for you if you need to kedge and wait out a foul tide.

You'll have a far more interesting time when cruising the East Coast if you have a boat with only a modest draught. Then the marinas will be available to you, but so too will those remote creeks, shortcut swatchways and nights with just the haunting calls of curlews beneath a panoply of stars.

Each of the many rivers has its own special appeal, whether it's the broad expanse of the Blackwater or the widely admired rolling, wooded shores of the Orwell, which runs inland from the busy container port of Harwich. Take extra care crossing the shifting bars of the rivers Deben and Ore, but do so and you'll find yourself in a magical world surrounded by history, such as the Viking ship buried at Sutton Hoo opposite the marina at Woodbridge, or the Norman Keep at Orford. For an atmosphere that gets no saltier, visit the Butt and Oyster pub on the hard at Pin Mill on the Orwell. Sup your pint, eat your meal and watch all kinds of craft enjoying the beautiful river. Take care though, it creeps into your soul.

SEALS AT MABLETHORPE

BURNHAM MARSHES

ORFORD NORMAN KEEP, SUFFOLK

FURTHER NORTH along the east coast lie the Norfolk Broads, famed as the setting for part of Arthur Ransome's *Swallows and Amazons* series.

CORK'S RUGGED coastline is strewn with great bays, coves, and rocky headlands.

South-west Ireland
Cork to Bantry Bay

CHART 2184, 2129, 3725, 2092, 1777
BEST FOR CRUISING June – September
AVERAGE TEMPERATURE 18ºC 64ºF
PREVAILING WIND SW
TIME ZONE GMT + 0
LANGUAGE English and Irish Gaelic
CURRENCY Euro (€)

NAVIGATIONAL DIFFICULTY
FAMILY FRIENDLY
DIVING/SNORKELLING
SHORE-SIDE EATING
SIGHTSEEING

If straight coastlines are boring, then few will be as stimulating as west Cork. It is a similarly "drowned" coastline as those of north-west Spain, Brittany, south-west England and Scotland's west coast, so the sea has slashed deep cuts into the land to create endless bays and coves.

PERHAPS THIS IS WHY the area is so popular with French yachts, often flying their distinctive black-and-white Breton flags. Rather like Brittany, the coast is littered with rocks, not all marked or named, so pilotage skills will be tested.

This is a proper ocean seaboard and the land, vegetation and buildings have that tough, hunkered down feel about them. When it's beautiful, this Gulf Stream coast is superb; when it turns nasty the swell has a full-width-of-the-Atlantic send, visibility drops, fog is not uncommon and the serrated rocks created by uptilted strata are a vicious menace.

This is ground-tackle, fender-board, tender and jerry-can cruising. Pontoon berths are few and far between with Crosshaven, Royal Cork Yacht Club and West Ferry in Cork Harbour being the exception with three marinas in one location and Kinsale boasting a further two. These are also the two main yacht charter pick-ups in the area, both easily reached from Cork airport.

The Royal Cork at Crosshaven is one of the world's oldest yacht clubs. Founded in 1720, the locals insist it is THE oldest, and though the premises come up a little short as something to look at, this is a most welcoming club to be in. It also hosts the biannual Cork Week, which carries a five-star recommendation for sport afloat and ashore.

RUGGED COAST

BLARNEY CASTLE

KINSALE is well worth exploring by bicycle, on horseback or on foot. Walk the high road to Summercove for spectacular views of the town.

There are visitors' pontoons in Baltimore, Courtmacsherry and Skibbereen but this is about it. The pace of change is quickening, however, with development and the second-home market altering some parts of the coast. Who would have thought the Old Head of Kinsale (a dramatic, steep-sided promontory) would now sport one of the world's toughest golf courses?

You cruise this coast on its terms. The pleasures are simpler and purer, such as the greens receding in intensity and tone as headlands and hills dissolve into the distance; or a bowl of broth and glass of stout in Bushe's Bar in Baltimore, each a meal in itself.

This is an area steeped in history, not just the Anglo-Irish variety. Cork was the *Titanic*'s last port of call and the doomed *Lusitania*'s intended destination. The potato famine ravaged the population in the 1840s. And in 1631, pirates from Africa raided Baltimore and carried away the residents as slaves. There are buildings and ruins from Neolithic times onwards to reward a good walk ashore or tender-borne exploration.

I sailed these waters several times without actually stepping ashore thanks to the presence of the Fastnet Rock, which stands sentinel off the coast, and the biannual race around it. To go that far only to turn around and head for home…

For visitors, Cork is often the obvious point of arrival and departure, a huge natural harbour somewhat besmirched by an

COBH HARBOUR is where the Titanic made its last port of call, and where Sir Walter Raleigh first imported tobacco.

oil terminal and chemical plants, but fascinating with the old harbour town of Cobh to visit, and even the city of Cork itself.

Further west, Kinsale is the last major town before settlements become smaller and more beguiling until you turn the corner at Mizen Head and enter Bantry Bay. Kinsale now has something of a "foodie" reputation with a good choice of restaurants, cafés and shops. For over 300 years Kinsale was a garrison town and port of consequence, leaving a legacy of Georgian and Victorian architecture. Desmond Castle, especially, is well worth a visit.

Along the way to Mizen Head are many hidden gems, one of which you can only reach by dinghy. This is Lough Hyne, accessible from yachts anchored in Barloge Creek, on the top

COLOURFUL houses characterize the towns and villages of Cork. Kinsale is a treasure trove of Georgian architecture.

of the tide. It is a virtually landlocked, low-salinity lake of quite outstanding beauty.

Beyond Baltimore are both the evocatively named Roaring Water Bay and Cape Clear, which is an island. Sparsely populated and thin on buildings, its attraction is Danny Mike's, a pub that sells several varieties of stout plus the odd bag of sugar, box of Corn Flakes and packet of Persil. Time doesn't quite stand still, but it sure drags its feet here.

Roaring Water Bay is far from the only appealingly named place. Glandore's splendid little harbour has three rocks narrowing its approach called The Dangers. Parallel to Roaring Water is Long Island Bay, essentially the same stretch of water but with a dot-dash-dot string of small islands sub-dividing it. Here you'll find Schull and Crookhaven, both well worth a visit.

North and west from Mizen Head, the scale of the landscape increases. The bays, Bantry Bay and Kenmare River, get bigger and the hills aspire to be mountains. It is a whole new cruising ground.

Everywhere, however, it seems there is a "can't do enough for you" welcome.

GLANDORE is a very popular port of call for the yachting and boating fraternity, and has some excellent restaurants.

RICH FARMLANDS, river valleys, and wild sandstone hills form a magnificent coastline carved by the Atlantic.

STRANGFORD LOUGH is an 18 mile by 3 mile (29 x 5km) arm of water.

Northern Ireland
Strangford Lough

CHART 2156, 2159
BEST FOR CRUISING May – September
AVERAGE TEMPERATURE 15ºC 59ºF
PREVAILING WIND SW
TIME ZONE GMT + 0
LANGUAGE English
CURRENCY Sterling (£)

NAVIGATIONAL DIFFICULTY
FAMILY FRIENDLY
DIVING/SNORKELLING
SHORE-SIDE EATING
SIGHTSEEING

Studded with 120 islands and shoals (pladdies), Strangford Lough has some of the most abundant wild- and sealife in Europe. Its palette ranges from vibrant green to the anthracite of wet granite with every mottled shade in between.

THE ISLANDS are distinctive tapered lozenges (Drumlins), pushed up and smoothed by the advance of an ice cap two million years ago. Global cooling we would call it now. 12,000 years ago, the ice melted and submerged what was left, leaving an exquisite sailing ground, but one with a nasty side to its character: the Narrows.

This is the Lough's umbilical cord to the Irish Sea, a mere 984ft (300m) wide, 197ft (60m) deep and a couple of miles long. Through it, some 12,360 million ft^3 (350 million m^3) of water is ingested and ejected on each tide. The bar at the seaward end and the collision of waters is enough to earn respect and demand careful assessment of the times just either side of slack water. The white water is visible from space.

For added measure there is always a whirlpool, the most notable being the Routen Wheel. As teenagers, sailing dinghies through the Narrows and learning to use the ribbon of counter-currents and eddies running along either jagged shore, we were fed stories of the Routen Wheel's boat-swallowing menace. Rather like Corryvreckan between the Scottish islands of Jura and Scarba, it is the stuff of legend more than fact. It is also impressive and to be treated with the utmost respect.

The Vikings, it seems, gave Strangford its name for all these reasons – Strong Fjord – and not so much has changed since their longships ventured down Scotland's West Coast to Ireland's eastern flank.

It is only recently that lights, all two of them, have been established inside the Lough. In 2008, there was a further upgrade of navigation marks. Night sailing is not care-free but it is rewarding. There is only one tiny marina at Portaferry on the north side of the Narrows but there are many places to anchor.

For locally based boats Strangford Lough is all the sailing you'll ever need in a lifetime. But sailors aren't like that. The Isle of Man and Scotland are within easy reach, which also means that yachts passing through the North Channel can come and discover this extraordinary place for themselves.

MOORINGS

GREY ABBEY

HISTORIC SITES

TUCKED behind the Drumlins' humps are market towns, ancient monastic sites, castles, cairns and quiet bays. Mount Stewart is a protected 18th-century house with beautiful walled gardens.

THE LOUGH supports a staggering diversity of wildlife from grey seals, porpoises and otters to tens of thousands of birds.

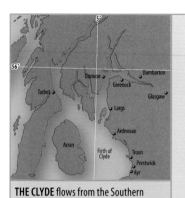

THE CLYDE flows from the Southern Uplands to the Firth of Clyde.

Scotland
The Clyde

CHART 2126, 2131
BEST FOR CRUISING May – September
AVERAGE TEMPERATURE 15ºC 59ºF
PREVAILING WIND SW
TIME ZONE GMT + 0
LANGUAGE English
CURRENCY Sterling (£)

NAVIGATIONAL DIFFICULTY ✸ ✸
FAMILY FRIENDLY 🍹 🍹 🍹 🍹
DIVING/SNORKELLING 🤿
SHORE-SIDE EATING 🍽 🍽
SIGHTSEEING 🏰 🏰 🏰

The Firth of Clyde is Scotland in miniature, bounded by the tendril-like Mull of Kintyre to the west and the low-lying mainland to the east. Green hills are deeply indented by sea lochs, and dark waters are occasionally broken by the silhouettes of submarine conning towers from the Royal Marines' base on Gareloch.

THERE ARE once-again-fashionable resort towns such as Rothesay on the Isle of Bute with its quite magnificent marble pierhead WCs. If civic pride extends to a "cathedral to convenience" then you know this is a town developed with heart, soul and a conscience.

Of remote anchorages, there are plenty, such as Lamlash Bay on Arran, or Loch Ranza on the north-western corner of the island. Protected in the sense that the hills that surround it can also generate downdraughts and quite severe squalls. Anchoring is done with care and with decent ground tackle.

So deep does the sea penetrate the land as you go west from Glasgow that even nearby places as the crow flies,

become quite remote. Movement by boat is often quicker and vastly more satisfying. North of Bute are the Kyles, the two ribbons of water that form a chevron above the island. At their intersection are the Burnt Isles, Scottish sailing in microcosm, with narrow channels, plentiful shoals and islands and tide to consider. Diligent pilotage is rewarded by a beautiful anchorage or, at the very least, a rewarding safe passage.

This is if you are in a hurry, which would be a shame. There is enough cruising in the Clyde to satisfy repeated visits. To the east, there are the marinas founded in old gravel workings (Inverkip) or industrial ports (Troon). They are rarer further west, so good-sized fenders are needed, though Campbeltown and Tarbert now offer visiting pontoon berths.

There is good hill walking, golf galore from the links around Troon to Tarbert's little nine-holer with its honesty-box for green fees, and enough castles, ruins and gardens to add real variety to a cruise.

Should you wish to leave the Clyde, you'll pass "Paddy's Milestone" Ailsa Craig on the way towards the North Channel and Irish Sea, or join the Crinan Canal at Ardrishaig on Long Fyne, which saves the 80-mile (129km) passage around the Mull of Kintyre for those heading west.

CLYDE PUFFER

EASTERN SHORE OF BUTE

SPECTACULAR VIEWS

TARBERT Castle sits on a hill in Tarbert overlooking the bay and offers a stunning view of the harbour below. A path leads to a point where there are great views looking east over Loch Fyne.

Slip in and out of countless sea lochs, slide around the islands, sally through the Kyles, sidle into west-coast harbour towns.

THERE'S GOLF GALORE from Troon to Tarbert, hills to hike, or pick up a mooring and dine out on Loch Fyne oysters.

THE HEBRIDES is a group of more than 500 islands in the Atlantic Ocean off the western coast of Scotland.

Scotland
West Coast and Hebrides

CHART 2474, 1785, 1794, 1757, 1795, 1796, 2208, 2207, 2724

BEST FOR CRUISING May – September

AVERAGE TEMPERATURE 15ºC 59ºF

PREVAILING WIND W to SW

TIME ZONE GMT + 0

LANGUAGE English

CURRENCY Sterling (£)

NAVIGATIONAL DIFFICULTY

FAMILY FRIENDLY

DIVING/SNORKELLING

SHORE-SIDE EATING

SIGHTSEEING

"The best cruising waters on the planet, when the weather serves," enthuse West Coast aficionados. Only Antarctica, the inlets of Chile, and the fjords of South Island New Zealand elicit the same knowing smile of pleasure. "This is the world's finest sailing. For heaven's sake don't let the secret out."

NOSING INTO THE FAR recesses of a sea loch or scattering rainbows in a brisk thrash between islands, Hebridean sailing can be challenging, but never dull. Navigation is more often intriguing, rather than tricky. From a yachtsman's guide to the Isle of Mull comes this classic example of West Coast pilotage: "From southeast steer with Lagavulin [whisky] distillery bearing 315 degrees… so that only the letters ULIN are visible on the wall to the right of the castle."

Though often it can be wild, protection lies never more than an hour away. Whether a pub and a warming dram awaits, let alone a village shop, is another matter; self-sufficiency is the name of the game.

Beyond mainland Britain's most westerly point, Ardnamurchan, facilities become even fewer and farther between. But those who venture past Cape Wrath can look forward to a warm welcome in Orkney and Shetland whose investment in marinas and yachting infrastructure have made them popular cruising destinations for adventurous yachtsmen from all over Europe.

May to September are the best months, when oilskins and thick sweaters will most likely be the rig of the day, even in high summer when darkness never quite falls. Daunting under

WILD LANDSCAPE

CALLANISH, LEWIS

PORTREE

TOBERMORY is the main village on the island of Mull and is a must-see destination on any trip to the West Coast.

lowering skies in a rising gale, the colours of sea and sky, heather and machair, sand and rock enrich the spirit when caught by a shaft of sunlight.

Fortunately it will be many years before the "Harbour Full" sign appears in Portree, Tobermory, Tarbert…let alone that enchanting little anchorage on the west side of South Rona – Acarseid Mor, marked only by a white arrow on an adjacent rock. There we anchored a sturdy old wooden cutter in clear water on a blazing day in June and, bottle of Famous Grouse in hand, wandered to the high point above the anchorage, as the setting sun turned the surrounding rocks rose-pink.

Scavaig, a sea loch on Skye, is a typical example of the West's dual personality, described in the *Sailing Companion to the West Coast* as "one of the darkest frowns on the coast face of Skye", where at midnight, we sat on deck, and listened to the sound of a waterfall tumbling down from the crags. That apart, all was still.

Cruising the waters is always weather dependent. The choices are huge: through the dog-legged Sound of Harris bound for Taransay, Loch Roagh or remote St Kilda; alongside the fishing boats in Stornoway or anchored off Ullapool; snugged up on Canna – the best anchorage in the Small Isles – or tucked behind

LERWICK HARBOUR is the principal port for the Shetland Isles and a major fishing port. At the crossroads of the North Sea and the North-east Atlantic, it is also the most northerly commercial port in Great Britain.

BEAUTIFUL BEACHES and magnificent bays abound on the Island of Mull, from Calgary and Kilninian in the north to Loch Buie and Carsaig in the south. Bird life includes sea eagles, golden eagles, divers, merlins, peregrines and hen harriers.

a rock in a pool between two tiny Outer Hebridean islands, reachable only at high water with seals alone for company.

Corryvreckan, the Grey Dogs Channel, Cuan Sound, Iona, Staffa, little Muck and mighty Rum have strong resonances in legend and literature – the Torran Rocks, for example, on which Robert Louis Stevenson's hero David Balfour in *Kidnapped* was wrecked. Tinker's Hole is a classic Highland anchorage, protected from all but the worst the westerlies can fling. Inevitably, a rock drying 7.5ft (2.3m) lies dead centre of the best approach. RLS came here while his uncle Alan the "lighthouse Stevenson" was building Dubh Artach, and immortalized it as Fiddler's Hole.

On one occasion, skirting the basalt cliffs of Staffa, where a boatload of tourists were picking their way around the edge of Fingal's Cave, we made for Muck, the

smallest of the Small Isles. It lies about five miles (8km) north of Ardnamurchan point, its name from the Gaelic *muc-mahara*, sea pig, or porpoise. During the Napoleonic wars the islanders made potash for gunpowder from the kelp that carpeted the shore before they were all cleared in the 19th century to make way for Lord and Lady Muck's sheep. Today it is as if time stopped in the 1950s.

From little Muck's highest point, 451ft (137m) above sea level, its heather moors and green fields, its surrounding islands and the mountains of the distant north make a dramatic panorama. The summer air is warm and soft. That day, in the bay below me a trawler circled. I probably heard a skylark. Over to the north the island of Eigg rose above the sea, and beyond – its twin peaks Hallival and Askival rising to a Muck-humbling 2,000ft (610m) – brooding Rum. There, in the eccentric Edwardian castle of Kinloch, long before the world at large had such things, Lord and Lady George Bullough enjoyed hot sea-water baths, air conditioning to clear the billiard room of cigar smoke, an orchestrion (a kind of mechanical juke box), and a private telegraph linking his lordship to the racing at Newmarket.

From the heights of Muck I descended through the fields of wildflowers, stopping to chat with a family, baling hay. "It

ORKNEY is a group of islands situated off the north-east tip of Scotland with rugged cliffs and pinnacles rising out of the sea.

certainly is a lovely place," I said. "Yes, on a day like this," they laughed. Perhaps not in a south-westerly winter gale, their eyes told me. Which seemed to sum up cruising along the West Coast of Scotland.

THE AUGUSTINE NUNNERY on the Isle of Iona is one of the best-preserved medieval nunneries in Britain.

THE FAROES lie in the North Atlantic between Scotland, Iceland and Norway.

Denmark
The Faroe Islands

CHART 117

BEST FOR CRUISING June – August

AVERAGE TEMPERATURE 11ºC 52ºF

PREVAILING WIND W

TIME ZONE GMT + 1

LANGUAGE Faroese, English widely spoken, Nordic languages widely understood

CURRENCY Faroese Króne, Danish Krone (kr)

NAVIGATIONAL DIFFICULTY ✪ ✪ ✪ ✪ ✪

FAMILY FRIENDLY 👤 👤

DIVING/SNORKELLING 🤿

SHORE-SIDE EATING 🍴

SIGHTSEEING 🏰 🏰 🏰 🏰

Tall emerald-green witches' hats of islands anchored mid way between Cape Wrath and Iceland where unpredictable weather, fog and strong tidal currents pose a true challenge for small yachts. Midnight sun and awesome anchorages are the just rewards.

ONE GLANCE at the Faroes tidal atlas will scare you witless: no prim numerals, the power of the water bursting from the Skopunarfjørdur channel between Hestur and Sandoy, is indicated by angry dragon's fire, as the tide gathers strength in a headlong race from Scandinavia towards the Atlantic at the moon's starting gun.

When sailing in the lee of the islands' sea cliffs, you do so under sufferance. At the north tip of Viðoy, Cape Enniberg, they rise sheer to 2,476ft (754m), the highest vertical cliffs above sea in the world.

The puffins (the Faroese stuff them for souvenirs) will amuse you, the fulmars, which bank like Spitfires, will impress, but the wild grandeur of the place, emerald green against deep blue, and the fragile-looking, colourful villages – white, blue, ochre, black and yellow turf-roofed,

houses and clapboard churches – clinging to the steep, conical hillsides, will leave the deepest imprint.

Peopled by the pure-bred descendants of Hrafna-Flóki and Thrandur of Gata who arrived around 860, and named by the Vikings Færeyjar, or islands of sheep, the Faroes boast the smallest capital in the world, Tórshavn, a pretty city of some 18,000 souls, and surely the only one to have a turf-roofed parliament, or a sign on an (unguarded) door inscribed "Prime Minister's Office".

Strong tidal currents and lack of wind in summer explain the reliance on oar-power and horsepower. The quickest way upwind, the Vikings knew, was under oar. In Klaksvik the women's rowing team look pretty scary. Norse power?

Unsurprisingly the Faroese are insatiably curious about visiting boats. Tie up in one of the massively protected fishing harbours and people will gather. We often swapped fresh cod for lager with local fishermen (beware the price of alcohol).

On a dark sand beach on Vidavik, we built a huge fire and played skittles with storm-taken fishing floats until the tide sucked at our feet and we scrambled for the dinghy. On board, whisky in hands, we watched the flames sizzle and die. It was just past midnight; the sun was rising.

TURF ROOF

"WITCH'S HAT" HILLS

BIRD LIFE

ALONG with the 50,000 Faroese who inhabit the isles, fulmars, puffins, black guillemots, shearwaters, storm petrels and the rare red-throated divers (15 pairs), also cling to these rocky Atlantic outcrops.

THE FAROE Islanders are renowned sailors and fishermen. The fishing industry is an important source of income for the islands.

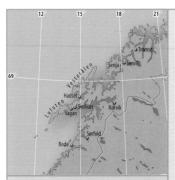

LOFOTEN is a mountainous archipelago to the north of the Arctic Circle. Principal islands include Austvågøy and Gimsøy.

Norway
North-west Norway and the Lofoten Islands

CHART (routeing charts) 4010, 2321, 2327

BEST FOR CRUISING May – July. The nearer to June 21 you get, the more midnight sun

AVERAGE TEMPERATURE 13ºC 55ºF, but with the Gulf Stream with 27ºC 80ºF by no means unusual

PREVAILING WIND Varies: generally W

TIME ZONE GMT + 1

LANGUAGE Norwegian, but English widely spoken

CURRENCY Norwegian Krone (NOK)

NAVIGATIONAL DIFFICULTY ✹ ✹ ✹ ✹

FAMILY FRIENDLY 🍹 🍹

DIVING/SNORKELLING 🤿

SHORE-SIDE EATING 🍽 🍽 🍽

SIGHTSEEING 🦷 🦷 🦷 🦷 🦷

I suppose I could justly claim to have seen some of the wonders of the maritime world. I've been astounded by the impossible islands of Thailand, I've swum from tropic beaches of dazzling coral sand and I've watched Pico rise from the Atlantic after weeks at sea, but, if it's scenery you want, for my money you should head straight to Norway. Turn your back resolutely on temperate latitudes and sail ever-northwards until finally you fetch Lofoten.

THE FIRST TIME I made it up there we took so long cruising from Bergen that two of my crew were obliged to downsize their personal ambitions. They settled instead for chilling a rare bottle of vodka in the depths of the Svartisen glacier as it grinds its way almost to sea level at around 68° north on the mainland shore. This goal was achieved after anchoring up exactly on the Arctic Circle (nominally 67° 30') by an island inhabited only by circling eagles and their in-house larder of woodland creatures. Here, we had our first experience of the weird magic of the midnight sun. It did not sink below the skyline again for three weeks. Night after night, it rolled with infinite patience around the horizon, its shadows thick and black, its light an endless red-gold so intense it hurt the eyes.

Pressing onwards through the Northlands, the mountain scenery had been growing systematically more spectacular, but it was all set to naught as we burst out of the coastal islands, reaching hard in a strong breeze up to the town of Bodø. Fifty

MIDNIGHT SUN

LOFOTEN MARINA

DRYING FISH

THE LOFOTEN TRADITION of preserving cod naturally by hanging it to dry in the wind has survived for hundreds of years.

LOFOTEN SEAS are teeming with life, including, from October until January, killer whales in pursuit of herring.

miles (80km) away across the wide Westfjord rose the impossible pinnacles of the Lofoten Wall. Even at this extreme range the "Misty Mountains" were perfectly distinct, but first we had to put our crew onto the train.

Strolling home at midnight from Bodø station, my wife and I fell in with a man claiming to be a tax inspector whose idea of a quiet snifter was to impose a litre of home-distilled firewater on the foreign visitors. The result was unspeakable, but cruising teaches us to take our pleasures where we find them. When we finally broke the hangover, a gentle breeze wafted us across the sparkling blue sea to Svolvaer, capital of the Lofoten fishery in the days of sail and oar. Here, in the winter twilight, men in open boats long-lined for cod four feet (1.2m) and more in length. The

BODØ (right) is known as the gateway to the Lofoten Islands and has a busy harbour, railway station and airport.

THE "MISTY MOUNTAINS" (below) of the Lofoten Islands provide some truly breathtaking scenery.

A STATUE of a fisherman's wife looking out to seas that can be treacherous.

storms could be beyond endurance, and the loss of life was shocking. The statue on the pier head of a fisherman's wife looking eternally seawards says it all.

The Norwegian coast is still rich in cod for the small-time line fisherman, and we caught our dinner every night under clear skies, stunned to silence by the vertical backdrop rising 3,200ft (1,000m) and more straight from the windy sea. The bays and inlets of the far north sheltered us each evening when we turned in for our nominal night's sleep until the breeze, which had powered us so far from the soft-edged coasts of home, veered round into a wild north-easter to drive us back to reality and the grey tides of the English Channel.

SVOLVAER was the capital of the Lofoten fishery in the days of sail and oar when men in open boats long-lined for cod four feet (1.2m) and more in length.

GOTHENBURG is Sweden's chief seaport and second-largest city.

Sweden
Gothenburg Archipelago

CHART 857, 873, 870, 869, 879; plus Swedish charts and Swedish Cruising Club guides

BEST FOR CRUISING June – September

AVERAGE TEMPERATURE 18ºC 64ºF

PREVAILING WIND W

TIME ZONE GMT + 1

LANGUAGE Swedish, English widely spoken

CURRENCY Swedish Krona (Kr)

NAVIGATIONAL DIFFICULTY

FAMILY FRIENDLY

DIVING/SNORKELLING

SHORE-SIDE EATING

SIGHTSEEING

Where fertile Bohuslän, Sweden's westernmost farming province, pulls on its seaboots and sou'wester, and braces itself to meet the Kattegatt the coastline is shattered by Ice Age and weather. Yet, so protected from the North Sea are the indentations of fjord and vik by a barrier of granite islands that you can be sailing in full oilskins outside the shelter of breaking skerries while children in little open boats are trolling for mackerel in spray jackets inside.

ONLY PARTS of Scotland's Western Isles come close to Gothenburg archipelago's perplexing complexity. The largest scale charts are spattered with dots as if the Great Designer, having drawn as many islands as he could in an afternoon, rested his writing arm and flicked his fountain pen, idly filling the gaps with rocks. There is no navigation as such here, only careful pilotage; one eye on the chart, the other ticking off the marks, buoys, lights, leading lines, cairns, rocks and transits.

This tale of wrecks and shoal waters should not in any way deter even the most timid of yachtsmen. The skerries that took their toll on fishing boats on snow-stormy nights, or when thick fog blotted out the high lights and leading marks, are a magnificent playground in summer for Swedish yachtsmen.

What you see (or rather what you don't see) is what you get. These waters are virtually tideless; that 1.3ft (0.4m) skerry over there (marked by a slight darkening) never quite dries, so you can forget pretty much everything in Tom Cunliffe's chapter on tidal heights. You touch, you stick, and skerries are hard and unforgiving foes.

LOBSTER FISHING

SKERRIES

Warm, skerry-scattered waters under clear blue northern skies offer an adrenaline fizz in spume and spray with shelter ever-present in the myriad passages.

BOHUSLÄN is a rugged maritime province of south-west Sweden with a wild, steep coast fringed by rocky, bare islands and skerries.

Every rock has been charted – well, maybe the Swedish Maritime Administration in Norrköping hasn't quite found them all – the folio charts are comprehensive, the Swedish Cruising Club's guides excellent

FISHING HUTS and boat houses are ubiquitous in Gullholmen. Nameboards of long-decayed trawlers hang above the white doors of red fishing huts.

GULLHOLMEN is the oldest fishing village in Sweden and one of the most picturesque. Reminders of its seafaring past delight you at every turn.

and chart plotters make it all easy. It becomes wholly pleasurable to tick off the stick buoys, line up for the next channel and wonder at the scenery. Even the evidence of man's work, the houses and lighthouses, seamarks and beacons, enhances the work of nature rather than detracts from it.

Swedish yachts, by and large, do not anchor, preferring to lie to the same iron rings that held their ancestors' boats. These natural harbours are packed in summer, pale Swedes on flat rocks basking like seals, children playing.

MARSTRAND is a principal summer resort and hosts Sweden's largest international sailing event: the Swedish Match Cup.

And it gets better the further north you sail. The rocks take on a pinkish tinge, the islands become more remote; the villages more picturesque, clinging to the bedrock like a collection of coloured seashells. In Gullholmen the streets are simply paths through the exposed granite. Reminders of its seafaring past delight you at every turn: the lace-curtained window, a carved seagull on the sill, a ship model, a bunch of flowers left by departing summer guests. The names of the houses reflect the connection with the sea and fishing. Nameboards of long-decayed trawlers hang above the doors of red fishing huts. For every house there's a boat shed; through the windows a glimpse of hemp and tarred rope, sails hanging in the rafters, a skein of fishing net, lobster pots, fluorescent marker buoys and children's lifejackets, neatly piled for the next time their owners are up from Gothenburg.

For these are quiet places in the winter, now the herring have gone, along with the summer visitors, and often battered by storms and isolated for days on end. The sea dictates life here now as it has always done. Mollösund was once the biggest fishing station on this coast. On a hill above the town stands a wooden figure, carved in the form of a stooped, grey-shrouded fishwife. She looks seaward, hoping to catch a glimpse of her man's boat, slipping between the skerries, smothered in foam, laden with herring, longing for home.

A coast with such strong associations, such sadness, so much hardship, does not, surprisingly, make for depressing sailing. Quite the opposite; something to do with the light, and the profusion of Swedish flags which reflect the predominant colours of nature: yellow and blue, fresh, hopeful, happy colours. Under clear blue skies, the wind piping up from the west, the skerries blown to smithereens and spume, raking waves piling in from the North Sea, this is a magnificent coast, where the air invites you to gulp deep. So it's cold in those icy clear, blue, Swedish waters? Not in August. The spray that fired over our bows felt lukewarm from the last gasp of the Gulf Stream as it peters out somewhere in the Kattegatt. And the hardship is soon over. An hour's adrenaline sailing in the open sea north of Marstrand then scurry back behind the shelter of the islands. Invigorating, exuberant – enough to feel tough, not long enough to be rugged.

In late August you will have the place to yourself; the little wooden summer houses that dot the shore mostly deserted, just the crack of Swedish pennants flying from gold-topped poles, and a candle stump on the table marking the owners' last meal, invariably including some sort of herring, before packing for the big city.

Yachtsmen can dine well here, if expensively, and beware the alcohol prices. At Salt & Sill, a waterside restaurant on Klädesholmen, centre of the canning industry, each herring dish comes with an accompanying aquavit: Aalborg Dill, flavoured with dill and aniseed; Hallands Fläder, elderflower and so on, and with rough bread, Vasterbotten cheese, rye crispbread and local beer. Sweden's traditional foods are fresh, good looking and healthy – like the stereotypical image we hold of its people.

TRADITIONAL SWEDISH FOOD is famously fresh and healthy. Herring dishes are a regional speciality in Gothenburg.

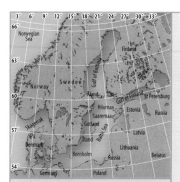

The Baltic
Kiel Canal to St Petersburg

THE BALTIC SEA is situated right in the middle of Europe – halfway between the west coast of Ireland and the Urals.

CHART 259, 2816, 2817; Local charts are essential in the archipelagos.

BEST FOR CRUISING May – September

AVERAGE TEMPERATURE 16ºC 60ºF

PREVAILING WIND Variable

TIME ZONE Summer, GMT + 1

LANGUAGE German, Danish, Swedish, Finnish, English widely spoken. German is useful in Russia, although an English speaker will find ways of surviving

CURRENCY Germany Euro (€); Denmark Danish Krone (DKK); Sweden Swedish Krone (SEK); Russia Rouble (RUB)

NAVIGATIONAL DIFFICULTY ⏲ ⏲ ⏲

FAMILY FRIENDLY 👤 👤 👤

DIVING/SNORKELLING 🤿 🤿

SHORE-SIDE EATING 🍴 🍴 🍴

SIGHTSEEING ♜ ♜ ♜ ♜ ♜

Mention the Baltic to an average cruising sailor and I guarantee you'll hear something along the lines of, "Sounds lovely, but I'd rather go somewhere warm…"

NOBODY CAN ARGUE that a decent Baltic cruise will reach 60° north, which also happens to be the latitude of Southern Greenland and Hudson's Bay. Put like that, it's understandable that people fear the cold, yet there's more to climate than your apparent proximity to the Pole.

I've sailed for two summers in the tideless, saltless Baltic and each has delivered as much sunshine as anyone could wish. The place is remote from the North Atlantic weather systems and temperatures regularly make the high 70s. There's also the bonus of almost 24-hour daylight. The natives are more than friendly and the man who sold me a ticket for the underground train in Stockholm spoke better English than his counterpart at London's King's Cross.

The Baltic is the true centre of Europe. Denmark, Sweden, East Germany, the Baltic States, Finland and Russia are soaked in history. Quaint waterfront buildings reflect the distinctive tastes of the merchant adventurers who formed the Hanseatic League back in the 13th century, but away from the towns, vast tracts of unchanged nature remain to be explored. The enclosed sea was once a world in itself, and its islands, beaches and surprisingly amenable rockscapes seem endless to the wandering sailor. With only one life to play with, can you really afford not to visit the Baltic?

ST PETERSBURG, RUSSIA

ISLE OF FENMARN, GERMANY

COPENHAGEN, DENMARK

LÜBECK is the largest German port on the
Baltic Sea. The water-enclosed Old Town has
been declared a world cultural heritage site.

From points north, the Baltic is entered by way of the Sound at Copenhagen after traversing the Kattegat between Denmark and Sweden. Most boats, however, come in from west and south through the mighty locks of the Kiel Canal. This main gateway was cut across the root of the Danish peninsula by Kaiser Bill himself in 1895 to give his battleships ready access to the North Sea and a crack at the Royal Navy. Today, huge cargo ships and hundreds of yachts make the one-day passage from the Elbe to Kiel.

Once through the canal, you're "in", so to speak, and can day-sail anywhere that takes your fancy. The ancient ports and wildlife marshes of Eastern Germany or the southern Danish islands are on the doorstep, while an easy "over-nighter" brings you into the Swedish islands around Karlskrona. A further ten hours sees a six-knot boat arriving under the walls of Kalmar Castle whose quasi-

THE KIEL CANAL (right) is a 60-mile (100km) canal running from the mouth of the Elbe River to the Baltic Sea.

KALMAR CASTLE (below), in the east of Sweden, is the best-preserved Renaissance castle in northen Europe.

STRALSUND is a medieval jewel on the Baltic coast of northern Germany that was a major trading centre of the Hanseatic League in the 14th and 15th centuries. The fabulous brick architecture is characteristic of the Hanseatic towns.

onion towers have a distinctly Eastern whiff. Two more days island-hopping in smooth water and you've made it to the vast Stockholm Archipelago, which, when the Almighty declares his favourite cruising grounds at the Last Trumpet, will surely ride high on his list. From here, it's Finland and wall-to-wall islands almost all the way to St Petersburg in another world altogether called Russia.

Eastern Germany offers a long, low coastline of little apparent interest until you realize that it's indented with rivers hiding Hanseatic cities such as Lübeck and Stralsund. These communities are now full-on German "metrops" with medieval waterfronts, cobbled streets, vast cathedrals and modern European people. Wide inland waterways lead eastwards past Peenemunde and the eerie remains of the Nazi V1 and V2 rocket sites. The local museum shows how these were pounded by RAF Lancasters in 1943, but leaves no doubt that the gigantic, echoing buildings housed the precursors of today's space technology.

Setting the past firmly astern, you can cruise straight from World War II into timeless inland seas that are the wide, silent "Boddens", sultry with heat. Flights of birds shimmer in the haze, the island paradise of Rugen shelters it all from the

HOLSTEN GATE with its fabulous conical spires is a remarkable example of the Gothic architecture that characterizes the medieval town of Lübeck in East Germany. It houses a museum of local history.

THE SWEDISH ARCHIPELAGO poses some serious navigational problems, but the rewards include sensational seascapes.

sea and, just over the Eastern horizon, Poland waits in the half-light that has followed years of Soviet occupation.

Day has long since dawned in the Swedish archipelago when I wake up and grope for the bunkside lamp to read my watch. There isn't much in the way of night in July, so my last job before turning in is always to dump a load of clutter on the skylights to fool myself it's actually bed-time. 0800 already! Time to show a leg and rouse the shipmate. With no tides to kick-start our passages there's no hurry. It just seems rude to rot in the sack on yet another lovely morning.

Coffee next, then breakfast in the cockpit and a good peer around the island anchorage of Grönskär. We're landlocked and there's ample depth, but the entrance gave us a fright yesterday afternoon. "Three metres", (9.8ft) the chart said. We found two (6.6ft) and we draw 1.98 (6.5ft). We crept in anyway, heart in mouth, waiting for the dreaded "Baltic bump" that lurks at every turn. Lack of water doesn't seem to bother the Swedes one bit. A dozen or so boats are moored close by. Several followed us through that terrifying gap under sail, then berthed in classic Nordic style. These guys have sang-froid in buckets. They just run straight in towards the smooth, glaciated rocks and heave a pick over the stern when they're 30 yards (27m) out. Then they nose up to the granite, hop off and secure their lines to a tree.

At 1030 the first of the "sun-wind" stirs the pines. The Swedes are clearing out now, but we're in no rush, so we take a fresh-water swim then go ashore for a stroll and a rubbish run. Our chart indicates a bin tucked away in the trees; we scrunch up through the pine needles with our well-stuffed supermarket bag and the dumpster is right there. It isn't full to bursting either.

These remarkable facilities are emptied regularly, though it's hard to imagine by whom.

Back on board in the midday sun there's a grand breeze blowing. This'll be useful when we get outside, if we ever make it over that boulder. It's a shame that the chart's not as accurate with rocks as it is with garbage collection.

Somehow, we keep clear of the bricks as we heave up the main, unroll the jib and bear away on a four-hour pilotage bonanza towards a rock anchorage in the outer skerries. The wind's fair as we jink and gybe through the unmarked reefs until, punch-drunk with the challenge of it all, we sound gingerly in

ST PETERSBURG is a city of incomparable architectural, historic and artistic interest.

THE HERMITAGE occupies six magnificent buildings along the embankment of the River Neva, in the heart of St Petersburg.

among the "stones" to where Bottskär is killing the surge of the sea. The shelter's perfect, but there's a lot less swinging room than we'd hoped. In the end I stop chewing my nails, launch the dinghy and row a long line over to a stout-looking bush. All around me, the tiny skerry is alive with wild flowers. The shipmate heaves the boat round to lie securely between the hook and the foliage. Problem solved.

The sun-wind dies as I light the cockpit lamp and lay out supper – cured herring, caviar, boat-baked bread, crisp Polish vodka and strawberries. It's too bright for stars. As Venus follows the sun down below the northern horizon a flock of geese tag along behind to see where they've gone. To seaward, there's only the rocks, the fading blue Baltic, the Finnish Gulf and Russia.

I have not visited St Petersburg since the overthrow of communism, but I remain one of the very few yachtsmen to have berthed there while it was soviet Leningrad. The political obstructions for casual sailors were substantial and in the end I bought my visa from a shady character behind a bus station in Helsinki. The deal worked like a charm and I was permitted to sail

my 100-year-old pilot cutter into the heart of Russia's second city. Here, my crew and I were greeted by the bemused members of the Central Yacht Club of Trade Unions who finally came to accept that anyone owning such a vessel did not have to be royalty. Once this misunderstanding was sorted out, we were recognized as humble journalists, piled into a trolley bus and transported in true Russian fashion to see the manifold sights of this remarkable city.

We marvelled at the Hermitage and the golden domes of the palaces, we were enchanted by the ancient singing in the few surviving churches, we queued up to buy beetroot and we trudged up Nevsky Prospekt looking for a clothes shop with something to sell. We breakfasted on cabbage pasties with rough-hewn taxi drivers and dined with Kirov ballerinas whose Slavonic beauty breathed mystery and faraway Steppes, but the over-riding memory of any red-blooded man who visits this tragic land will always be one of love and brotherhood. As the white night blazes through until morning behind the grimy windows of a communal apartment high in a tenement, the toasts of eternal comradeship drunk in mind-numbing vodka ring louder and more frequent as you embrace workers, artists and stubble-cheeked poets alike. And never forget that somewhere deep in his soul, every Russian is a poet.

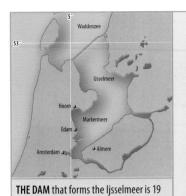

THE DAM that forms the Ijsselmeer is 19 miles (31 km) long.

Holland
Ijsselmeer

CHART 126, 1546 (covers only North Sea approaches), plus Dutch Hydrographic Office charts or Imray C25, C26

BEST FOR CRUISING May– October

AVERAGE TEMPERATURE 18°C 64°F

PREVAILING WIND Seabreeze in summer

TIME ZONE GMT + 1

LANGUAGE Dutch, English widely spoken

CURRENCY Euro (€)

NAVIGATIONAL DIFFICULTY

FAMILY FRIENDLY

DIVING/SNORKELLING

SHORE-SIDE EATING

SIGHTSEEING

Holland is home to some of the world's great explorers. Abel Tasman preceded Captain Cook to Australia and New Zealand, and Willem Schouten named Cape Horn after his home town, Hoorn. This Ijsselmeer town, with a harbour entered between two majestic towers, highlights why sailing here is a special experience.

THESE TOWNS on the Ijsselmeer, with their neat houses made from small bricks and wafer-thin mortar joints and Old Dutch Green painted doors, grew from the sea inwards. If you arrive by boat, you enter straight into the heart of the towns and avoid the modern low-rise suburbs that extend inland. The same is true of Amsterdam: here is a capital city you can sail into, cutting through from the North Sea and joining the Ijsselmeer through the Oranjesluizen.

In a sense the towns have been turned inside out, an impression created when the Dutch sealed off the former saltwater Zuider Zee and made it into the freshwater Ijsselmeer in 1932. Rather than

dying through being cut off, the Ijsselmeer towns have prospered for recreational boaters.

Seemingly, the Dutch never cease trying to control the sea. In 1975, the Ijsselmeer was cut in half by another dyke to form the Markermeer to the south, and then an entire new area poldered, drained and filled to create yet more land – Flevoland – in 1986.

But there is still an extensive area to cruise. A week would cover the most picturesque towns such as Enkhuizen, Hoorn, Medemblick, Urk, Stavoren and Workum. Better still, because this country is dotted by rivers, canals and lakes, if you have a yacht of moderate draft you can penetrate the lifting bridge and cruise inland amongst the cows and herons.

Most towns have cafés and bars – some are the fabled "brown bars" with carpeted tables – by the water. There is always a wonderful show of bluff-bowed traditional Dutch sailing vessels to watch. Most give masterly displays of single-screw boat-handling in the tightest of spaces.

Yachts can also enter the Ijsselmeer through the 20-mile-long (32km) Afsluitdijk with locks at either end. Alternatively, this is also the way out to the shoal waters of the Friesian Islands.

ENKHUIZEN

MUIDEN MALL

TRADITIONAL SAILING BOATS

HOORN is a historic town with a rich maritime history that is set in rural surroundings on the shore of the Ijsselmeer.

THE SEA has carved innumerable gorges in the north of France, and the coastline is deeply indented.

France
North Brittany and Tréguier

CHART 3674, 3670, 3668, 3669, 3345, 3427

BEST FOR CRUISING May – September

AVERAGE TEMPERATURE 19°C 66°F

PREVAILING WIND SW, variable

TIME ZONE GMT + 1

LANGUAGE French

CURRENCY Euro (€)

NAVIGATIONAL DIFFICULTY

FAMILY FRIENDLY

DIVING/SNORKELLING

SHORE-SIDE EATING

SIGHTSEEING

North Brittany's rugged coastline is challenging even for those who enjoy intricate pilotage and tidal mathematics, but its rewards are rich. Of its many harbours Tréguier is not only one of the most attractive but also one of the few ports offering access at all states of tide. The town is several miles from the sea and so the marina is very well sheltered and there are good transport connections to the ferry port of St Malo for anyone wanting to change crew or leave their boat there.

ONCE SECURELY tied up, Tréguier – typically of the ports along this coast – offers the gourmet plentiful choice: seafood, of course; Breton country food such as boudin noir (blood sausage) or andouillette (though this particular type of charcuterie has a very strong taste and smell), washed down with the local cider or the flinty dry Gros Plant white wine – which, incidentally, does not travel well; or fine French cuisine at one of several excellent restaurants. And there's good shopping here, too. The cathedral with its 15th-century cloisters and distinctive Pleubian spire – holed like a Swiss cheese – is well worth a visit, or you could just take a coffee or aperitif, sitting in the town square watching the games of boules.

The first time I visited Tréguier was at the end of the first leg of the twohanded Torquay, Tréguier, Crosshaven, Torquay Triangle Race in the late 1980s. Having left Torquay the previous afternoon we closed the Breton coast as dawn approached, revealing, on

DINAN

ST MALO

BRITTANY'S wildly beautiful coast presents a challenge for navigators, a paradise for gourmets and a plethora of impossibly pretty ports.

the horizon, the jagged teeth of North Brittany's hard coast. Even though the weather was fair with a moderate breeze it was not difficult to image the dangers of fast running tides, an onshore gale and those oh-so-sharp rocks.

I had recently fitted Decca – the forerunner of GPS in Europe – and was fascinated to match our course over the ground in the four-knot east-going tide with bearing to waypoint, the Basse Crublent buoy. We were sailing some 30 degrees above our course. In due course we found the landfall buoy and were in amongst those rocks in the deceptively wide entrance of La Grande Passe, one of three approach channels. The flood carried us quickly up the river, past the La Corne Tower and the narrows at Le Taureau and quite suddenly the lunar-like hostile landscape

PORTRIEUX (below) is a pretty resort with superb panoramas over the islands, fine sandy beaches and a deep water harbour.

TRÉGUIER (above) repays exploring on foot to take in the natural scenery, beautiful flowers and authentic Breton architecture.

gave way to gentle, rolling hills with pretty cottages and farms on the riverbanks.

Finally, round the last bend in the river, the town of Tréguier opened up with the marina straight ahead. As has happened each time I have visited since, the harbour master came out in his dory to help us to berth; much appreciated assistance as the tide can run at several knots through the marina and yachtsmen are advised to arrive near slack water.

The weather on the North Brittany coast is similar to that in the English Channel; variable winds, warm under sunny skies one day, cold and wet, even in summer, the next – it is not until beyond the Isle of Ushant and into South Brittany that light winds and reliable sunshine really predominate. And crews need to be alert to strong tidal streams, a large tidal range, the Atlantic swell and numerous rocks. The coast is extremely well marked but, even in summer, there is often a haze – and fog is not uncommon – so it can be difficult to identify leading marks. That said, the large tidal range, for example, also has the distinct advantage of

BREST hosts the Festival of the Sea every four years – a maritime gathering of hundreds of boats from all around the world.

transforming the look of your chosen anchorage in a most exciting way – it is also likely to renew your respect for the multitude of rocks and skerries it reveals through its cycle from high to low.

Sailing west from St Malo to the Isle of Ouessant, each and every mile of this wild coast offers contrast and interest – steep rugged cliffs indented by golden, sandy bays, jagged skerries and smooth, rose-red granite islands – and small, secluded deep-water anchorages are plentiful.

North Brittany's ports are, pretty much without exception, attractive and a pleasure to walk, eat, drink and provision in – Lézardrieux, Portrieux, Ploumanac'h, L'Aber-Wrac'h, to name but a very few of the many gems. Closely connected to the sea, Bretons play host annually to a number of excellent maritime festivals to which visiting boats are always made very welcome.

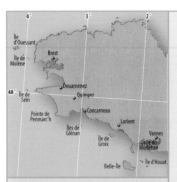

France
Ouessant to the Golfe du Morbihan

THE GULF OF MORBIHAN is sheltered from the Atlantic Ocean by the peninsula of Rhuys.

CHART 2358, 2643, 2646, 2358, 2663

BEST FOR CRUISING May – October (although very busy July & August)

AVERAGE TEMPERATURE 24ºC 75ºF

PREVAILING WIND SW, variable

TIME ZONE GMT + 1

LANGUAGE French & Breton

CURRENCY Euro (€)

NAVIGATIONAL DIFFICULTY

FAMILY FRIENDLY

DIVING/SNORKELLING

SHORE-SIDE EATING

SIGHTSEEING

The passage via by the Four Tower and inside the rugged island of Ouessant – sailing south-east along the glorious coasts and islands of South Brittany – exacts a high entry fee: the rock-strewn tidal maelstroms of the Chenal du Four and the infamous Raz de Sein. The key is getting the tides right and in not attempting them, especially the Raz de Sein, in strong winds, which is potentially one of the most dangerous headlands in the world.

THE CHENAL DU FOUR is, in clear weather, well marked and fairly straightforward, even if one of its main landmarks, Les Platresses Tower, was destroyed in winter storms in early 2008. Arrive off the Four Tower no earlier than high water Brest and no later than two hours after and you'll carry the tide right through the Four, across L'Iroise, the wide bay off Brest, and 30 miles (48km) further on you should, if you can average five to six knots over the ground, arrive at the Raz shortly before slack water when the stream will be less ferocious and still get a small helping hand south towards Pointe de Penmarc'h.

At Penmarc'h the world changes. The ragged rocks of north Brittany give way to an altogether gentler landscape, still with fast tides and hard rocks, and the weather is kinder. Following the coast round, you'll see the dotted rocky Îles de Glénan, home to France's top sailing school, on your starboard bow whilst Loctudy slips by to port and the River Odet opens up ahead, an ideal stopover. Moor up in the marina at Sainte Marine on the left

VAUBAN CITADEL

VANNES MARKET

SEAFOOD

THE GULF OF MORBIHAN is a paradise for seafood lovers. Vannes, the 'capital' of the Morbihan, smells of holidays. Its quays are lined with seafood restaurants and sunny café terraces full of tourists in summer.

PORT TUDY, on the Île de Groix, is the main port and was once a centre of tunny fishing. The island is just five miles (8km) long.

with kicking langoustines to take back on board, cooked and eaten piping hot with a hollandaise sauce and bottle of Muscadet.

From Benodet, Les Glénans are worth a lunch stop and a scramble ashore but, other than the sailing school, there is little to see except wildlife, seaweed and rocks, threaded by dozens of channels. It is possible to island hop in 20 or 25 mile (32–40 km) stages: first to Port Tudy on the Île de Groix, then on to Belle Île where, if the weather allows, you can try your luck in the tiny fjord of Ster Wenn on the island's north west coast, lying to anchor and with a long line ashore, making sure to keep well clear of the overhead power cable. The main harbour on Belle Île is Le Palais, a brightly coloured, walled town with tall harbourside buildings, overlooked by the Vauban citadel. In high season it gets very busy with boats moored several deep, bashing and clashing from the wash of the regular ferry to the mainland.

A few miles to the east of Belle Île are the twin, sandy islands of Houat and Hoëdic. Whilst it is possible to anchor or moor up here overnight it will probably be more comfortable to head for the mainland harbours of Port Haliguen, a rather soulless marina, La Trinité-sur-Mer, or the Golfe du Morbihan.

THE ÎLE DE OUESSANT presents formidable obstacles to navigation in rough seas.

bank, or at the Benodet Port de Plaisance a little further up the river on the right but be warned, the tide runs very fast here.

Although Sainte Marine has basic facilities and a couple of restaurants, Benodet offers much more so it is a toss up between the easier mooring and taking your tender across the river or sharpening your boat handling skills. I kept my boat in Sainte Marine for a year, which cost me about 10 per cent of the cost of a UK marina berth. Take a carrier bag to the evening fish market and fill it

BENODET, at the mouth of the River Odet, is a popular family resort with a large harbour and a long, sheltered beach on the ocean side, with amusements for children.

BELLE ÎLE is the largest island off Brittany, 12.5 miles (20km) at its widest, and is deserving of its name. The island has been immortaliszed in the paintings of Claude Monet and Henri Matisse, and the Australian Impressionist John Peter Russell who lived there for two decades.

HOUAT, west of Belle Île, is a relatively small island, just 3 miles (5km) long, but it has a rugged beauty with enchanting, sandy beaches, clear blue water and chalk-white houses. Houat is a treasure trove for bird lovers.

Better still to stay on the mainland shore. There are half-a-dozen good harbours between here and the Morbihan: Port la Forêt with its excellent yachting facilities and Corncarneau's medieval walled town, or my favourite, a mecca to seafood lovers, the Belon River, home to the finest oysters in the world.

Both the Belon and Aven Rivers are quite shallow so larger yachts should anchor or pick up a mooring on the west side of the entrance by Port Manec'h. But smaller boats can head carefully up the Belon, keeping clear of the many oyster farms, and anchor or pick up a visitor's mooring about half-a-mile (1km) upstream where the famous Chez Jacky restaurant awaits...

From Belon to the River Etel is about 30 miles (48km), past the busy port of Lorient. Etel is a fishing port with a well-sheltered marina. The entrance is best described as "interesting". The shallow approach channel and drying bar shift frequently and traditionally fishing boats were guided back by a pilot using the semaphore tower on the west side of the entrance. Today it is well buoyed, but even so it is eerie to enter on a strong flood, hearing the sound of shingle shifting through the hull.

The final destination is the magical Golfe du Morbihan, an inland sea dotted with hundreds of islands and islets where the

OYSTER FARMING is an important traditional occupation in the Gulf of Morbihan.

THE QUIBERON PENINSULA (below left) in the Morbihan is separated from the mainland by a narrow isthmus.

THE RIVER LOCH (below) at Auray is spanned by a lovely 17th-century stone bridge, affording a great view of the harbour.

tide does not so much ebb and flood as sluice in and out. Tides are the key to successful navigation and it is not worth the effort to fight the streams, just go with the flow.

Go up the Auray River and anchor or moor off Le Rocher, then dinghy up to the old town of Auray. Listen to the whispering pines on Île Longue and wonder at the standing stones, or menhirs, on Er Lanic. Anchor off Île aux Moines and go ashore in early evening, after the vedettes and tourists have left for the day, and wander through summer meadows the like of which have all but vanished in most of Europe. Finally, follow the winding channel up to the picturesque Conleau Narrows before entering the narrow canal up to the marina right in the heart of the medieval city of Vannes. And don't do what I did once, which was to run aground on the sill between the single lock gates that are the only barrier to prevent the whole of the Vannes Basin draining. And it was on a falling tide. I've never seen a lock keeper move so fast and, yes, we did get off.

VANNES has some of the finest traditional half-timbered houses with steep roofs and wood carved facades.

BRITTANY'S ROCK-STREWN COAST is carved by the untamed Atlantic with tides that, in places, stream as rapidly as "a galloping horse".

THE ARCHIPELAGO of the Azores is composed of nine volcanic islands.

Atlantic Islands
Azores

CHART 1950, 1959, 1956, 1895
BEST FOR CRUISING June – August
AVERAGE TEMPERATURE 22°C 71°F
PREVAILING WIND Variable
TIME ZONE GMT – 1
LANGUAGE Portuguese, English widely spoken
CURRENCY Euro (€)

NAVIGATIONAL DIFFICULTY
FAMILY FRIENDLY
DIVING/SNORKELLING
SHORE-SIDE EATING
SIGHTSEEING

Reputed by many to be the remaining fragments of Plato's fabled Atlantis, the Azores are a popular landfall for yachts heading east from the Caribbean, Bermuda or US. Although more than 1,000 yachts call here every year, very few of them cruise around the islands and the majority stop only in Horta, on the island of Faial.

THE AZORES comprise five islands – Faial, Pico, São Jorge, Gracioca and Terceira – which form a close, central cluster, with outlying Corvo and Flores to their north-west, and São Miguel (the largest of the islands) and Santa Maria to the south-east.

All nine of these volcanic islands have a scenic landscape of cones and craters, where the rich soil is covered in lush vegetation – both sub-tropical and temperate – with vividly coloured flowers growing in abundance. Conifer forests, hot springs and high waterfalls in the mountains give way to sweet, green lowland pasture and pretty villages by sheltered bays. The islands' once-important whaling industry has developed into an equally important whale-watching industry; more than eleven species of whale and dolphin frequent the waters here. Around Pico and Faial between May and October are considered the best locations and months in which to see cetaceans likely to include sperm whales, beaked whales, striped and bottlenose dolphins, or, more rarely blue, fin and sei whales and humpbacks have been sighted off São Miguel.

With their secluded bays, uncrowded anchorages and protected harbours, the Azores are still waiting to be discovered as a cruising destination in their own right. Besides their natural beauty, the relaxed pace of life in the islands is their main appeal. The islanders are as welcoming and hospitable to today's visiting sailors as they were to one Joshua Slocum, who stopped here in 1895 during his singlehanded circumnavigation.

The climate in the Azores is dominated by the mid-Atlantic area of high pressure which bears their name. The position of the Azores high varies with the season, being more northerly in the autumn and more southerly in the spring, usually lying to the south or south-west of the islands. In winter the area can be stormy and wet, while in summer the Azores high can be stationary with prolonged periods of calm weather.

PICO

SÃO MIGUEL

DOLPHINS

IN THE AZORES it is not uncommon to encounter pods of dolphin of between 50 and 200, leaping with astonishing exuberance and vitality, often riding close in the boat's bow wave.

HORTA, with its marina, convivial bars and restaurants, and convenient provisioning, is a perennial favourite of long-distance sailors.

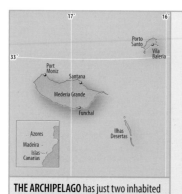

THE ARCHIPELAGO has just two inhabited islands: Madeira and Porto Santo.

Atlantic Islands
Madeira

CHART 1685, 1689, 1831
BEST FOR CRUISING April – October
AVERAGE TEMPERATURE 24ºC 75ºF summer
PREVAILING WIND NE
TIME ZONE GMT + 0
LANGUAGE Portuguese, English widely spoken
CURRENCY Euro (€)

NAVIGATIONAL DIFFICULTY 🧭
FAMILY FRIENDLY ⛱⛱⛱⛱⛱
DIVING/SNORKELLING 🤿🤿
SHORE-SIDE EATING 🍴🍴🍴🍴🍴
SIGHTSEEING 🏰🏰🏰🏰🏰

Disputing with the Azores the claim to being part of the lost continent of Atlantis, only two islands of Madeira's volcanic archipelago are inhabited, the largest, Madeira Grande, which gives its name to the entire group, and Porto Santo to the north-east.

TO THE EAST are the three smaller Ilhas Desertas while further south, halfway to the Canaries, lie the Ilhas Selvagens (Savage Islands). The largest of the Selvagens, Ilha Selvagem Grande, is a protected bird sanctuary – access to this nature reserve is prohibited and yachts wishing to visit them need permission from the authorities in the capital Funchal on Madeira Grande.

Discovered by the Portuguese in the early 15th century, the Madeira archipelago is one of those places whose geographical position means that it is usually visited by yachts en route to somewhere else. Yet these islands have much to be enjoyed and many sailors regard Madeira with special affection.

The tourist industry here remains low-key and Madeira retains its unique character and atmosphere. Food is based on fine peasant traditions; delicious fresh fish, meat and fruit simply prepared, and with sugar once an economic staple, sweet cakes and biscuits are a tempting feature. It goes without saying that the famous Madeira wine should be sampled – try dry varieties such as Verdelho, served chilled, as a refreshing aperitif; sweeter wines are served with puddings and Malmsey, the richest, is just right after dinner. As they did in the days of the great cruise liners, visitors continue to arrive by ship in Funchal's natural harbour and, since the Sixties when the island gained an airport, the number of hotels, restaurants and shops in the capital has seen a steady increase. Outside Funchal, rural life meanders along at a gentle pace, and true to their farming origins, most islanders work the fields on their smallholdings.

The majority of yachts arrive here during October and November on their way to the Canary Islands and the Caribbean. Yachting facilities are steadily improving with a much-needed new marina now operating at Caniçal on Madeira Grande. The islands have a pleasant and mild climate all year round, the air temperature rarely falling below 16°C (61°F) in winter or rising above 25°C (77°F) in summer.

PORTO SANTO

MARKET PRODUCE

SMALLHOLDINGS

More than 600 miles (1,000km) apart
but sharing a common language and
a claim to being Atlantis, Madeira
and the Azores will reward those
who stay awhile.

MADEIRA'S dramatic landscape has been shaped
by millions of years of volcanic activity: majestic
mountains, rich valleys and a vastness of green.

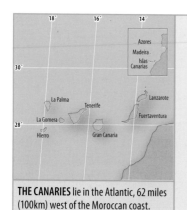

THE CANARIES lie in the Atlantic, 62 miles (100km) west of the Moroccan coast.

Atlantic Islands
The Canary Islands

CHART 1869, 1870

BEST FOR CRUISING Year-round

AVERAGE TEMPERATURE 22ºC 72ºF (winter), 26ºC 79ºF (summer)

PREVAILING WIND NE

TIME ZONE GMT + 0

LANGUAGE Spanish

CURRENCY Euro (€)

NAVIGATIONAL DIFFICULTY

FAMILY FRIENDLY

DIVING/SNORKELLING

SHORE-SIDE EATING

SIGHTSEEING

Every autumn well over 1,000 yachts, most of them en route to the Caribbean, call at this archipelago perched on Africa's north-western shoulder. For centuries the people of the Canaries have welcomed sailors to their shores, including Christopher Columbus in 1492.

THE RELATIVELY short distances between the archipelago's main islands are such that it is only a day's sail between most of them. From the north, the logical route to follow would start with visits to Lanzarote and Fuerteventura, then sail west towards Gran Canaria, Tenerife, La Gomera and Hierro and complete your cruise at La Palma. The north-east trade winds blow over the archipelago almost without interruption and the sailing here can be challenging, as some of these high volcanic islands cause wind acceleration zones in their lee that can catch the unwary with sudden, violent gusts. Otherwise the climate is gloriously benign throughout the year.

Described as a continent in miniature, every island has its own distinctive character: those closest to Africa, such as Lanzarote and Fuerteventura, are dry and arid; those further west – La Palma, La Gomera and Hierro – are lush and green; while on Tenerife you will see Mount Teide's snowy cap towering 12,198 feet (3,718m) above the ocean. The two largest islands, Gran Canaria and Tenerife, lie in the middle and are much more developed than the rest.

Being intrinsically linked with the sea and sailing, facilities for visiting yachts are of the highest order with well-endowed marinas on every island. The best provisioning and repair facilities are in Las Palmas de Gran Canaria, the starting point of the annual (end of November) Atlantic Rally for Cruisers (ARC). Ashore, Gran Canaria, like its neighbours, lives up to its "little continent" reputation, offering sun, sea, sand, mountains, the buzz, culture and nightlife of its capital and peaceful hideaways.

For good reason, the islands are now regarded as an all-year cruising ground as well as a year-round tourist destination, but if you want to steer clear of the crowds avoid chartering during the busiest months, December to March – especially the popular, and thus jam-packed, carnival season in February/March – and during the summer influx from July to September.

MOUNT TEIDE, TENERIFE

HIERRO

GRAN CANARIA

THE THIRD LARGEST island of the Canaries boasts 147 miles (236km) of coast with sandy beaches, mostly located on the south-east coast, including the famous Playa del Inglés and Maspalomas beaches.

THE CANARY ISLANDS are a sub-tropical paradise complete with swaying palm trees and many pristine beaches.

PARADISE FOUND: steady winds; warm, sparkling, crystal-clear seas; minimal tidal ranges; white, soft sand; and (sometimes) splendid isolation.

The Caribbean

Haunt of buccaneers, squabbled over by the French, Dutch, English and Spanish, the islands in the Caribbean Sea hold a special allure to those who count Robert Louis Stevenson's *Treasure Island* among their favourite books. Yet their dark and troubled history serves only to enhance the romance that surrounds them. For some time the Caribbean has been *the* charter destination, a playground that promises steady trade winds, warm seas, sparkling colours and, of course, as many variations of rum punch as there are beachside bar tenders to mix them. Yet there is more than enough adventure for those seeking to get away from the crowd. Head for Belize or the San Blas Islands, and you'd be (un)lucky to see a dozen yachts all week.

THE CARIBBEAN SEA is framed by myriad islands, from tiny uninhabited islets to island nations, such as Jamaica.

BAHAMAS

ST VINCENT AND THE GRENADINES

THE CARIBBEAN

The islands and adjacent countries of the Caribbean Sea are a vast cruising area that is the most popular offshore destination for both North American and European sailors. The Lesser Antilles and Virgin Islands in the Eastern Caribbean attract most of the cruising and charter yachts, although the Greater Antilles and countries of the Western Caribbean have seen a steady increase in the number of visiting yachts. Also gaining in popularity are Venezuela and the San Blas Archipelago as well as the ABC Islands of Aruba, Bonaire and Curaçao.

In spite of the large number of yachts, cruising the Lesser Antilles is as attractive as ever, with perfect sailing weather during the balmy winter months, clean waters, pristine beaches and picturesque well-sheltered anchorages. Beside the delights of cruising, there is also an active racing programme with the Heineken Regatta held in Saint Maarten in March and Antigua Sailing Week, at the end of April, being among the most famous regattas anywhere in the world.

The popularity of the Caribbean is well deserved as the winter weather is mostly fine, the trade winds reliable and the facilities

For some time the Caribbean has been <u>the</u> charter destination, a playground that promises steady trade winds.

are being continually improved to cope with a constant demand. The weather during winter – particularly from Christmas until the end of April – is very good, with steady easterly winds and not much rain; these are the best months during which to book your charter. Winds are usually from the north-east at the beginning of winter and become south-easterly with the approach of summer.

The hurricane season lasts from June through November, the most dangerous period being from the middle of August until early October. While the majority of cruising yachts leave the area, either to sail home or continue their voyage around the world, those that stay behind have a choice of places to lay up their boats during the off season. The entire region can be affected by hurricanes, with the exception of the southern part where tropical storms are very rare – and chartering is restricted accordingly. It is possible – and also cheaper – to charter during the low season (August through October) and, while weather may put some destinations out of bounds, those you do visit will be less crowded. Rainstorms are likely, too, but air and water temperatures remain warm and such storms often pass through quite quickly.

DOMINICA

BELIZE

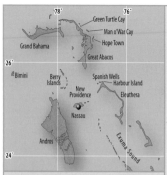

The Bahamas
Bimini to the Exumas

CHART NOAA 11013
BEST FOR CRUISING December – May
AVERAGE TEMPERATURE 24°C 75°F
PREVAILING WIND E
TIME ZONE GMT – 5
LANGUAGE English
CURRENCY Bahamian Dollar (B$)

NAVIGATIONAL DIFFICULTY
FAMILY FRIENDLY
DIVING/SNORKELLING
SHORE-SIDE EATING
SIGHTSEEING

For decades, the Bahamas have been every skipper's dream of a tropical island getaway. Starting just fifty miles (80km) off the Florida coast and then stretching for 500 miles (805km) and 700 islands, the Bahamas are a legend in their own time.

ERNEST HEMINGWAY gave us wanderlust with his *Islands in the Stream*, which he wrote above a rum-soaked bar in Bimini, but the Bahamas were a part of American life as early as Prohibition, when William McCoy, arguably the most successful rumrunner, used the Bahamas as a base of operations to bring in liquor that became known as "the real McCoy" for its quality.

For years, these islands have dozed in the warm sun, known to fishermen for world-class sportfishing and to cruisers for palmy anchorages and gin-clear waters. Ashore, the facilities have run heavily toward quaint towns with seedy waterfront bars where old men played dominoes and anglers told tall tales, and where the words luxury and resort couldn't be used in the same sentence.

But that has all changed and today the sound of the Bahamas isn't a steel drum band or the yowl of a fishing reel, but the clatter of earthmovers and the sound of hammers. The Bahamas have awakened.

Just a short hop from Miami, Bimini is the gateway to the Bahamas and is a superlative sportfishing capital as record-sized gamefish feed off the nutrient-laden Gulf Stream. You'll find Hemingway memorabilia at the restored Big John's Hotel, as well as a new marina and boardwalk.

Once you've cleared customs, the possibilities are endless: north-east to Grand Bahama, a bit more easting to the Abacos, due east to the Exumas, south-east to Nassau.

CRYSTALLINE WATERS

REMOTE ANCHORAGES

WORLD-CLASS FISHING

BIMINI is the deep-sea fishing capital of the world; its coastal waters yield giant tuna and enormous white and blue marlin, along with amberjack, bonefish, barracuda, and tarpon.

From Hemingway to Jimmy Buffett, through fish-rich snorkelling and world-class sportfishing, to conch burgers at Ma Ruby's, there's something for everyone and it's the real McCoy.

ISLAND PARADISES in the Bahamas come in sizes to suit all: 700 in fact, from rocky outcrops to Grand Bahama, and everything in between.

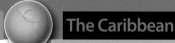

NASSAU is the capital of the Bahamas. Neighbouring Paradise Island is dominated by the huge Atlantis Royal Towers Hotel.

Grand Bahama is another entry point, and a $4.9-billion (£2.5 billion) resort is underway with everything from Venetian waterways to a Monte Carlo casino to a megayacht marina. For a quieter stay, the Old Bahama Bay Resort and marina is close to great fishing and snorkelling.

The Abacos have long been a popular destination for cruisers and for bareboat charters, with the shallow and protected sea rimmed by gorgeous beaches and villages populated by the remnants of British Loyalists who fled the American Revolution. Take time to explore Hope Town and the oft-photographed striped lighthouse with its 138-year-old kerosene light. You'll find brilliantly painted clapboard houses that managed to survive Hurricane Floyd's 229-mph (368kph) winds, and be sure to top off with rum or your booze of choice.

ABACOS is home to Hope Town and the famous and oft-photographed red-and-white striped lighthouse that was built in 1864.

Next stop is Man O' War Cay, which is a dry island so there are no pubs. Visit Albury's canvas shop instead, which has been making sails and canvas boat bags (great gifts!) for centuries. At Green Turtle Cay, cruising tradition dictates a stop at Miss Emily's Blue Bee Bar, where you can sample the legendary Goombay Smash and add your business card to the millions covering the walls and ceiling.

New Providence is the political and social centre of the Bahamas but, to be blunt, the main city of Nassau is a tourist trap designed to lure thousands of cruise ship passengers. Use Nassau for provisions and as an air entry point, and then leave.

Heading north-east across the island chain takes you to Spanish Wells, where treasure galleons once filled their casks, and wise skippers will hire a pilot to tiptoe through the reefs of the Devil's Backbone on Eleuthera. (Suggestion: ask for the pilot named just "A-1". He's a hoot.)

Harbour Island ("Briland" to insiders) has always been synonymous with laid-back island life. I prefer the Harbour Island Club marina, because it doesn't have the party atmosphere (and noise) of Valentine's marina. Rent a golf cart to explore Dunmore Town, admire the colourful homes covered with brilliant bougainvillea, and swim on the famed

ANDROS ISLAND has some spectactular, blinding white sand beaches that you can have entirely to yourself.

DUNMORE on Harbour Island is sprinkled with charming white-painted clapboard houses.

pink sands, but, whatever you decide to do, don't miss a conch burger at Ma Ruby's café.

If you head south from Nassau, you'll be able to enjoy Staniel Cay, which singer songwriter Jimmy Buffett calls the best place in the world for a waterside drink. This island still feels like the 1950s. Nearby is Thunderball Grotto, where two James Bond films have been shot. Plan to snorkel here at slack water, because the current through this fish-filled grotto can make swimming difficult.

The Exumas are known for great diving and snorkelling at the Land and Sea Refuge Park and at Stocking Island, with undersea caves and coral gardens.

Sail, swim, fish, loaf, snorkel, beach comb, explore tiny villages and empty cays (islands): the Bahamas have something for everyone. As the lyrics to Kenny Rogers' *Islands in the Stream* say: "Sail away with me…to another world".

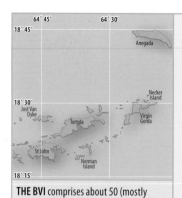

THE BVI comprises about 50 (mostly uninhabited) islands and cays, of which Tortola is the commercial centre.

The Leeward Islands
Tortola and the British Virgin Islands

CHART 130, 2020, 2452
BEST FOR CRUISING December –May
AVERAGE TEMPERATURE 26ºC 80ºF
PREVAILING WIND NE
TIME ZONE GMT – 4
LANGUAGE English

CURRENCY Dollar (US$)
NAVIGATIONAL DIFFICULTY
FAMILY FRIENDLY
DIVING/SNORKELLING
SHORE-SIDE EATING
SIGHTSEEING

Columbus first sighted these islands and named them for the 11,000 virgins who followed Saint Ursula, daughter of a British king, to their deaths at the hands of the Hun on a pilgrimage to Cologne in 383AD. Former haunt of pirates, of whom Blackbeard is the most notorious, the Virgin Islands have been fought over by the English, Dutch, French, Spanish and Danish.

THESE DAYS THE ISLANDS attract yachtsmen by the thousand to their crystal clear waters, white sand beaches and promise of steady, if boisterous at times, trade wind sailing. A developed infrastructure of restaurants and marinas, plus line-of-sight navigation between the 33-odd islands still make the British Virgin Islands (BVI) a sailor's paradise; windy, but not too windy, and never far from a rum punch. This is quintessential chartering territory, a playground for American visitors, for whom this is their backyard, and a winter getaway for sun-starved Europeans. So don't expect to find solitude. Do expect a certain laid-back Britishness that is largely absent in their nearby US equivalents, St Thomas and St Croix.

Tortola is the most developed and the largest island at 21½ square miles (35km²). It is the hub of this chain of islands and has an airport plus a bustling capital, Road Town, with plenty of well-stocked shops selling provisions and souvenirs. As darkness falls the sound of steel bands may well enliven your attempts to sleep.

Cane Garden Bay, a sweeping beach on the north-west coast is just one of many palm-fringed, white sand beaches all around the coast offering a wide variety of water sports. And the

SOPER'S HOLE WHARF, TORTOLA

SANDY BEACHES

SHOPPING, BVI-STYLE

TORTOLA is the hub of the island chain and there are plenty of activities to enjoy: scuba-diving, snorkelling, horse riding, shopping...

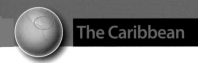

sheltered bays on this lush, volcanic island provide protected anchorages as well as good snorkelling and superb diving, including the wreck of the Royal Mail steamer Rhone, the setting for the movie *The Deep*, starring Nick Nolte and Jacqueline Bissett. Although there are few industries in the BVI, other than holiday resorts, the art of brewing rum is still going strong. The Callwood Distillery in Tortola is one of two in the BVI.

The small tidal range – a mere 12in (30cm) – and the sheltered waters mean that even novice sailors can enjoy island hopping from Tortola, although many more experienced sailors also travel to the islands each year to relax and lazily crisscross the Sir Francis Drake Channel without the hassles of customs clearance. Passages between the islands can take as little as half an hour and rarely more than three hours.

Norman Island, for example, just seven miles (11km) south of Road Town, is within easy reach. A world-renowned site for snorkelling, the sea here teems with life, including turtles, exotic sponges and corals. The island was a favourite haunt of legendary pirates and is said to have inspired Robert Louis Stevenson's *Treasure Island*. To the west of Norman Island is a safe, sheltered anchorage if you decide to drop anchor for the night and party,

NORMAN ISLAND is a world-class snorkelling site whose natural wonders include the Green Sea Turtle. Weighing in at up to 705lb (320kg), they rank among the world's largest sea turtles.

JOST VAN DYKE is the smallest of the four main islands of the BVI. It harbours some fantastic sealife – and sea food, Jost Van Dyke's lobster is reputed to be the best in the Caribbean.

Caribbean style, aboard the famous Willy T, a converted 1915 schooner.

Other must-see islands include Jost Van Dyke, named after a Dutch pirate. This island, three miles north-west of Tortola, is worth exploring on foot and rewards with many stunning views. The island's notorious "painkiller" cocktail originated at the Soggy Dollar, a bar so-named because sailors would dive from their boats to swim ashore from its perfect anchorages and hang up their wet dollars to pay for their drinks.

Seven miles south-east of Tortola is Virgin Gorda, or the "fat virgin" from the Spanish, with its labyrinth of boulders, caves and natural pools, known as "The Baths". Swim ashore, wade between the huge boulders and you may chance upon one of the Caribbean's finest beaches while round the corner – passing the extraordinary island they call Fallen Jerusalem – and through

ANEGADA is protected by the Horseshoe Reef and has several stunning beaches including Bones Bright and Cow Wreck.

into Gorda Sound at the Bitter End yachtsmen can pick up a mooring and dine ashore in noisy conviviality.

Celebrity spotters will know that Sir Richard Branson's Necker Island is a boat-hop away, but well protected from prying eyes behind fringing reefs. Mysterious Anegada lies low on the horizon for those who enjoy eyeball navigation. Just don't leave it too late in the day: dark blue water is deep, powder-blue shallow and if you find yourself in brown water, the coral heads are just below the surface, so it's time to retrace a course to safety.

Not surprisingly, there are many reputable yacht charter companies based in the BVI. Some even allow one-way chartering so that you can pick up a yacht in Tortola and disembark on a more distant Caribbean Island, such as Grenada, before flying home.

THE BATHS, VIRGIN GORDA, are a popular anchorage where you can snorkel in the clear blue water around the boulders.

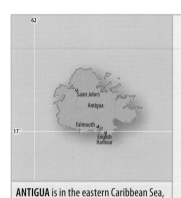

ANTIGUA is in the eastern Caribbean Sea, on the sea's boundary with the Atlantic.

The Leeward Islands
Antigua

CHART 2064, 2065; Imray Iolaire A27
BEST FOR CRUISING December – May
AVERAGE TEMPERATURE 25ºC 77ºF
PREVAILING WIND NE to SE
TIME ZONE GMT – 4
LANGUAGE English and Creole
CURRENCY East Caribbean Dollar (EC$)

NAVIGATIONAL DIFFICULTY
FAMILY FRIENDLY
DIVING/SNORKELLING
SHORE-SIDE EATING
SIGHTSEEING

English Harbour could claim to be the cradle of yacht charter in the Caribbean. When the Nicholson family sailed in soon after World War II, yachts were rare and it did not take them long to establish their business, Nicholson's Charter. The company still exists today and organizes the hugely successful Charter Show each December – the start of the Caribbean season – with some of the world's most stunning superyachts on display.

ENGLISH AND the neighbouring Falmouth Harbour offer excellent shelter as well as good yachting facilities, with a large marina at the Yacht Club in the latter. Certainly these were the British Navy's main bases in the Caribbean when the historic Nelson's Dockyard, now restored, was built. Today, the nearest Antigua comes to war are the two big annual regattas, Antigua Classics and Antigua Sailing Week, both held in April (at the end of the season) before many of the boats head out across the Atlantic to the

Mediterranean. Classics attracts some of the world's more beautiful restored and recreated classic sailing yachts, such as the mighty J Class, while Sailing Week, although not the biggest Caribbean Regatta, is the oldest and the most prestigious, attracting world-class boats and crews.

The resort beaches – Dickenson Bay and Runaway Bay, for example – are mainly on the north-west coast, with those on the hilly south and south-west quieter and less developed but, for palm-fringed white sand, on Antigua you are well and truly spoiled for choice.

The coral reefs, once the bane of navigators, now attract snorkellers and scuba-divers from all over the world. And the neighbouring island of Barbuda is now a major bird sanctuary.

Two things not to miss in Antigua. A drink at the Mad Mongoose at Falmouth Harbour, especially late evening when the yacht crews are ashore hell bent on having a good time. And the second is to visit Shirley Heights on a Sunday evening for the jump up and to watch the sun set. With a rum punch in your hand and listening to the steel band playing, the sound rolling down the hill to Galleon Beach below, you could almost imagine you were in – the Caribbean.

FALMOUTH HARBOUR

CRUISE LINERS

CLASSIC YACHTS

THE ANTIGUA CLASSICS REGATTA hosts around 50 yachts every year including traditional craft from the islands, classic ketches, sloops, schooners, yawls, J Class yachts, and spectacular Tall Ships.

ENGLISH HARBOUR originally served as the headquarters of the British fleet of the Leeward Islands in the late 18th century.

A 109FT HERRESHOFF SCHOONER making waves at the Antigua Classics Regatta in the sparkling Caribbean Sea.

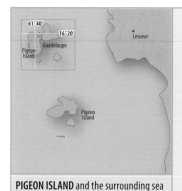

Guadeloupe
Pigeon Island

PIGEON ISLAND and the surrounding sea to the north are part of a marine park.

CHART 593; Imray Iolaire A28
BEST FOR CRUISING December – May
AVERAGE TEMPERATURE 27°C 80°F
PREVAILING WIND NE to SE
TIME ZONE GMT – 4
LANGUAGE French and Creole, English widely spoken

CURRENCY Euro (€) (US$ widely accepted)
NAVIGATIONAL DIFFICULTY
FAMILY FRIENDLY N/A
DIVING/SNORKELLING
SHORE-SIDE EATING
SIGHTSEEING N/A

Situated on the west coast of the French island of Guadeloupe, at first sight Pigeon Island has very little to mark it out as anything much different from the many islets in the Leewards. But it is not what is above the water that is the attraction. For the island and an area of sea and the coast for about a mile (1.5 km) north comprises the Cousteau National Marine Park.

ANCHORING HERE IS FORBIDDEN as is fishing, both of which dicta have helped to preserve the abundant sealife and fragile corals. In the little bay on the west side of the island there are a number of mooring buoys. The blue-and-white ones, coloured the same as the "A" flag used to indicate divers down, are reserved for dive boats but the yellow or orange buoys can be used by visiting charter or cruising yachts. So get out those masks, snorkels and flippers and go swimming. A word of advice here, it's very easy to get sunburnt when snorkelling, so if you are prone to burning it's best to wear a T-shirt.

There is a wide variety of sealife from brightly coloured fish, octopus and corals and if the water is clear, which it usually is, you're in for a feast. Some parts of the Park are too deep for snorkelling and scuba-divers might like to go to one of several dive gear hire shops along Malendure Beach and possibly go out on one of the dive boats and they will know the best hot spots to dive on.

This is not a particularly comfortable overnight anchorage, and there may be some doubt as to the strength of the mooring, so it's probably best to cross to the main island and anchor in Malendure Bay. There is a dinghy dock here and a variety of snack bars and restaurants to round the day off with a tasty seafood supper.

If there is much swell both Pigeon Island and Malendure Bay can be uncomfortable and much better shelter is afforded in Anse a la Barque, which is just over five miles to the south. Entry is straightforward although there are shoals on both the north and south sides of the bay so you should stay in the centre. There is a yellow lighthouse on the northern headland and a white one at the head of the bay. You can anchor just outside the fishing boats. Although quieter here there is little ashore and it is somewhat spoilt by the main coastal road that loops round the bay.

LAWKSKILL TURTLE

RED STARFISH

COUSTEAU MARINE SANCTUARY

HOT SPRINGS flow in to the waters, creating a warm haven for fish and other marine wildlife that can be viewed by snorkelling, scuba-diving, or cruising on a glass-bottom boat.

PIGEON ISLAND enjoys a colourful underworld described by the great Jacques Cousteau as one of the world's top ten dive sites.

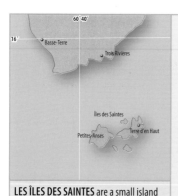

The Leeward Islands
Les Îles des Saintes

CHART 5642 (Folio charts), 618; Imray Iolaire A281

BEST FOR CRUISING December – May

AVERAGE TEMPERATURE 27°C 80°F

PREVAILING WIND NE to SE

TIME ZONE GMT – 4 hours

LANGUAGE French

CURRENCY Euro (€)

NAVIGATIONAL DIFFICULTY ⏱ ⏱ ⏱

FAMILY FRIENDLY 🍹 🍹 🍹 🍹

DIVING/SNORKELLING 🤿 🤿 🤿

SHORE-SIDE EATING 🍽 🍽 🍽 🍽 🍽

SIGHTSEEING 🏰 🏰 🏰

Les Îles des Saintes, made up of four islands and a number of islets, lie between Dominica and Guadeloupe, some 18 miles (29km) north of Portsmouth. Like Martinique and Guadeloupe the islands are French, though in their way they are far more Gallic than either of the other two islands.

WALKING THROUGH the main town – albeit a very small town – of Bourg des Saintes on the island of Terre d'en Haut, on wide walkways and past neat cottages with low fences and wicket gates, you could almost be in a small South of France seaside village. It's utterly charming.

When I was last there we anchored first under the steep-sided Pain de Sucre hill, impressive but not nearly as tall as its Rio de Janeiro namesake. Space is tight here and we had to re-anchor more than once to avoid longer established residents (remember the rule, last in is always the first to move if there's a problem). The main anchorage is in the bay off Bourg des Saintes and there are also anchorages on two of the other islands.

As on the other French islands, in Les Saintes' restaurants and supermarkets you can be sure of good, if pricey, food or wine – a treat for anyone whose palate is jaded by too much Caribbean cooking.

August 15, commemorates the first expulsion of British invaders in 1666 and the following day honours those lost at sea. There are speeches and parades, and various rituals related to fishing and the sea, which support the bulk of the island's economy. It is also, of course, a time for wining and dining.

During any day, Terre d'en Haut can get very crowded with day-trippers coming over from Guadeloupe but come the evening and everything calms down a bit. It's worth a walk across the island in early evening to the Baie de Pompierre (sometimes confusingly called Baie de Pontpierre in pilot books) on the windward side, a gentle stroll of just under a mile (1.6km). Here you'll find the classic white sand, palm-fringed beach, even if the water is less clear than on the leeward side, churned up a bit by the onshore breeze. Anchoring here was banned in the 1990s as the authorities were concerned about pollution from yachts blowing ashore. Sit down and enjoy a cold beer before heading back to town and some fine French cuisine for dinner.

BOURG DES SAINTES

TERRE D'EN HAUT

FRENCH FOOD

Proud of their Breton and Norman ancestry the islanders are more French than the French and are, they claim, the best fishermen in the West Indies. Vive la France, bon appétit.

TAKE A STROLL up to Fort Napoleon on Terre d'en Haut, the most populated of the islands, to enjoy the spectacular views over the harbour.

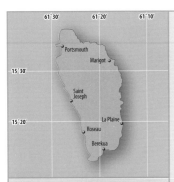

The Windward Islands
Dominica

CHART 5642 (Folio charts), 697; Imray Iolaire A29

BEST FOR CRUISING December – May

AVERAGE TEMPERATURE 27ºC 80ºF

PREVAILING WIND NE to SE

TIME ZONE GMT – 4

LANGUAGE English

CURRENCY East Caribbean Dollar (EC$), £, € and

US$ widely accepted

NAVIGATIONAL DIFFICULTY 🧭 🧭 🧭

FAMILY FRIENDLY 🍹 🍹 🍹

DIVING/SNORKELLING 🤿 🤿 🤿

SHORE-SIDE EATING 🍽️ 🍽️ 🍽️

SIGHTSEEING 🏰 🏰 🏰 🏰

DOMINICA sits just a few miles north of Martinique and south of Guadeloupe.

Batman, our guide for the day, proudly pointed out landmarks in Roseau, capital town of this small, independent island that lies between the French islands of Martinique and Guadeloupe. We were standing in the lush botanical gardens on the hills above the town. "This island is peaceful," said Batman, "we have little crime here."

DOMINICA MIGHT be described as the forgotten island of the Leewards. Steep and mountainous with several volcanoes, bubbling sulphurous pools and spectacular waterfalls, it has avoided the tourist exploitation suffered by some of its neighbours because it has few good beaches. The result is that it's great for its fauna and flora.

Roseau is a bustling town with a thriving market, and if you are going to take a minibus tour of the island this south-west corner is the best place to start from. In our case we secured Batman's service and the skipper of our charter boat, Robin (really!), sat up in the front with him. On the way up the island hills we stopped and he showed us lemongrass, coffee beans and many other spices growing by the roadside.

Eventually, after inspecting a few bubbling volcanic springs, we arrived at the start of the trail to Trafalgar Falls, one of the most spectacular in this part of the Caribbean. It's quite a hike but well worth it for the refreshing dip in the pool under the falls.

At the northern end of Dominica are the wide and open Prince Rupert Bay and the town of Portsmouth. There was, until recently, a lot of aggression from the boat boys here which put a lot of yachts off from visiting but they have cleaned up their act now. Ashore are the rusting hulks of several ships blown onto the beach during hurricanes, a few restaurants and shops for most stores – you should find fresh fruit and vegetables in abundance. But one thing not to miss is a trip up the Indian River. You need to hire an Indian River Guide as you cannot take your own tender nor are motors permitted. He will row you up this tropical river and tell you just what you are seeing (all of them have to be qualified), whether it's bloodwood trees, herons or iguanas.

Off shore, Dominica has received increasing recognition as an ideal destination for whale watching, including the spectacular sperm whales.

TRAFALGAR FALLS

INDIAN RIVER

WILDLIFE HAVEN

IN THE FORESTS of Dominica there is an abundance of wildlife, including the manicou, agouti, mountain chicken (actually a frog) and green iguanas.

DOMINICA is the lushest, most verdant of the Caribbean islands, with rich rainforest, raging rivers, hot springs and sulphur pools.

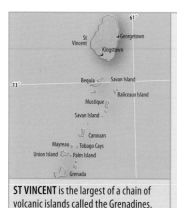

ST VINCENT is the largest of a chain of volcanic islands called the Grenadines.

The Windward Islands
St Vincent and the Grenadines

CHART 5643 (Folio charts), 793
BEST FOR CRUISING December – May
AVERAGE TEMPERATURE 27ºC 80ºF
PREVAILING WIND NE
TIME ZONE GMT – 4
LANGUAGE English
CURRENCY Eastern Caribbean Dollar (EC$), US$

widely accepted
NAVIGATIONAL DIFFICULTY
FAMILY FRIENDLY
DIVING/SNORKELLING
SHORE-SIDE EATING
SIGHTSEEING

You have a week's sailing holiday, would you spend it in the Grenadines? Be warned. Flight, transfers, jetlag, acclimatization all take their toll and by the time the crew has shaken down, begun to turn from white to pink to mahogany, the week's half gone, and the second half always goes quicker than the first.

THE WORD "UNSPOILT" might just have been accurate ten years ago; today the best anchorages are well used to charter yachts, and some – such as Salt Whistle Bay on Mayreau, and Tobago Cays themselves – are choc-a-bloc in high summer.

Outside the hermetically sealed charter bases, you quickly find yourself in the real Caribbean: shabby, vibrant and colourful. Hitch a ride to Kingstown and lose yourself in the market. In Market Square, stall holders will sell you anything from cheap trainers to home-made spicy sauce. And if you are tempted to buy those ripe bananas, check first that they are not plantains.

St Vincent is worth a good look before you head down island. It has coconut groves and a few good beaches, also an active volcano to climb (last eruption 1902), botanical gardens (where Captain Bligh was bound with his breadfruit), rainforests, gorges and wild countryside, some of which is given over to the cultivation of marijuana and into which we were advised not to venture. Kingstown port is a hub of inter-island trade, as far removed from a scrubbed marina as the rusty ferry is to a superyacht.

St Vincent is authentic, and thus in pleasant contrast to nearby Mustique where the rich have built their version of an ideal Caribbean island of swaying palm trees, white sand beaches and

TOBAGO CAYS

SHABBY, VIBRANT AND COLOURFUL

COCONUT GROVE

KINGSTOWN, the main port on St Vincent, is a charming antidote to characterless marinas, and is at the centre of inter-island trade.

lush greenery. After rubber-necking the villas of the rich – Mick Jagger has a pad here – we slipped into Basil's Bar, one of *Newsweek*'s Top Ten Bars in the World.

The best sunshine and sailing conditions are from November to May. The rest of the year is quieter and still hot, but with more rain. Sailing is boisterous and exhilarating outside the lee of the islands. Unlike Greece's Ionian, for example, you'll find proper, full-blooded sea breezes here; enough to satisfy all but the most hardened sailor. Bowling along under the trade winds, beneath a cloudless sky, is the classic Caribbean experience, warm spray and no question of oilskins. We did have several days when the skies were overcast, and several torrential downpours, which came as quite a relief, for it is hot in high season. Navigation is untaxing, but currents can throw you downwind of your destination, and no-one likes beating, even in these conditions.

Tobago Cays, a national park, was to be the highlight of our week. Divers will tell you that the reef is spectacular despite the damage done over the years by careless anchors, illegal fishing and clumsy flippers. Reef to reef with charter boats hanging on anchors, it was a mild disappointment; however, the view of the coral reefs from the Catholic church atop the highest hill on

MAYREAU ISLAND offers ample opportunities to enjoy the magical white sand beaches so emblematic of the Caribbean.

TOBAGO CAYS is a group of five beautiful and uninhabited Grenadine islands surrounded by coral reefs.

TOBAGO CAYS offers world-class scuba-diving among extraordinarily beautiful reefs.

nearby Mayreau was breathtaking. Mayreau, with its little village reached by climbing a steep concrete road from Saline Bay, was the true highlight of the week, along with a simple tuna salad at the Paradise Island Restaurant. The Mayreans appear to have life down to a slow art. This is quite a hot spot for yachties in high season, yet of a yellow wellie or Sperry Topsider there was no sign.

For those in search of pirates, the islands never seem to have appealed to the likes of Morgan and Kidd, Blackbeard and Bonny, so you are left to chase the Hollywood version. And so it was that, on the last day, we discovered *The Black Pearl* alongside a quay on the west side of St Vincent, Jolly Roger at the masthead, decks swarming with film extras, riggers and carpenters. That evening we rounded a vertiginous bluff they call Indian Gallows off which the Caribs preferred to leap rather than be captured by the British, and slipped into Wallilabou. There we dropped anchor off an old storehouse. Outside lay stacked huge bales of cotton, molasses, cannonballs and barrels of rum.

Alas, it was all a sham. After dining ashore in the delightful old storehouse, with its collection of antique bakelite telephones, suits of armour and curiosities, we concluded that for all the fakery, Wallilabou was the best anchorage of the week. We raised a glass to Hollywood and the scurvy crew of *The Black Pearl*.

SERENE BEACHES IN THE GRENADINES are the ideal place to relax and watch the world, and the odd yacht, go by.

The Windward Islands
Bequia

CHART 791	widely accepted
BEST FOR CRUISING December – May	**NAVIGATIONAL DIFFICULTY** ⏱ ⏱
AVERAGE TEMPERATURE 27°C 80°F	**FAMILY FRIENDLY** 🍹 🍹
PREVAILING WIND NE	**DIVING/SNORKELLING** 🤿 🤿 🤿
TIME ZONE GMT – 4	**SHORE-SIDE EATING** 🍽 🍽
LANGUAGE English	**SIGHTSEEING** 🏰 🏰 🏰
CURRENCY Eastern Caribbean Dollar (EC$), US$	

BEQUIA is a relatively small Caribbean island with less than 6,000 inhabitants.

Would Barclays Bank, Bequia branch, still stand beside the beach, and would the Frangipani still serve rum punches, indeed even exist? These were the questions uppermost in my mind as we dropped anchor off Bequia. As a footloose 24-year-old I first set eyes on the island in 1977 from the deck of a 34 foot (10m) wooden sloop, 21 days out of the Canaries, desperate to cash a cheque, and thirsting for a drink.

EVEN THEN the Admiralty Bay anchorage was thick with boats, the majority wooden like ourselves. Bumboats bearing mangoes hove alongside; dreadlocks and a ready line in banter. Bequia in those days felt to us young adventurers lately off the high Atlantic seas, like the real Caribbean; islands of pirates and rum, slaves and wild mulatto women, spices and the pulsating rhythms of the steel band. Treasure islands.

The boats are now of glassfibre and villas dot the lush hillsides, that's all. Across the island they still hunt the humpback whale by harpoon from open boats, and there's every chance you'll get overcharged a wee bit at the market, but enjoy every moment of the bargaining.

This time we anchored off Princess Margaret's Beach – away from most other boats – dinghied ashore and walked round to the town which hugs the shoreline. Catch the Sargeant Brothers famous model makers' shop, but walk over the hill towards Friendship Bay and take a look at Kingsley "Prop" King's little boats, carved from coconut fibres and local hardwoods, which sail with an uncanny balance and authenticity. Kingsley's wife Lucy makes the sails and also sells her own unique artworks. This side of the island has an altogether more laid-back atmosphere, if that could be possible.

My attention was taken more by the whaleboat drawn up on the beach below, in which every detail from the leather-bound oarlocks to the razor-sharp harpoon blade, in its wooden cover, served a deadly, efficient purpose. The apogee of my time on Bequia was nevertheless the offer of a straight swap for my leather Dubarry seaboots for Ras' fruit and vegetable stall on the quay, an offer made, it has to be said, through a haze of suspiciously aromatic smoke from beneath a huge rasta bonnet…

ADMIRALTY BAY

BEQUIA BEACH

HUMPBACK WHALES

HUMPBACK WHALES have longer fins than any other species and it is a remarkable sight when they breach. Whaling in Bequia has long been a tradition.

PORT ELIZABETH is the centrepoint of Bequia, where yachtsmen stop for supplies, repairs or just plain fun.

The Grenadines, Union Island
Chatham Bay

UNION ISLAND is the largest island in the southern part of St Vincent's Grenadines.

CHART 794; Imray Iolaire B311
BEST FOR CRUISING October – May
AVERAGE TEMPERATURE 26ºC 79ºF
PREVAILING WIND NE
TIME ZONE GMT – 4
LANGUAGE English
CURRENCY East Caribbean Dollars (ECs)

NAVIGATIONAL DIFFICULTY
FAMILY FRIENDLY
DIVING/SNORKELLING
SHORE-SIDE EATING
SIGHTSEEING

In his useful handbook *Sailor's Guide to the Windward Islands* author Chris Doyle says of Chatham Bay: "On the lee side of Union is a large protected anchorage. The best spot to anchor is the northeast corner. The wind tends to come over the hills in shrieking gusts."

INDEED, ON MY FIRST VISIT there in the mid-90s on a charter boat, his words rang all too true. All night, bullets of wind fired down from the high, tree-covered surrounding hills as we veered around our anchor, keeping a night-long anchor watch and ducking the rain squalls.

Subsequent visits have been less dramatic. Union's inhabitants live almost exclusively on the east coast of the island to benefit from the cooling trade winds and in Chatham you have the impression of being anchored close to an uninhabited island. There are a few fishermen out seine netting and living in a small camp on shore, no road, no houses and a handful of other yachts, although in high season it can be crowded. There are tracks through the wooded hillside but when the sun goes down, apart from dim cockpit and cabin lights from other yachts and perhaps a fire from the fisher camp there is total darkness and on a moon-free night the swathe of the Milky Way pulsates in the sky and the planets shine bright.

One good reason for visiting Chatham is Shark Attack, an entrepreneurial Union Islander. Unlike in some Caribbean anchorages, Shark Attack will not come and hassle you while you set your anchor and sort the boat out. He will come later and offer you one of the most memorable barbeques you'll ever have. The menu is simple. Fish or lobster.

You take your own crockery, cutlery, salads, glasses and drinks ashore where Shark Attack will guide you to the pitch-dark beach by torch. Your meal will follow soon and you eat by the light of a guttering paraffin lamp, the occasional possum dropping from the trees and scampering into the darkness, sometimes chased by the fishermen looking for their supper. It's not cordon bleu perhaps, but it's certainly memorable.

The energetic can go ashore early the next day for some of the better trekking in the Grenadines, or perhaps don mask and snorkel, as fish life is good here.

NEWLANDS REEF

FISHING IN CHATHAM BAY

REEF LIFE

SQUIRRELFISH teem around the coral reefs that shelter the island. Soldierfishes and the saber squirrelfish, with their rich oily flesh, are are important subsistence fish on the island.

UNION ISLAND is a relatively mountainous island with secluded anchorages. Its highest peak soars some 900ft (275m) above sea level.

TRINIDAD lies off the coast of Venezuela. It has an area of 3,190 sq miles (5,130km²).

Trinidad
Scotland Bay

CHART 477; Imray Iolaire D10
BEST FOR CRUISING November – May
AVERAGE TEMPERATURE 28ºC 82ºF
PREVAILING WIND NE
TIME ZONE GMT – 4
LANGUAGE English and Spanish
CURRENCY Trinidad and Tobago Dollars (TTs)

NAVIGATIONAL DIFFICULTY
FAMILY FRIENDLY
DIVING/SNORKELLING
SHORE-SIDE EATING N/A
SIGHTSEEING

Trinidad is well off the Caribbean's cruising track but every year thousands of yachts head south to the island for good reason, firstly to get south of the hurricane track between May and November and secondly for the excellent lay-up, service and repair facilities at Chaguaramas in the north-west of the island

THE CROSSING to and from Grenada is some 80 miles (129km), a dawn to dusk passage for most yachts, and rather than arrive at Chaguaramas after dark, or if leaving for an early start heading north, one very attractive overnight option is Scotland Bay.

Sailing south towards Trinidad, you'll get a clue to the very different Caribbean you are headed for half-way across from Grenada when the clear blue seas give way to translucent blue-green waters, muddied by the mighty Orinoco.

You enter the Gulf of Paria, home to Trinidad's thriving offshore oil industry, at the Bocas. The fearsomely named Dragon's Mouth is divided by three rocky islands with mainland Venezuela a few

miles to the west. The widest channel, the Boca Grande, runs between Venezuela and the three islands, but take the easternmost of the three channels (Boca de Monos) between the islands and Scotland Bay opens up on your left: well sheltered with high, wooded banks, no sign of habitation except a fisherman's camp at the head of the bay. This is more Amazon rainforest than Caribbean anchorage.

The water here is a soupy green and what fitful breeze reaches into the bay comes from any direction so you finish up with your anchor cable ranging in circles. The air too feels soupy, heavy with humidity and stiflingly hot, and from time to time walls of water advance across the jungly slopes and deluge the anchorage.

And yet this is a magic spot. At dusk, like an acoustic Mexican wave, the birds and parrots start screeching at one end of the bay and this carries on round to the other. Then, as it gets darker, so the howler monkeys add to the chorus. Their grunts and growls, more like a lion or tiger, echo round the hills, make the hairs on the back of your neck stand up. As suddenly as they started, so they stop as if on some secret signal and there is silence. If you look up, above the hills you may just see the twinkle of the evening star.

BLUE-HEADED PARROT

RAINFOREST

HOWLER MONKEYS

Navigate the Dragon's Mouth to a magical "Amazonian" jungle in the Caribbean, accessible only by boat. Here be turtles in soupy green water, parrots and howler monkeys.

TRINIDAD is tiny by North American standards, but it harbours unequalled species diversity when compared to other Caribbean islands.

THE SAN BLAS archipelago lies off the northeast coast of Panama.

Panama
San Blas Islands

CHART 2417; NOAA digital chart 26042, 26063; Tom Zydler's pilot *The Panama Guide* (ISBN 0-9639566-3-9) is extremely useful

BEST FOR CRUISING March – May

AVERAGE TEMPERATURE 24ºC 75ºF

PREVAILING WIND Light easterlies

TIME ZONE GMT – 5

LANGUAGE Kuna

CURRENCY Balboa and US$

NAVIGATIONAL DIFFICULTY

FAMILY FRIENDLY

DIVING/SNORKELLING

SHORE-SIDE EATING

SIGHTSEEING

When the girl at Panama's domestic airport check-in desk asked my body weight, as well as weighing my baggage, I guessed I was in for something different. Reportedly, it's 40 years since any white person found ashore in the San Blas islands after dark was ceremoniously put to death.

THE SAN BLAS archipelago lies off the Caribbean coast of Panama on the blue-water highway to the Panama Canal in an area not much bigger than the UK's Solent. There's an island for almost every day of the year – cartoon islands with pearl-white sand beaches and coconut-laden palm trees – and most of them are uninhabited. There are no roads here. You arrive by boat or small plane. It's straight out of *Robinson Crusoe*.

Aeroperlas Flight No 211, a 30-year-old De Havilland Twin Otter with 20 seats, rattled down the runway. Minutes later we were skimming the Darien Jungle that separates North and South America. My fellow passengers – an exotic assortment of Kuna Indian men and women, sporting multi-coloured bangles

and ankle bracelets – broke into spontaneous applause as we bounced down a tiny airstrip on the island of Corazon de Jesus. Eventually, we landed at Playon Chico. A cayucos (dugout canoe) took me to the island of Sapibenega, formerly known as Iskardup, to join my charter yacht.

San Blas is a gringo name. The region is known as the Kuna Yala (Land of the Kuna) who have lived here since 400BC. Not much has changed since the time of Columbus, or the Conquistadors who followed in his footsteps. The second smallest race of people in the world after African pygmies, the Kunas live on the fish they catch and the crops they grow on the mainland – plus the molas (embroidered panels) they sell to passing sailors.

Despite their violent history, the Kunas are quite shy. Some will only be photographed if you brandish dollars, but the kids will follow you everywhere and pose endlessly for the camera with genuine smiles. Only a few miles separate most of these tiny islands where you can walk in and paddle up river into primary rainforest, or dine out on the catch of the day at a table set on sand as you slip between village life and splendid isolation.

TRADITIONAL DRESS

BEACH HUT HOMES

TRADITIONAL MOLA

THE SAN BLAS archipelago is "straight out of *Robinson Crusoe*": a scattering of small islands dotted with swaying coconut palms.

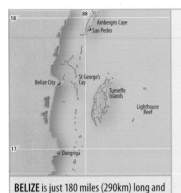

BELIZE is just 180 miles (290km) long and 68 miles (109km) at its widest.

Central America
Belize

CHART 522, 959, 1797
BEST FOR CRUISING February – May (rainy season June – August)
AVERAGE TEMPERATURE 28°C 82°F
PREVAILING WIND NE
TIME ZONE GMT – 6
LANGUAGE English

CURRENCY Belize Dollar (BZ$)
NAVIGATIONAL DIFFICULTY
FAMILY FRIENDLY
DIVING/SNORKELLING
SHORE-SIDE EATING
SIGHTSEEING

If you're looking for perfect sailing off the beaten track, the tropical cayes of Belize, protected by one of the world's longest barrier reefs, should be on your list. Belize, formerly British Honduras, gained its independence in 1981. A colourful mixture of Creole, Caribbean and Latin cultures, Belize shares a border with Mexico and Guatemala. It is one of the least populous Central American countries but it has a long history of democracy.

WE TOOK OFF OUR SHOES to be X-rayed at Belize International Airport, and hardly put them back on for the next ten days. Sand and salt water would be the only things underfoot as we became "castaways".

We joined our yacht in Placencia (population 600), a village at the very tip of a long, narrow sandy peninsula, 60 miles (96km) south of Belize City. Long considered a backpackers' hideout, Placencia is fast becoming one of Belize's worst–kept secrets. It's a three-hour drive from the capital and the peninsula road is a dirt track, so we opted to fly in a twin-engined plane, landing 45 minutes later on a tiny airstrip which ran into the Caribbean Sea. The arrivals and departure lounge was a wooden hut, though it did have air-conditioning. And so did the mini-bus, which drove us into town and the yacht charter base.

The good news for sailors is that Belize's east coast is fringed by one of the longest coral barrier reefs in the world acting as a buffer against the ocean swell and allowing cruising in comfort. There's a choice of 200 cayes (pronounced keys), or islands, to explore. Most of the cayes are uninhabited, a few privately

INVITING BEACHES

LOCAL FISHERMAN

BIRD PARADISE

BELIZE is a birdwatcher's paradise due to the diversity of habitats. It is home to over 550 species of bird, including the jabiru stork (the largest bird in the Western Hemisphere) and the rare harpy eagle.

THE MAINLAND boasts many beautiful beaches ideal for swimming, diving, snorkelling, kayaking, fishing, surfing or just taking a gentle stroll.

owned, with cabanas (palm-thatched huts with wooden walls) rented out to adventurous holidaymakers. Some are home to local fishermen and their families.

This is get-away-from-it-all wilderness cruising country. "If you want to eat ashore, you'll need to radio ahead, so they can get supplies in, or ask the local fisherman to catch your supper," we were told. We dined ashore at The Inn at Robert's Grove, nestling in 15 acres (6ha) between Placencia's lagoon and the Caribbean Sea, with swimming pool, tennis court, beachfront bedrooms and rooftop hot tubs. It was Belize's 2008 hotel of the year.

The charm of the cayes is that tourism hasn't reached these parts. Other than one or two other charter yachts, the only other folk we met on our travels afloat were a handful of long-term live-aboard cruisers and backpackers, canoeing down the barrier reef and sleeping in cabanas or tents.

In six days we'd visited some 12 cayes, but another 188 beckoned, and south lay Guatemala's Rio Dulce (Sweet River), a favourite stopover for blue water cruisers. We'd tasted the sweet life, but we'd only scratched the surface of what Belize – home to one of the greatest ancient civilizations, the Mayans – has to offer.

BELIZE CITY hosts over 40 per cent of all cruise passengers that come ashore in Belize. Tourism is growing rapidly.

AMBERGRIS CAYE is the main dive island in Belize, less than a mile away from the Belize Barrier Reef.

THE TEMPLE OF THE JAGUAR (above) is a spectacular Mayan temple situated along the New River Lagoon, in Lamania.

VICTORIA PEAK (top) is the second highest mountain in Belize, looming high above the tropical rainforest.

THE CORAL REEF (left) stretches for the entire length of Belize. Only the Great Barrier Reef is larger.

PORTLAND HEAD, where Longfellow wrote his famous lighthouse poem, is one of Maine's most popular tourist attractions.

North America, East Coast

American and Canadian sailors are blessed with a wealth of cruising destinations on their own doorstep, a vast area which stretches all the way from the icy fjords of Greenland to the sun-kissed beaches of Mexico. It is a land of contrasts: from the quaint, historic charm of the towns of New England; the bustle and excitement of the world's most vibrant city, New York; to the mysterious and exotic splendour of the Florida Keys. Surprisingly, the western reaches of the North Atlantic attract relatively few European sailors who are obviously deterred by the short sailing season at its northern extreme, the risk of hurricanes in the south and stringent formalities imposed on visiting yachts by the US authorities.

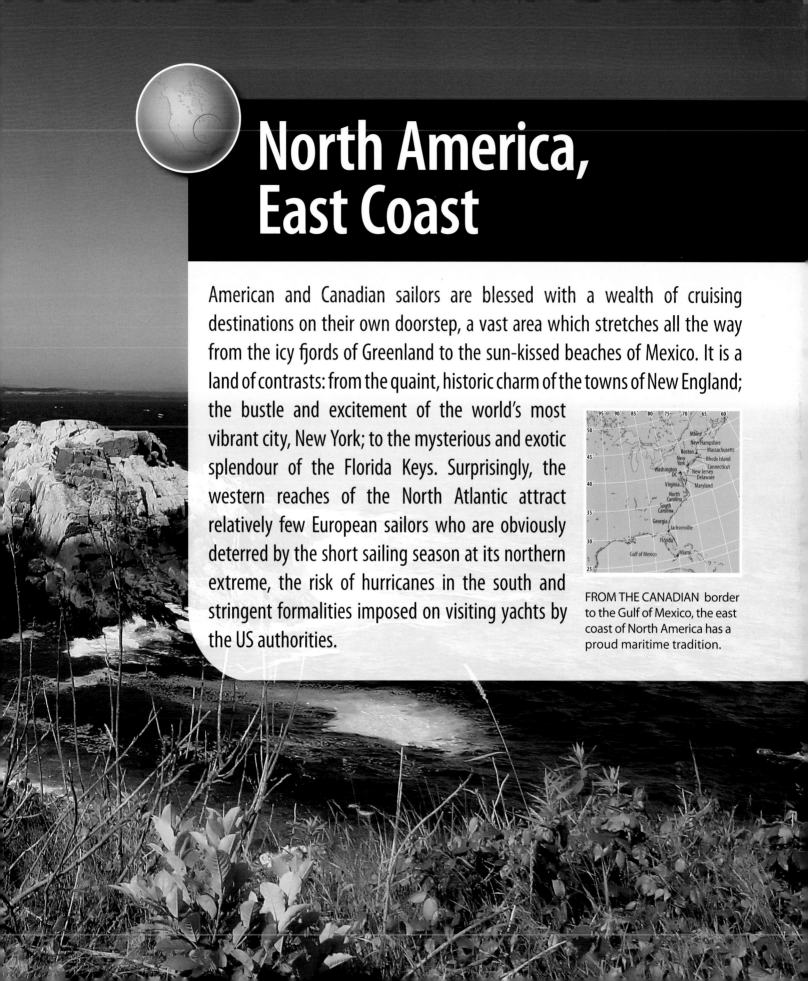

FROM THE CANADIAN border to the Gulf of Mexico, the east coast of North America has a proud maritime tradition.

MAINE

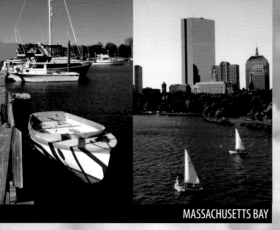

MASSACHUSETTS BAY

EXPLORING THE NEW WORLD

Besides the opportunities provided by coastal cruising, much of the interior of the United States and Canada is accessible by a large network of navigable rivers and canals. The Great Lakes can thus be reached either from New York or the St Lawrence River, providing a unique opportunity to reach the largest inland cruising area in the world. A cruise along the US East Coast has the added attraction of the Intracoastal Waterway, an ingenious system of canals, rivers and estuaries, which stretches along the eastern seaboard from Florida to Maine and offers the chance of sailing in sheltered waters almost within sight of the ocean. The waterways of the southern states wind their way through old cities, deserted estuaries and ancient woods to reach Chesapeake Bay. This large landlocked bay with its secluded anchorages and snug harbours is within striking distance of some of America's main cities, including Washington DC and Baltimore.

Further up the coast lies New York, one of the few major cities in the world where one can sail right through its centre. Passing almost within touching distance of Manhattan's skyscrapers and

Much of the interior of the United States and Canada is accessible by a large network of navigable rivers and canals.

under the many bridges is an experience that cannot be replicated. The Long Island Sound leads into the heart of New England where much of modern America's history was made. Further north, beyond the coast of New Hampshire, is the island world of Maine where many summers – the best time to visit – could be spent exploring the countless bays, rivers and anchorages that stretch right up to the Canadian border.

At the other extreme, Mexico's Yucatan Peninsula used to be an attractive cruising area but a massive tourist development has blighted the previously deserted beaches and bays with large hotels where for centuries the tallest buildings were the Mayan temples. A visit to the Mayan sites, within easy reach of the coast, still justifies including this area in one's cruising plans.

The entire region can be affected by tropical storms that can reach as far north as the Canadian border. The season lasts from June to November and the worst affected areas are those in the south. There are sheltered ports and marinas throughout the area but those who wish to cruise during the summer will find it safer to stay north of the Chesapeake.

NEWPORT

THE KEYS, FLORIDA

NEW ENGLAND consists of six states in the north-eastern United States.

New England
New York to Maine

CHART 2492, 2754; plus numerous NOAA charts
BEST FOR CRUISING June – September
AVERAGE TEMPERATURE 25ºC 77ºF
PREVAILING WIND SW
TIME ZONE GMT – 5
LANGUAGE English
CURRENCY US Dollar (US$)

NAVIGATIONAL DIFFICULTY ⊕ ⊕ ⊕ ⊕
FAMILY FRIENDLY ♈ ♈ ♈ ♈ ♈
DIVING/SNORKELLING 🤿
SHORE-SIDE EATING 🍴 🍴 🍴
SIGHTSEEING ♖ ♖ ♖ ♖ ♖

From the skyscrapers of New York City to the gingerbread towns of New England, the north-eastern seaboard of the United States offers a remarkable diversity for cruisers. Pull up a lobster pot off Nantucket, see a Broadway show in New York, wake to a misty, rockbound cove on the coast of Maine: there's something for every taste.

COLONIAL HOUSE, NEW ENGLAND

IT IS, IN FACT, quite too much to do in a lifetime. A better approach would be to pick and choose from the offerings, just as you'd pick berries along a country road on Block Island. Choose a starting point and, in a radius of a week's cruising, you'll find more than enough to satisfy you.

New York is, well, New York, and from North Cove Marina you can take a bite of the Big Apple. It's one of the busiest harbours in the world, but swing past the Statue of Liberty and Ellis Island.

Long Island Sound is lined with coves and commuter villages, all with marina facilities and the attractions of small town life. Pick either the mainland or the Long Island side, and harbour-hop at your own pace. Near the end of Long Island, Sag Harbor has a famous whaling history and some pricey nightlife, but sailors gather at the Corner Bar for burgers and beer.

Just a short hop across the sound is Mystic Seaport, a Disneyworld for anyone who loves boats. There is a 19th-century village, a preserved shipyard, nautical exhibits and a waterfront packed with historic vessels to explore, but call far in advance for dock reservations.

Stop in at the Great Salt Pond on Block Island, one of the best natural harbours on this coast and completely landlocked for all-weather protection. Rent a bicycle to visit the 150-year-

MYSTIC SEAPORT

MISTS

NEW ENGLAND is a cruising paradise with consistent wind and awesome scenery. However, it is notorious for its fast fog and changeable weather, which can be challenging even for experienced sailors.

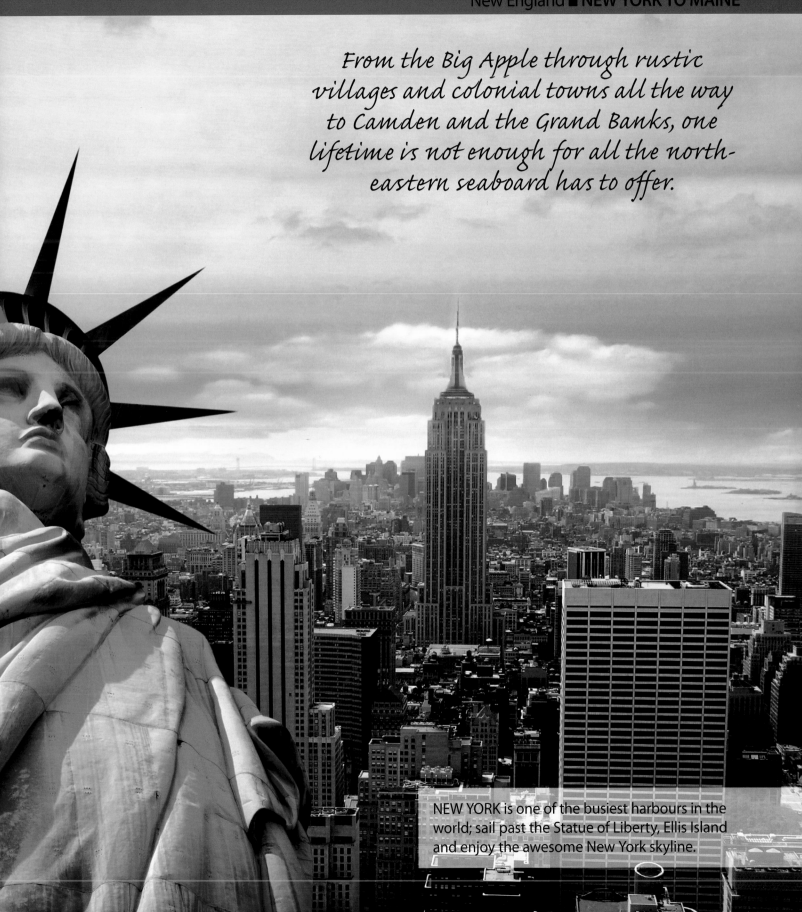

From the Big Apple through rustic villages and colonial towns all the way to Camden and the Grand Banks, one lifetime is not enough for all the north-eastern seaboard has to offer.

NEW YORK is one of the busiest harbours in the world; sail past the Statue of Liberty, Ellis Island and enjoy the awesome New York skyline.

MENEMSHA HARBOR on Martha's Vineyard is famous as the setting for the Steven Spielberg monster hit *Jaws*.

old lighthouse at the south-west corner of the island and enjoy the spectacular scenery.

Near the head of Narragansett Bay, Newport, Rhode Island is clearly the yachting centre of the north-east, and rightfully so. Whether you're going north or south, or just exploring this area, you'll stop in Newport. This was where the America's Cup was contested for decades and, after it was lost to the Aussies, Newport reinvented itself.

Bannister's Wharf (with the famed Candy Store restaurant/bar of Cup fame) is the centre of the action and a bowl of chowder at the Black Pearl on Thames Street is always essential. Take a tour of the grandiose "summer cottages" of early business tycoons and, if you visit in August, enjoy the events during the annual Newport Jazz Festival.

Stop to savour Cuttyhunk, at the western end of the Elizabeth Island chain that stretches from Woods Hole on the elbow of Cape Cod toward Block Island. This tiny island has just 50 residents, a few buildings and one schoolhouse, as well as a rustic charm and solitude, not to mention a good anchorage.

From here, it's a short hop down Vineyard Sound to Edgartown Harbor, which looks just as it did in colonial days, with streets lined with the homes of whaling captains. Opt for a guided tour of the island to see Menemsha (where *Jaws* was filmed) and don't

EDGARTOWN was a whaling port in the 1800s, and the harbour is lined with stately homes built by whaling captains.

OAK BLUFFS, on the north-east shore of the island of Martha's Vineyard, operates the largest marina on Martha's Vineyard and boasts the unique and colourful Victorian "gingerbread" cottages.

miss the Victorian, gingerbread architecture at Oak Bluffs.

Finishing the islands is Nantucket, which was the busiest whaling port in North America and, aside from cars and cell phones, not much has changed since the 17th century. Old-fashioned lamps line the streets and yachts now have secure moorings where whaling ships once set out on year-long voyages. Inland, the wild moors are protected and, in springtime,

are lush with flowers. If you're feeling more active, play a round on one of the island golf courses.

Tourism and art have replaced whale oil on Nantucket, which now boasts an array of good restaurants and streets lined with art galleries and museums. For a lovely meal in a historic home, sample the seafood and fresh produce at Oran Mor on Beach Street.

One of my fondest North-east memories is sailing aboard a perfectly restored Concordia yawl into Hadley's Harbor, tucked just off Woods Hole. This is one of the prettiest harbours in the world, and we arrived just as one of the dense New England fogs descended. With the hook set and a fire in the little tiled fireplace,

CAPE COD BAY offers good protection from the Atlantic, and there are a number of quaint villages with excellent marinas.

we spent a quiet night reading at anchor. The next morning, we were awakened by a gentle tapping on the hull. In a lobster boat alongside, a fishermen held up a couple of huge (and angry) lobsters and, in a slow drawl, asked, "You folks need a couple of big bugs? Dollar apiece?"

To save a long haul offshore, the Cape Cod Canal was created so that yachts and ships can transit easily between Buzzard's Bay and Cape Cod Bay. More than 17 miles (27km) long and 500ft (152m) wide, there is considerable current when the tide is running and yachts over 65ft (19.8m) must wait for the red-and-green "traffic signals" for their passage.

Cape Cod Bay offers good protection from the Atlantic, and there are a number

CAPE ANN is the oldest fishing village in the country and home to the Rocky Neck Art Colony.

of quaint villages with marinas or anchorages scattered along the cape to Provincetown.

On the mainland is Plymouth, where the Pilgrims landed in 1620, and the town is filled with museums and sites commemorating the Plymouth Colony.

Further north is Boston, home of the historic Charlestown Navy Yard and the USS *Constitution* (Old Ironsides). Boston's Logan Airport has good international connections for starting or ending cruises.

Nearby Marblehead is famous as a sailing town, and here you'll find homes from the 1800s and great baked scrod (young cod or haddock) at The Landing pub on Front Street, just a walk from the marina. The crème caramel is to die for, too.

Cape Ann is the oldest fishing village in the country and Gloucester was the site of the filmed (and, in October 1991, the real-life) *Perfect Storm*. The rugged coastline is an artist's dream, which has led to the Rocky Neck Art Colony – and there's a little marina here, so you can explore the galleries and enjoy a meal ashore at the Studio Restaurant.

Portland is a good launch pad to explore "Downeast" Maine, so named because the eastern coast of Maine, from Penobscot Bay to the Canadian border, is generally downwind for square-riggers

BOSTON is home to the historic Charlestown Navy Yard and the USS *Constitution* (Old Ironsides).

BOOTHBAY HARBOR is a charming town in Lincoln County, Maine, with plentiful and varied restaurants serving delicious local seafood dishes.

sailing from Boston. Today, it's come to mean a whole world of lobster boats, rocky islands, and traditional boatbuilders.

Round the 18th-century Portland Head Lighthouse and head for Boothbay Harbor to dine on fresh Maine lobster and Damariscotta oysters. Yum!

Explore Penobscot Bay, stopping at the picturesque ports of Camden and

PORTLAND HEAD and its lighthouse were said by historian Edward Rowe Snow to "symbolize the state of Maine – rocky coast, breaking waves, sparkling water and clear, pure salt air".

Rockport. If you have time, visit the Farnsworth Museum in Rockland, which shows three generations of Wyeth family art. Once a granite-quarrying capital, the island of Vinalhaven provided stone for skyscrapers in New York. Carver's Harbor has the largest fleet of lobster boats in Maine, with their traditional lines now being adapted to yachts.

At Islesford in the Cranberry Isles, you'll find a museum with nautical artefacts, and nearby Swans Island has miles of scenic bike trails leading to the picturesque Bass Harbor Light.

Mount Desert Island is the gateway to the Acadia National Park, and you might want to linger in Bar Harbor for char-grilled lobster or a movie at the historic Criterion theatre.

At Camden you'll see the six schooners that carry on the traditional world of sail, now with tourists rather than fish from the Grand Banks, and this is a good point to end your cruise of the north-eastern coast.

CAMDEN (right) is famous as the setting as the setting for classic 50s movie *Peyton Place*. In the popular harbour today, you're likely to encounter the odd classic schooner too.

STUNNING AUTUMN COLOURS (left) adorn the granite coastline near Otter Point, Acadia National Park. Otter Point is breathtaking at any time of year and a paradise for rock-pool enthusiasts.

NEW ENGLAND (below) is synonymous with lobster. Tenants Harbor is a tranquil village that has some great restaurants selling fresh, locally caught lobster and fish dishes.

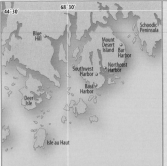

ACADIA National Park is located off the coast of Maine on Mount Desert Island.

Maine
Acadia National Park

CHART 4746
BEST FOR CRUISING June – September
AVERAGE TEMPERATURE 23°C 74°F
PREVAILING WIND SW
TIME ZONE GMT – 5
LANGUAGE English
CURRENCY US Dollar (US$)

NAVIGATIONAL DIFFICULTY
FAMILY FRIENDLY
DIVING/SNORKELLING
SHORE-SIDE EATING
SIGHTSEEING

"Mainers" are fond of telling visitors to this most north-eastern of the New England states that they have three seasons; summer, winter and mud. If you're lucky enough to be sailing in the Acadia National Park you can add "beauty" to that list.

THE SNAGGLETOOTHED Maine shoreline that shoves its rocky fingers into the Atlantic for hundreds of miles is blessed with a multitude of breathtaking views and great cruising grounds, but Acadia encapsulates the drama and the glory in a neat, accessible package.

This isn't a national park in the sense that that it is completely devoted to nature. There are many small villages and harbours. Most of the parkland is on Mount Desert Island and a host of small islands that surround it, with some on the Schoodic peninsula to the east and, to the south-west, Isle au Haut.

It's possible to touch the main points of Acadia in a week's cruising, for distances between anchorages and harbours are not great; it is equally possible to spend a month here, dividing your nights between snug coves with not a single light visible on shore and townships with evocative names like Bass Harbor, Bar Harbor and Southwest Harbor. There's as much to do on land as there is on the water, providing you are a nature lover.

Hike along the granite cliffs, along the sand and cobblestone beaches, or beside the many deep lakes and enjoy the splendour of glacier-carved mountains rising from the sea. Habitats range from meadows and marshes to dense evergreen forests. The ocean is omnipresent.

A trip to Bass Harbor lighthouse is a must. A path on the right takes you to a vantage point for a fabulous ocean view.

Some of America's finest boatbuilders make their home in and around Acadia. You'll see their work in every anchorage; Hinckley, Morris, Sabre, along with dozens of older classics. They like their boats pretty up here.

The season starts late, but by the end of May most boats are in the water. In July and August unpredictable fogbanks can leave you harbourbound for a day or two at a time, and a combination of currents, lobster pots and rocks mean you have to keep your wits about you. But once you've sailed here, you'll be planning the next time before you've got your gear off the boat.

CADILLAC MOUNTAIN

SCHOODIC PENINSULA

AUTUMN SPLENDOUR

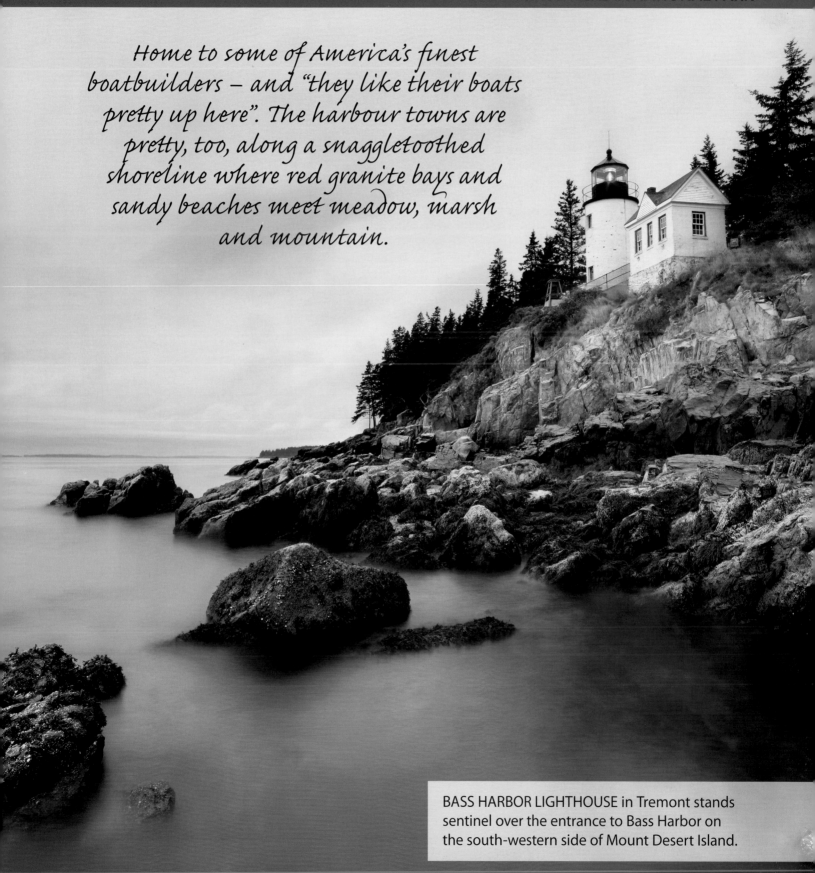

Home to some of America's finest boatbuilders – and "they like their boats pretty up here". The harbour towns are pretty, too, along a snaggletoothed shoreline where red granite bays and sandy beaches meet meadow, marsh and mountain.

BASS HARBOR LIGHTHOUSE in Tremont stands sentinel over the entrance to Bass Harbor on the south-western side of Mount Desert Island.

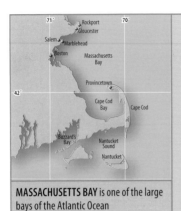

MASSACHUSETTS BAY is one of the large bays of the Atlantic Ocean

Boston
Massachusetts Bay

CHART 1227, 3096, 1516, 2891, 2487, 2427
BEST FOR CRUISING June – October
AVERAGE TEMPERATURE 23°C 74°F
PREVAILING WIND SW (June – September)
TIME ZONE GMT – 5
LANGUAGE English
CURRENCY US Dollar (US$)

NAVIGATIONAL DIFFICULTY
FAMILY FRIENDLY
DIVING/SNORKELLING
SHORE-SIDE EATING
SIGHTSEEING

Poor old Massachusetts Bay; stuck in the same state as the delectable cruising grounds of Martha's Vineyard, Nantucket, the Elizabeth Islands and Buzzard's Bay, it tends to be overlooked when planning a New England cruise.

MASSACHUSETTS BAY is highly populated, and some of its harbours are shallow and hard to get into. And yet, it offers a fine sailing and cultural experience of its own.

Let's start from Gloucester, still the working fishing port portrayed in *The Perfect Storm*. It's one of the most sheltered harbours on this piece of coast, and a good place to be in a north-easter. Sail around the corner of Cape Ann to charming Rockport. From there, you could get up at daybreak, and take advantage of the typical south-westerly breeze to make the 40-mile (64km) open water passage to Provincetown, just inside the clenched fist of the long, curled arm of Cape Cod. You'll wince at the mooring fees, but enjoy a day on the white sand beaches, and marvel at the nightlife – it's the gay capital of New England.

Then it's a solid, close reach to Boston, and its cluster of harbour islands. Many of these have moorings, and there are some good anchorages. If you're into 18th- and 19th-century fortifications, these are for you. It's easy to spend a couple of days poking around here. In Boston itself, you can get a berth at Constitution Marina and walk into the friendly, laid-back city. There's excellent dining here, and almost everywhere else along the coast. I recommend the seafood – hey, you're in New England.

Heading north the next day, if you call ahead to the harbourmaster you can generally pick up a visitor's mooring in the lovely town of Marblehead, 20 miles (32km) up the coast. If the harbour's full, as it often is on weekends or during regatta weeks, motor around the corner to Salem, where there's always a berth or a mooring to be had. Salem is full of museums, most of them to do with pirates or witch burnings, but the Peabody Essex, a stone's throw from the waterfront, is well worth visiting if you want a real sense of the area's history.

Wind up your cruise with a daysail around the outlying islands, followed by a visit to Manchester and its singing beach. What next? How about a good daysail down to the Cape Cod Canal, and then slipping into Buzzard's Bay…

PROVINCETOWN

CAPE COD BAY

BOSTON

ROCKPORT HARBOR is one of the most picturesque little harbours you'll find in a region chock full of picturesque little harbours.

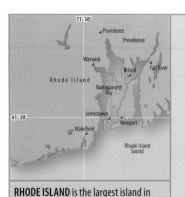

RHODE ISLAND is the largest island in Narragansett Bay.

Rhode Island
Newport

CHART 2730
BEST FOR CRUISING May – September
AVERAGE TEMPERATURE 20°C 68°F
PREVAILING WIND S
TIME ZONE GMT – 5
LANGUAGE English
CURRENCY US Dollar (US$)

NAVIGATIONAL DIFFICULTY
FAMILY FRIENDLY
DIVING/SNORKELLING
SHORE-SIDE EATING
SIGHTSEEING

As a witness to yachting history, Newport has few peers. These days it's short of piers, too, as many of the wooden walkways suspended between rows of piles, have gone. Water frontage is much more lucrative as business and apartment space than yacht docking.

SO NO MORE can you wander down Bowen's Wharf or Bannister's Wharf and see an America's Cup 12-metre hanging up in its hoist as you could until 1983. That was the September when Australia II turned the America's Cup upside down, this light and nimble white boat with her inverted winged keel ending sport's longest winning streak.

All this is recent history. As an English colony, Newport was founded in 1639, by settlers moving south from the Boston area. Aquidneck Island (Rhode) was bought from Native Americans who had been on the land for 5,000 years.

This deeply indented coast of bays, rivers and coves remains a treat, softer and lusher than Maine to the north. The white weatherboard houses look right at home.

When it comes to houses, Newport has a stock of something special, the so-called cottages built by the banking, steel and railroad barons of the 19th century. Newport's residents had an artistic and cultural mien until the Golden Age when the ostentatious mansions were built for the likes of the Vanderbilts.

No surprise then that when the America's Cup races moved away from New York, in 1930 they came to Newport. For 50 years, the town was the Cup Capital of the World.

The loss of the Cup changed Newport, but is still one of prime yachting centres in America. The harbour throngs with desirable yachts, is lined by clubs from the highest (the New York Yacht Club's out-station at Harbour Court) to the humble, hosts the Bermuda Race start, still sees 12-metres race actively throughout the season and is home to many in the business of boats. It also has a magnificent Museum of Yachting at Fort Adams and not far away, at Bristol, the Herreshoff Museum and America's Cup Hall of Fame is unmissable.

Though highly developed, and in parts industrialized, Narragansett Bay is scenic and in places, tranquil. Sail out past Beaver Tail Point to Atlantic and you'll see Brenton Reef Tower, longtime the finish line for the solo transatlantic race from Plymouth.

BOWEN'S WHARF

NEWPORT COASTLINE

NEWPORT MANSIONS

NEWPORT boasts many superb examples of 18th–19th century architecture. Some of its famous "summer cottages" were acquired by the Newport Preservation Society and are open to the public.

NEWPORT HARBOR is been acclaimed as one of the finest small boat harbours in the world, and its surrounding shoreline is exquisitely beautiful.

NEWPORT HARBOR BRIDGE is a spectacular landmark, and is especially beautiful viewed from the water during a splendid sunset.

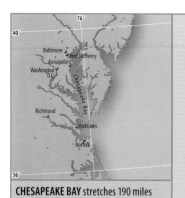

CHESAPEAKE BAY stretches 190 miles (306km) into Maryland and Virginia.

Maryland and Virginia
Chesapeake Bay

CHART 2861, 2921, 2920; NOAA 12280
BEST FOR CRUISING Spring and autumn
AVERAGE TEMPERATURE 24ºC 75ºF
PREVAILING WIND SW (summer); NW (winter)
TIME ZONE GMT – 5
LANGUAGE English
CURRENCY US Dollar (US$)

NAVIGATIONAL DIFFICULTY
FAMILY FRIENDLY
DIVING/SNORKELLING
SHORE-SIDE EATING
SIGHTSEEING

Chesapeake Bay has an amazingly serrated shoreline of more than 5,000 miles (8,047km). There are more than 500 harbours, plus uncounted coves, villages and islands to explore in a region that time seems to have passed by.

THE BAY is also a slice of American history, with plantation-era homes on the eastern peninsula and battlefields on the western shore, from Fort McHenry at the head of the bay to Yorktown near the mouth.

Though the tide is negligible, keep a careful eye on the charts. Locals say there are two kinds of skipper on Chesapeake Bay: those who have run aground and those who are about to. The good news is that the bottom is mostly soft mud or sand so, unless you were very unwise, you can usually slide free easily. Another warning: the Chesapeake Bay is a minefield of lobster pots; keep a sharp lookout to avoid wrapping the stretchy nylon around your prop.

Annapolis is the pride of the bay and, as an important crossroads of culture, finance and politics since the 18th century, it was called the "Paris of America". It was once

the capital of the United States, and is home to the US Naval Academy. Visitors enjoy a variety of treats: fresh oysters on the city docks, the small shops along Main Street and houses dating back to the 1700s that are painted in bright, nautical colours.

The City Marina is the centre of action (for dockage, fuel and great ice cream cones), but the surrounding area has good moorings and full marine services. Take a tour of the Naval Academy and its museum by stopping at the visitor centre at Gate 1. A great starting point for exploring the vast cruising grounds of the Chesapeake, Annapolis also hosts two annual in-water boat shows in October that occupy every inch of dock space, so plan your visit around them. Chesapeake weather is often steamy in the summer, but the spring and autumn are mild and pleasant.

Before leaving the Annapolis area, take time to explore the quiet Severn River, as well as Spa, College and Back Creeks, with tree-lined estates and waterfront homes.

Head across to the eastern shore to visit St Michael's, a pre-Revolutionary town with a pretty waterfront, and home to the Chesapeake Bay Maritime Museum. You can overnight in the fine harbour of Oxford or, if it's quiet you're seeking, you might prefer to drop a hook in Gibson Island's protected harbour.

ANNAPOLIS

SPA CREEK

CHESAPEAKE CRABS

THE CHESAPEAKE BAY CRAB seems to be ubiquitous in the summertime: crab quiche, crab cakes, crab chowder, crab gazpacho – the choice is endless but always delicious.

THE CHESAPEAKE BAY MARITIME MUSEUM is well worth a leisurely visit to see exhibits that include vintage oyster-dredging skipjacks.

Smith Island is a time warp to another era. Just 12 miles (19km) offshore, it has existed for three centuries on commercial fishing, and it is still populated by watermen. The most unusual feature, however, is that the locals still speak in a remnant of Elizabethan-Cornwall English left from the early English settlers.

You won't find any waterfront bars or pubs (this is a "dry" island, so bring your own) in Ewell, the primary village, but you can find wonderful jars of preserves in the 1920s-era Driftwood General Store, which is also known far and wide for crab cakes. Don't miss a chance to try a piece of Smith Island cake, either. And if you leave without sampling the famed blue crabs at the Bayside Inn, well, it's your own fault. Enjoy them steamed with a peppery sauce and washed down with plenty of icy beer.

A word to the wise: the Smith fuel dock has limited space and the watermen usually fill up in the late afternoons, so do your refuelling early. If you're looking for souvenirs, retired boatbuilders make scale replicas of lighthouses and other nautical items.

Worth watching are the summer log canoe races along the eastern shore, where long narrow double-enders from the 1800s pile on mountains of sail and balance them with crews piled on outriggers.

OXFORD was home to the celebrated Robert Morris, and the inn that bears his name is itself something of an institution.

FABULOUS FOOD, numerous anchorages and marinas, awesome scenery and mild weather: Chesapeake Bay has it all.

DOGWOOD HARBOR (above) brings to life the tradition and heritage of the Chesapeake Bay watermen. Visitors can view the day's harvest and chat with watermen of three generations.

CHESAPEAKE (right) houses are colourful and steeped in history, most located on George Street and Bohemia Avenue, which are on the southern side of the Chesapeake and Delaware canal.

BLUE CRAB CAKES (far right) are a celebrated local delicacy. Plenty of places claim to produce the best but wherever you are, check with the locals and you'll enjoy a real culinary delight.

THE AIW stretches from Chesapeake Bay to the Florida Keys.

Atlantic Intracoastal Waterway
Chesapeake Bay to Key West

CHART 2861, 2864, 2865, 2866; plus numerous NOAA charts

BEST FOR CRUISING Spring and autumn

AVERAGE TEMPERATURE 24ºC 75ºF

PREVAILING WIND Summer S; winter NE

TIME ZONE GMT − 5

LANGUAGE English

CURRENCY US Dollar (US$)

NAVIGATIONAL DIFFICULTY

FAMILY FRIENDLY

DIVING/SNORKELLING

SHORE-SIDE EATING

SIGHTSEEING

American drivers have Route 66, but boaters have the Atlantic Intracoastal Waterway (AIW), a 1,200-mile (1,931km) string of protected waterways that stretches from Chesapeake Bay to Key West, Florida.

TWICE EVERY YEAR, in the spring and the autumn, thousands of skippers take their boats down this combination of natural and man-made waterways that provide a safe route away from the open Atlantic Ocean. They're called "ditch-crawlers" or "snowbirds", and their goal is to escape the onset of winter in the north-east. Yachts come from as far as the Great Lakes to reach the balmy winter in Florida, staying until the hurricane season approaches and the northern waters thaw enough for the return trip.

Created in the 1930s for commercial shipping, the AIW (there is a Gulf Intracoastal from Key West to Texas, too) used natural waterways when available, and dredged out channels through marshes and solid earth elsewhere. The AIW has become a political hot potato: as commercial usage declined, funds for maintenance and dredging also dried up, resulting in shallow spots.

This has created an infrastructure of annual charts, guidebooks and Internet sites that alert skippers to the danger areas. Me? I've gone aground 11 times, if you skip those times when we didn't come to a full stop. Watch the channel markers, keep the chart handy, use the range markers and talk to other skippers on VHF radio (or while you're waiting for bridge openings).

Just south of Mile 0 in Norfolk, Virginia, is the Dismal Swamp, which is a jungle cruise through wildlife-filled marshes. Nearby Elizabeth City has a welcoming committee that brings a rose for the women and throws dock parties for transient snowbirds.

North and South Carolina are pleasant, and I like Topsail Island (NC) and Charleston (SC) for overnight stops, as well as Hilton Head (SC). There are more than 100 public golf courses close to marinas in one 60-mile (97km) stretch on the border between the Carolinas.

The "Rock Pile" is a difficult stretch near Myrtle Beach (SC): try to pass through at low tide so you can see the rocky outcrops. When you reach Georgia, Jekyll Island is a good stopover. Florida is boating country, with good marinas in Jacksonville, St Augustine, Stuart (a sport-fishing centre), Palm Beach, Fort Lauderdale and Miami.

NORTH CAROLINA MARSHES

BALD HEAD ISLAND GOLF

CHARLESTOWN

Meander along mile upon mile of sheltered, interconnecting rivers, canals and estuaries, almost within sight of the Atlantic surf.

MURELLS INLET is a historic fishing village sited on a stunning estuary south of Myrtle Beach. It is known as the "seafood capital of South Carolina".

THE FLORIDA KEYS archipelago begins at the southeastern tip of the Florida peninsula.

Florida
The Florida Keys

CHART 1097, 1098; NOAA 11442, 11452
BEST FOR CRUISING November – April
AVERAGE TEMPERATURE 24ºC 75ºF
PREVAILING WIND Summer SE; winter NE
TIME ZONE GMT – 5
LANGUAGE English
CURRENCY US Dollar (US$)

NAVIGATIONAL DIFFICULTY
FAMILY FRIENDLY
DIVING/SNORKELLING
SHORE-SIDE EATING
SIGHTSEEING

The Florida Keys are as much a state of mind as a string of islands. Called America's Caribbean, they are more than that. They are Humphrey Bogart and Ernest Hemingway, Margaritaville and Key Largo, pirates, galleons, smugglers and Conquistadors, and rum drinks with umbrellas.

BUT MOST OF ALL, they are miles of empty sand beaches, palm trees blowing in the warm trades, and aqua waters that turn cobalt as they deepen.

Most people are surprised to see on a map that the Keys curve like a long stinger from Florida and much of the time you'll be heading more east than south. There are, by official count, some 1,700 islands that stretch 130 miles (209km) from the Florida mainland, all stitched together by the Overseas Highway, a long ribbon of concrete with 42 bridges including the accurately named Seven Mile Bridge. It is a beautiful drive, but it's even more spectacular by water.

There's no trick to navigating in the Florida Keys: keep your boat in deep water and don't try to go where birds are standing. With a little experience, you'll learn to gauge water depth by colour but, until then, pay close attention to the charts, the depth sounder and the buoys. The dangers are well marked, but you need to keep track of where you are in relation to the buoys. This is the IALA "B" system of buoys, so always remember: "Red, Right, Returning". The trick, when you seem to be going parallel to land, is to figure out which way is "returning".

Charter cruises often start in Miami, so you can sample the nightlife and art-deco architecture of South Beach or the hot-blooded Cuban restaurants before heading down Biscayne Bay toward the Keys.

THE SEVEN-MILE BRIDGE

MIAMI

CORAL REEF

THE FLORIDA KEYS archipelago is home to the continental United States' only living-coral barrier reef. The reef teems with marine life and runs the length of the Keys about five miles (8km) offshore.

A long crescent of green and gold on cobalt blue, this chain of more than 1,500 islands offers everything under the sun.

BAHIA HONDA BEACH is rated among the finest anywhere in the United States. It's a fabulous spot for snorkel trips and ocean kayaking.

KEY LARGO is the gateway to the 21-mile-long (34km) John Pennekamp Coral Reef State Park.

STOP AT HAWK'S CAY RESORT on Duck Key to swim with dolphins in a saltwater lagoon or play a round of golf.

To get acclimatized, stop at Elliott Key, where the notorious pirate Black Caesar once harboured, but you'll be snorkelling instead of walking the plank.

Key Largo is the gateway to the 21-mile-long (34km) John Pennekamp Coral Reef State Park. Call ahead on VHF-16 for moorings in Largo Sound, which are administered by the park. This is some of the best diving and snorkelling in the Keys because the reefs are pristine and bright as the sunlight filters through the clear and shallow waters.

A word about rules: the Florida Keys are a National Marine Sanctuary, meaning that you can boat, fish, snorkel, dive or play in the waters, but you must protect the environment. Anything that might damage coral, such as anchoring, is prohibited so you'll find mandatory mooring buoys in many areas. You must fly a red-and-white dive flag if you are snorkelling or diving, you can't remove any marine life and you can't create a wake near residences, anchored boats or diver flags. Trust me, these rules are strictly enforced and carry sizable penalties.

You'll have a choice when exploring the Keys. The Intracoastal Waterway ducks from the Atlantic side to the Florida Bay (west) side of the Keys at Jewfish Creek Bridge. Continuing down the eastern side is Hawk Channel, which is deep water inside the barrier reef. The Intracoastal is more protected but harder to navigate. Hawk Channel is less protected so there may be swells, but it is clearly marked and deep. Your choice.

Stop at Little Palm Island, a superluxe resort with an expensive marina, but you can use their facilities and enjoy five-star cuisine.

KEY WEST is the southernmost point in the United States.

At Looe Key, dive a wreck from the 1700s on a reef with spectacular elkhorn coral. Key West is wild, exuberant and often bizarre. Try a conch fritter on Duval Street, watch the sunset (and street entertainers) from Mallory Square or explore Hemingway's house.

With temperatures around 24ºC (75ºF) year-round, and waters warmed like a bath by the nearby Gulf Stream, the Florida Keys are truly a tropical paradise.

ISLAMORADA is a fishing paradise; choose between offshore sport fishing or the challenge of bonefish on the flats.

SEATTLE is bounded on the west by Puget Sound, an inland arm of the Pacific Ocean, and on the east by Lake Washington.

The American West Coast to Antarctica

From chilly north to Chile south, via the warmth of Southern California, these waters are nothing if not varied in climate, culture and navigational challenges. Alaska and the Pacific North-west alone encompass a vast, intricate area that would take a lifetime to explore. Catalina Island is a favourite weekend stopover for those who feel drawn by the glamorous spell left by the great movie stars of Hollywood's heyday: Bogey, Bacall and the legendary John Wayne. Mexico offers some magical sailing in the relatively sheltered Sea of Cortez. For true adventurers, Cape Horn is the gateway to Antarctica, a white wilderness that has been explored by fewer yachts than there have been missions into outer space.

FROM ALASKA to Mexico, the western coast of America is a vast, inhospitable coastline with few natural harbours.

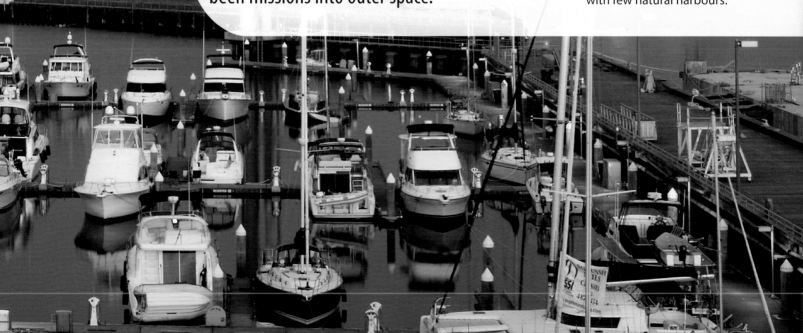

SAN DIEGO

KETCHIKAN

WEST COAST SAILING

The West Coast of the United States has fewer cruising opportunities than the East Coast, with the main attractions being concentrated at its two extremes. The most popular cruising area in the Pacific North-west is the San Juan Islands, an archipelago of some 200 islands, many of which are wildlife reserves or marine parks. Beyond those islands and through Canadian waters beckons the Inside Passage that links Puget Sound to Alaska, one of America's most tempting cruising destinations. Most sailors follow the inshore route to Alaska, but due to the prevailing north-west winds some boats setting off from Southern California opt for an offshore passage. For those who are not tempted by high-latitude cruising, there is all-year-round sailing in the San Francisco Bay area or the Channel Islands, off Southern California.

For West Coast sailors looking for an offshore challenge, Hawaii is the natural destination. The 2,000-mile (3,218km) passage normally benefits from favourable winds but the prevailing north-east winds that are generated by the North Pacific high

Every year, many yachts – both power and sail – make their way to Alaska for the short summer season.

are a permanent offshore feature that make the return voyage a real challenge. The accepted tactic is to sail north from Hawaii by skirting the area of high pressure and only turn east when an area of westerly winds has been reached. The other option is to leave Hawaii with a good reserve of fuel and simply motor through the calms until favourable winds are found closer to the coast.

The closest foreign destination is the Gulf of California, its main attraction being the diverse wildlife that inhabits the limpid waters of the Sea of Cortez. But Mexico also offers an ancient culture, a vibrant atmosphere and a landscape of varied scenery from the high mountains to the silvery beaches. Yachting facilities all along Mexico's west coast are of a good standard.

Tropical storms are a feature of the summer months, between June and late October, and affect the area between the west coast of Mexico and Hawaii. The unique scenery and abundant wildlife tempts a small number of sailors to head south for Chile and to take up the challenge of reaching Antarctica by sailing across the Drake Passage to the Antarctic Peninsula during the relatively safe season between December and early March.

CALIFORNIA

MEXICO

THE ARCHIPELAGO of more than 1,000 islands stretches for 300 miles (480km).

Alaska
The Alexander Archipelago

CHART 1499, 4970, 4971, 4972; NOAA 17420, 17360
BEST FOR CRUISING May – September
AVERAGE TEMPERATURE 17ºC 62ºF
PREVAILING WIND SE (panhandle)
TIME ZONE GMT – 9
LANGUAGE English
CURRENCY US Dollar (US$

NAVIGATIONAL DIFFICULTY
FAMILY FRIENDLY
DIVING/SNORKELLING
SHORE-SIDE EATING
SIGHTSEEING

It was the gin and tonic of a lifetime. We had eased our 40ft (12m) charter yacht up against the glacier at the end of a long fjord and, while we all listened warily for any creaks that might suggest a part of this wall of ice might calve away, we quickly knocked chunks of ice into a bucket and backed quickly into safer waters.

THAT NIGHT we toasted our Alaskan cruising adventure with G&Ts topped with ice that was old before the Wright brothers flew and perhaps even before Queen Victoria was born! I can tell you that it was very cold, very hard, and worth every effort we'd made to get there. It was such good ice, in fact, that we had several G&Ts.

No matter how prepared you are, or how blasé you wish to appear, your first glimpse of the immense blue-green hulk of a glacier is sure to take your breath away.

Alaska is America's last frontier and it is as much a land of dreams as when the pioneers were racing to the Yukon gold rush. It is frontier towns and sheltered waters, abundant wildlife and surprisingly mild summers.

Marvel at the sight of a bald eagle soaring high above a ridge, or a humpback whale breaching in a welter of spray. Alaska is a synonym for outdoor adventure, from the towering waterfalls to the majestic snow-covered mountains and, over it all, the incredible solitude and magnificence of the far north.

Though the daring can venture as far as the string of Aleutian Islands stretching toward Russia, my vote for the best cruising is the 400-mile (644km) "panhandle" in the south-east. Warmed by the Japan Current and protected by a maze of islands, it is within

SEWARD HARBOR

BROWN BEAR

AUGUSTIN, ALEUTIAN ISLANDS

America's last frontier; an unforgettable adventure. Killer whales prey on humpbacks, otters and salmon; eagles rule the snow-white mountains. Glaciers calve away into the sea and "shooter" icebergs rocket skyward.

SITKA, nestled on the west side of Baranof Island, is flanked by majestic mountains in the east, and the Pacific Ocean in the west.

reach of North American skippers aboard even small boats who can harbour-hop the Inside Passage from Seattle.

The major towns are Sitka, Juneau, Skagway or Ketchikan, but these are just your starting point for grand adventure. With uncountable miles of serrated coastline, the problem is deciding where to go. There is, quite simply, too much to see in a lifetime.

From Juneau, you have immediate access to the fjords and glaciers of Tracy Arm to the south, home to the twin Sawyer Glaciers, both active reminders of the Ice Age. Visitors are often told that Glacier Bay is spectacular (and it is), but I think Tracy Arm is even better.

SAWYER GLACIER in Tracy Arm, Alaska, is a landscape that is jawdropping.

This is *Lord of the Rings* country, with mountain goats on nearly vertical hillsides and, at the end, the two glaciers moving two feet (0.6m) a day, grinding against each other and calving away huge chunks into the sea. En route, you're between mountains where waterfalls spill 5,000ft (1,524m) to the sea.

If it's humpback or orca whales you want to see, Frederick Sound is the place. Shut down the engines and drift as they breach out of the water, and watch for the 6ft (2m) fins of the orcas, too. There are two great anchorages nearby: the Brothers Islands are uninhabited and picture-perfect while Deep Cove on Baranof Island – where inhabitants include people, brown bears and sitka deer – has 4,000ft (1,220m) walls and dramatic waterfalls.

While you're dallying in this area, an absolute must is a stop at Baranof Warm Springs. Leave plenty of time to soak in the three natural pools of hot water next to a raging waterfall – a memorable experience. We stayed so long (even through a rain shower) that our fingers puckered up.

Further south is Petersburg. If you have time, walk the ancient boardwalks that make the streets passable in winter. If you're feeling like a splurge, this is the place: take an aerial tour via helicopter to the top of a glacier and have a gourmet picnic atop an ancient river of ice.

Nearby is the fast-moving Le Conte glacier, the southernmost tidewater glacier on this continent. Because Le Conte Bay is often filled with "bergy bits", it's best to anchor near the entrance and

PETERSBURG is a picturesque fishing village with a fair share of Norwegian descendants.

ALASKA is home to some of the earth's last pristine wildernesses, with craggy mountains, glaciers and verdant hills.

take your tender into the bay. This mile-wide (1.6km) glacier is notorious for "shooter" icebergs that calve underwater and then shoot high in the air from their buoyancy, so stay at least half-a-mile off the face and be prepared for some quite spectacular eruptions.

Whether your passion is to drop a Royal Coachman fly into a cold stream full of trout and salmon, heli-ski down untouched powder, or simply enjoy a fine bottle of wine and dinner in the cockpit as the sunset paints the mountains with a rosy glow, you'll never forget Alaska.

WATCHING HUMPBACK WHALES frolic in the Alaskan seas is unforgettable.

THE INSIDE PASSAGE stretches from Seattle to Ketchikan in southern Alaska.

Pacific North-west
Seattle to Ketchikan

CHART 4920; NOAA 18440, 18421, 17420
BEST FOR CRUISING May – October
AVERAGE TEMPERATURE Ketchikan 15ºC 58ºF;
Seattle 17ºC 63ºF
PREVAILING WIND W
TIME ZONE Washington and British Columbia GMT
– 8; Alaska GMT – 9
LANGUAGE English

CURRENCY Canadian Dollar (C$), US Dollar (US$)
NAVIGATIONAL DIFFICULTY 🕐 🕐 🕐
FAMILY FRIENDLY 🍸 🍸 🍸 🍸
DIVING/SNORKELLING 🤿 🤿
SHORE-SIDE EATING 🍴 🍴 🍴
SIGHTSEEING 👤 👤 👤 👤 👤

As the first grey light of dawn filtered through the cabin windows, I could hear the patter of raindrops on the cabin roof. It was a sound that would have ruined a vacation anywhere else in the world, particularly on a bareboat charter like ours, but I was unconcerned. In fact, I was pleased, because we were cruising in the San Juan Islands of America's Pacific North-west.

SEATTLE, WA

THE ONE PIECE of advice that we had received from everyone, fishermen to dockmasters, was that if it drizzled in the morning, it would produce a fine afternoon. So I snuggled back into the warm covers and dozed off for another hour. Later that day? It was absolutely perfect!

Called the Inside Passage, the 700+ miles (966+ km) from Seattle, near the American border, to Ketchikan, at the southern end of Alaska, is arguably one of the best – and most pristine – cruising grounds in North America. This serrated coastline spans the length of Canada's British Columbia from the American states of Washington to Alaska, and includes the coastal perimeter of 285-mile-long (459km) Vancouver Island.

But, and I give away my impartiality here, I think the absolute best cruising is in the San Juan Islands of America's Pacific North-west. Not only is it a veritable hotbed of bareboat charter activity (easily accessible through Seattle), but the San Juans are a democratic archipelago: there is something for everyone.

Without going more than a half-day's sail in any direction, you can find hundreds of small coves, wildlife to watch, fossils to hunt, good skindiving, small villages, resorts to enjoy, sandy beaches

ROOSEVELT ELK

KETCHIKAN

Pick a sheltered cove, trap a few prawns for the barbeque, forage for fossils, hook a salmon. Hundreds of islands, thousands of miles of coastline, limitless possibilities.

HORSESHOE BAY, north-west of Vancouver, serves as a gateway community to British Columbia's west coast.

set in pine forests, and protected waters suitable for boats of all sizes. Local residents claim there are 750 islands at low tide but only 450 at high tide, but that's really an unresolved question. At least 150 islands have names, so you can make your own estimate.

Carved into their present shape by the great glaciers of the Ice Age, the terrain bears the scars of the ponderous ice: deep slashes, smoothly planed rocks and piles of rocky litter. The summer offers the best weather with warm days and sunny skies, but the docks and anchorages are packed at weekends. I prefer the "shoulder" seasons of spring and autumn when kids are still in school: the weather is cooler but pleasant and the joy of empty harbours is worth an extra sweater.

Once you arrive in the islands, you can pick your cruising area by your moods and interests. If you like having shore power, some sort of civilization nearby and perhaps even some nightlife, you can choose from several large marinas and resorts. On the other hand, if you prefer to leave the madding crowd behind, you can enjoy the handful of isolated Marine Parks, with docks, moorings, and picnic facilities ashore.

The social and political centre of the islands, Friday Harbor has a large municipal marina only a short walk from the town's main

PODS OF KILLER WHALES can be encountered near San Juan Islands from March to October.

street where, except for the cars, you might have time-warped into a old fishing village. We saw a few salty fishermen striding along in knee boots and canvas jackets, the buildings were clapboard and elderly, the shade trees overhanging the small park were out of an old painting, and the proprietors in the tiny shops still had time to lean on their counters and chat.

FRIDAY HARBOR in the San Juan Islands has a large municipal marina only a short walk from the town's main street.

I always enjoy nearby Sucia Island, with dream-like shorelines moulded by glaciers into melted ice cream, where we usually pick up a mooring or tie up to the dock in appropriately named Fossil Bay. There are fossils here (so they say) but we've only found beautiful stones for souvenirs. And it's a beautiful cove in the evening, with steaks sizzling on the barbeque and the only sound being the splash of a fish jumping.

On San Juan Island, the Victorian buildings of Roche Harbor remain as a reminder of a grand past and, at sunset, the flag ceremony concludes with a loudspeaker listing of temperatures (always colder) in less fortunate cities worldwide. On summer nights, the lighted grounds become a miniature Tivoli Garden of the north-west.

At uninhabited Stuart Island, we stopped for lunch at the Marine Park, which had docks and picnic facilities ashore. A small raccoon approached us looking for handouts and, because he

THE SAN JUAN ISLANDS located in the Puget Sound, are renowned as the "jewels" of the Pacific North-west.

BONAVENTURE ISLAND is one of the Gulf Islands, which, geographically, are a continuation of the San Juans.

was limping, we took pity and gave him plenty. As he left, however, we realized we'd been conned: eager to race away with his booty, he forgot himself and his limp suddenly changed to another foot.

The Gulf Islands are really a northern continuation of the San Juans, but across the Canadian border. When crossing the border in either direction, be sure to follow the customs and immigration procedures to the letter: post-9/11 North America is stricter than ever before.

The Gulf Islands are also glacially carved and, because the clearance issues tend to keep the American cruising fleets at bay, the islands are generally less crowded. These are a jumping off point for a circumnavigation of Vancouver Island, which is stunningly attractive on the eastern side with hundreds of islands and harbours, but unprotected on the western side open to the North Pacific.

IN THE SAN JUAN ISLANDS raccoons in search of titbits are likely to approach visiting humans.

Two major entry ports into Canada are Vancouver, which is on the mainland, and Victoria, which is on Vancouver Island just offshore. Confusing, isn't it? Both are modern, cosmopolitan cities with extensive marine facilities for transient boats, although I prefer Victoria because it's so striking at night with the impressively lit Fairmont Empress Hotel looming over the Inner Harbor. But, to be honest, these cities are just starting or ending points for your adventure: spend your time elsewhere.

A word about north-west weather: morning drizzles aside, anyone cruising these waters should monitor weather forecasts regularly. Weather prediction is excellent, but storms and wind can roll in off the ocean and turn even the protected Inside Passage into a no-man's land for small boats.

When it comes to navigation, north-west waters are generally deep and well-marked, but a good companion is *Waggoner's Cruising Guide*, a comprehensive yearly tome filled with services and tips.

A cautionary note, primarily for powerboats: deadheads, or floating logs, are common on these waterways and can not only

VANCOUVER, a cosmopolitan city with extensive marine facilities for transient boats, is a major entry port into Canada.

VICTORIA, on Vancouver Island, is striking at night with the Fairmont Empress Hotel looming over the Inner Harbor.

ruin propellers but also hole your boat. Floating low in the water, they are almost invisible, so travel at safe speeds and keep a good lookout.

Circumnavigating Vancouver Island is an ambitious undertaking which, if you harbour-hop, can be a distance of more than 1,000 miles (1,609km) and easily take a month. And, of course, there's the possibility – even in summer – of having to wait out periods of bad weather on the unforgiving western coast.

A better plan would be to cruise the Straits of Georgia along Vancouver Island, where there are dozens of inlets and islands to explore. Inside the protection of Gabriola and Galliano Islands are dozens of islets where you can set crab and prawn traps and enjoy the solitude of beautiful anchorages.

Fancy landing a 30lb (14kg) salmon? The Campbell River empties from Vancouver Island into Discovery Passage, and this area is acknowledged as the "salmon capital of the world". The season runs roughly from July to October, and the fish are

EVEN IN SUMMER there is the possibility of periods of bad weather on the unforgiving western coast of Vancouver Island.

so plentiful that many anglers tire after a few hours. If you can't eat it all, there are shoreside services that will smoke, can and ship your salmon home as a tasty souvenir.

For those heading north up the Inside Passage, there are two segments: from Victoria or Vancouver roughly 250 miles (402km) inside the protection of Vancouver Island in the Straits of Georgia to Cape Caution, and then from Cape Caution to Ketchikan with unprotected waters in Hecate Strait. It's here that most skippers choose to thread their way through the usually calm passages between the dozens of islands rather than running directly up Hecate Strait.

Certainly the jewel of the Inside Passage is Princess Louisa Inlet, with its 120ft (36.6m) Chatterbox Falls tumbling into a pristine anchorage. About 90 miles (145km) north of Vancouver, it lies at the inner end of the long Jervis Inlet but it's a gorgeous passage between snow-capped mountains on calm water.

En route, you'll pass Sechelt Inlet where the Skookumchuck Narrows create the fastest ocean rapids in the world when the tide is ebbing or flowing. With water speeds as high as 17 knots, huge breaking waves are formed and you never, ever, want to transit this area except at slack water.

One good reason to go into Sechelt Inlet, however, is to overnight at Egmont Marina, where a short walk takes you to Wilderness Lodge, an outpost that is perhaps one of the last places in the world you'd expect to find five-star gourmet cuisine served by a French waiter – but that's what happens.

With thousands of coastline miles to explore, the Inside Passage is a charter cruising playground, which is why there are so many charter companies located in the North-west. One trip and you'll be hooked!

THOMAS BASIN is the home to Ketchikan's fishing and sailing fleets. Only single hooks are allowed within the Basin.

AERIAL VIEW of the Misty Fjords in Ketchikan in the Inside Passage, Alaska.

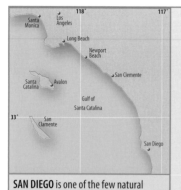

SAN DIEGO is one of the few natural harbours on this stretch of coastline.

California
San Diego to Los Angeles

CHART 899, 1063; NOAA 18740, 18720
BEST FOR CRUISING Year-round
AVERAGE TEMPERATURE 24ºC 75ºF
PREVAILING WIND W
TIME ZONE GMT – 8
LANGUAGE English
CURRENCY US Dollar (US$)

NAVIGATIONAL DIFFICULTY
FAMILY FRIENDLY
DIVING/SNORKELLING
SHORE-SIDE EATING
SIGHTSEEING

The Southern California coastline is basically inhospitable: there are few natural harbours, the prevailing winds want to push you onto an often rocky lee shore, and its emergence as a yachting centre is, frankly, quite surprising. The East Coast and the Pacific North-west are ideal for harbour-hopping but, unless you want to crawl from marina to marina, there isn't much here.

NEWPORT BEACH, CALIFORNIA

THAT SAID, Catalina is the prime cruising ground and, as the Four Preps sang in their 1958 hit, it's just "Twenty-six miles across the sea…". Avalon is the only city on the island, and it's memorable for its casino – never a gambling site but a huge dance hall and theatre where, for years, the big band sounds of Glenn Miller, Harry James and Artie Shaw beamed across America by radio "from the beautiful casino on Catalina Island". More important to skippers, however, is that its 12-storey white art-deco walls can be seen from the mainland on a clear day.

Avalon is red roofs, bougainvillea and whitewashed houses, with shops and restaurants elbowing each other for space on the waterfront promenade. Get there early because the mooring buoys go fast, and be prepared when the Harbour Patrol drops a blue dye pellet in your head: this is a no-discharge zone and woe betide any skipper with a blue underwater stain.

On the mainland, San Diego is just above the US border with Mexico, making it the starting point for this very different country and points south or west. The huge natural harbour is protected by Point Loma and if you can't find a yachting service or part here, well, it doesn't exist. Marinas and yacht clubs with transient facilities abound, and this is where the America's Cup resided for

TORREY PINES, SAN DIEGO

CATALINA ISLAND

SAN DIEGO is a diverse metropolitan city with skyscrapers, old turn-of-the-century buildings, serene parks and a vibrant, bustling harbour.

MISSION BAY is overlooked by the lighthouse on Point Loma peninsula, which wraps around the north end of Coronada.

several years. Shelter and Harbor Islands are the heart of the yachting scene. Local tip: for one of the world's great hamburgers (a favourite of America's Cup crews) try Rocky's Crown Pub in Pacific Beach. Also nearby, Mission Bay is a 4,200-acre (1,700ha) water playground with separate areas for sailing and waterskiing.

From a weather standpoint, San Diego is nearly perfect with temperatures averaging in the mid-70s °F (low-20s °C) in the summer and with only drop to the mid-60s (around 18 °C) in the winter, with sunshine on more than 75 per cent of the days.

Southern California weather is equally good, though cooling down as you move north. The only caveat is the notorious "Santana" wind of autumn, which blows hot and dry in a south-easterly direction from the desert and can cause havoc on the usual lee side of Catalina.

MISSION BAY, with its separate areas for sailing and waterskiing, is a popular destination.

BALBOA ISLAND is an enchanting area where you can explore the trendy shops and guzzle chili-cheese fries at Charlie's Chili.

Further north (and just south of Long Beach), Newport Harbor is one of the earliest California yachting centres and it is jam-packed with yachts of all sizes in front of opulent mansions: empty lots may sell for as much as $2,000 (around £1,000) a waterfront inch! Several yacht clubs and marinas provide transient moorings. You can explore the trendy shops of Balboa Island (don't miss the frozen chocolate bananas on a stick!) or drop in at Charlie's Chili, a no-glitz favourite of yachties who wolf down the chili-cheese fries (chips).

The Los Angeles/Long Beach Harbor area is notable for Alamitos Bay, a quiet backwater with winding residential canals and a yacht-racing reputation: the Long Beach area was the venue for the 1984 Sailing Olympics. Here, too, in common with the rest of the coast running south to San Diego, the year-round warm, sunny climate means charterers can always make the most of the wide sandy beaches and enjoy watersports from snorkelling to kiteboarding, or exploring the coast's numerous coves and caves by kayak.

Completing the Southern California boating scene is Marina del Rey, right up against the city of Los Angeles and the largest man-made small boat harbour in the world. With no commercial shipping, it is dedicated to marinas, yacht clubs and waterfront condominiums and has more than 5,000 slips as well as launching ramps.

Southern California is a world unto itself, and it only takes a weekend at Catalina to hook you for a lifetime.

MARINA DEL REY is the largest man-made small boat harbour in the world. It has more than 5,000 slips.

SAN DIEGO HARBOR is the southernmost port on the West Coast of the United States, and the gateway to Mexico and the south-west.

THE BAJA CALIFORNIA peninsula extends 680 miles (110 km) from the US border.

Mexico
Lower Sea of Cortez

CHART 2324; NIMA 21014, 21125, 21141

BEST FOR CRUISING Year-round, but in summer stay within 24 hours of La Paz or Puerto Escondido hurricane holes

AVERAGE TEMPERATURE 21ºC 70ºF

PREVAILING WIND Winter moderate NW to N; summer light S

TIME ZONE GMT – 8

LANGUAGE Spanish, but English in resorts

CURRENCY Mexican Peso

NAVIGATIONAL DIFFICULTY ◉ ◉

FAMILY FRIENDLY ♟ ♟ ♟ ♟ ♟

DIVING/SNORKELLING 🤿 🤿 🤿 🤿 🤿

SHORE-SIDE EATING 🍴 🍴 🍴 🍴

SIGHTSEEING ♜ ♜ ♜ ♜

Mix pristine desert landscapes with tropical turquoise coves and, presto, you're cruising the lower Sea of Cortez. November to June is the primary cruising season, but this region offers two hurricane holes to tide you over through the summer hurricane season as well.

BETWEEN THE HARBOURS of La Paz and Puerto Escondido, this cruising route provides adventurous yatistas (yacht cruisers) with more than 40 remote anchorages spread among 137 miles (220km) of Baja California desert and 12 uninhabited islands near shore. With wall-to-wall sunshine, you can explore dozens of blonde-sand beaches and lush mangrove estuaries. By night these skies, the darkest in the hemisphere, are ablaze with starlight. So few people live in this desert that yachts usually have all the coves and anchorages to themselves, for free, for days and weeks on end.

Overlooking this mystical coastline are the craggy peaks of La Giganta, the "Giant Woman", mountain range. With ancient benevolence, she shelters adventurous spirits from seasonal winds, sprinkling the route with colourful reefs to snorkel, dive or fish, offering sheltered bays for sleeping in the folds of her granite gown. Tranquility rules.

But before departing La Paz, be sure to provision your boat well with food, water and fuel, because no stores are available until you reach Puerto Escondido. La Paz has five full-service marinas, four floating fuel docks, four haul-out yards, two yacht charter fleets, one hurricane hole and excellent grocery markets and restaurants. It's the pleasant capital city of southern Baja.

First stop? The Espíritu Santos (Sacred Spirits) islands only 20 miles (32km) due north are where La Giganta first arises from the

LA GIGANTA

LA PAZ SLIPS

CORAL REEFS

*Barter for the pangueros' catch of the day,
find solitude under star-spangled skies
or join in pot-luck family beach parties;
all this and more on tranquil waters
protected by La Giganta's jagged peaks.*

THE LOWER SEA OF CORTEZ is sheltered by the
Baja California peninsula. The scenery is truly
spectacular and hidden coves are plentiful.

ISLA ESPÍRITU SANTOS and Isla Partida (above) are composed of layers of black lava and pink volcanic ash.

sea. This mountainous, 11-mile-long (18km) island chain provides 12 spectacular anchorages and no permanent residents. If you have only a weekend getaway, this is where you should go. But you can hide away for weeks, snorkelling the volcanic reefs, wandering the powder-white beaches and hiking the shady canyons. One trail leads to a natural red-rock amphitheatre, and another ends at a waterfall with dangling fig trees.

Each April, 30 cruising boats arrive here for Sea of Cortez Sailing Week – family fun races and beach pot-lucks. They anchor in Partida Cove, a huge bay inside the cleft between two islands. Only a tidal sandbar connects the islands, and at high tide kayaks and dinghies scoot through to the Back Side anchorage.

More than a dozen tiny anchorages line the 90 miles (145km) to our destination, but the must-see spots are the twin coves of Gato and Toro, and Bahia Agua Verde.

Whimsical sandstone formations in shades of pink, peach and oxblood-red line the Gato end of Gato and Toro (Cat and Bull)

THE ESPÍRITU SANTOS ISLANDS (below) are preserved as a national park, and spear fishing is prohibited.

Cove. Locals tell me that *gato* refers to a family of puma that live up that canyon, in the cactus-covered foothills of La Giganta. In the prevailing north-west winds of the cruising season, we anchor in the sheltered north end of El Gato, below pink cliffs. In the south end, we scuba-dive El Toro Reef, a black lava grotto of fans and sponges. During calm weather, a multihull can wriggle in behind El Gato Reef for the night.

In English, *agua verde* means turquoise or blue-green. Agua Verde village (population 100) is 35 miles (56km) from the nearest paved road and the only work is fishing from pangas, 18ft (5.48m) open skiffs with big outboards. As soon as you're anchored, friendly pangueros (panga fishermen) waste no time in zooming by to offer their fresh catch. And what are the best items to trade? Fresh water, fish hooks, children's clothing and sports shoes – any size.

Agua Verde has three anchorages, so no matter the weather there's usually one suitable. The north beach is so popular for yatista pot-luck parties – everyone takes along a dish of "something" to share – that we've dubbed it Agua Verde Yacht

THE SKIES over the Sea of Cortez are the darkest in the northern hemisphere.

Club. Each spring, rancheros and pangueros invite us yatistas to a goat roast and fish fry on this beach.

From offshore, Puerto Escondido's narrow entrance blends with La Giganta's loftiest peaks, so Spanish explorers named it "Hidden Port". But civilization is hiding inside: a full-service marina, fuel dock, haul-out yard, 119 moorings and Sunday brunch with Margaritas at Loreto's Hidden Port Yacht Club.

Each May, the club puts on Loreto Fest, a week of nautical fun and games. Yatistas who live aboard in Puerto Escondido year-round say they enjoy the 15-mile (24km) buffer zone from Loreto's busy downtown and international airport.

Like La Paz, Puerto Escondido is also a hurricane refuge, so it's popular year-round, not just during winter cruising season.

The area in general offers excellent diving and snorkelling for novices through to experts and there's plenty to see ashore, from prehistoric cave paintings and 1700s missions to the La Paz potters.

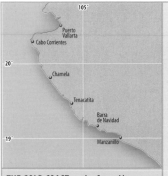

THE GOLD COAST on the Costa Alegre extends over 75 miles (121km).

Mexico
Gold Coast

CHART 2323; NIMA 503, 21017
BEST FOR CRUISING November – June
AVERAGE TEMPERATURE 27ºC 80ºF
PREVAILING WIND NW to WNW moderate
TIME ZONE GMT – 6
LANGUAGE Spanish and some English
CURRENCY Mexican Peso

NAVIGATIONAL DIFFICULTY
FAMILY FRIENDLY
DIVING/SNORKELLING
SHORE-SIDE EATING
SIGHTSEEING

For cruising sailors, Mexico's "Gold Coast" is a chain of 10 small bays dotting 75 miles (121km) of jungle-clad coastline – ideal for balmy winter conditions. And from Barra de Navidad – the crowning jewel here – you can easily hop up and down the coast to visit them.

STARTING AT THE north end, we enter Chamela Bay and head for its south end, to a little known anchorage in the middle of two tiny uninhabited islets (Pasavera and Colorado). You can snorkel from your swimming-step to hidden beaches on the islands. If the north-west winds pipe up, you scoot into Chamela Bay's north end for better shelter.

Careyes (eight miles (13 km) south) is where the endangered turtles nest. Anchor off the little hotel in the south lobe, dinghy ashore and ask their naturalist guide for a tour. Children can tend nests and launch hatchlings into the Pacific.

After I charted Tenacatita's estuary with GPS, I dubbed it the "Jungle River Dinghy Ride". In welcome shade, tendrils of flowering vines dangle from the canopy, mirrored in the crystal water. Friends in other

skiffs hide in the side channels to ambush us with water balloons. But wild crocodiles hunt iguanas here, so don't let Fido swim!

In early March, the village of San Patricio (across the bay from Barra de Navidad) celebrates their eponymous patron saint, with a seven-day festival of traditional foods, ranchero music and real whooping rodeos.

Sheltered inside Laguna Navidad you'll find Puerto de la Navidad, a full-service 200-slip marina, and behind it the stunning Spanish colonial arches and domes of the five-star Grand Bay Hotel climb the hillside. Wow! What a change from the (plentiful) beach cantinas and bay anchorages!

Puerto de la Navidad is the first megayacht marina – slips to 180ft (55m) – outside Puerto Vallarta, 140 miles (225km) north, so don't gasp when tuxedo-clad waiters deliver "room service" dinners right to your slip and the baker delivers fresh croissants every morning.

"Barra" as it's affectionately known, is not totally posh, however. Free anchorage is available in Laguna Navidad, and during the winter cruising season, I've seen 30 sailboats anchored here for weeks on end. The beach town of Barra de Navidad covers the lagoon's barrier island. It's my favourite destination in Mexico, and it's an ideal base for savouring the Gold Coast.

REPAIR SHOP

BARRA VILLAGE

RARE TURTLE

COSTA CAREYES is home to four species of endangered turtle: the leatherback, the olive ridley, the loggerhead and the hawksbill. The turtles lay their eggs in the golden sands of this beautiful bay.

BARRA DE NAVIDAD is a funky surfing mecca during summer, complete with cobblestone streets, shady banyan trees and cheap eateries.

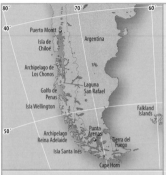

FROM NORTH TO SOUTH Chile extends for over 2,600 miles (4,184km).

Chile
Puerto Montt to Cape Horn

CHART 1289, 1288, 1287, 1286, 1282, 554
BEST FOR CRUISING December – March
AVERAGE TEMPERATURE 24°C 75°F (in north); 20°C 70°F (in south)
PREVAILING WIND W
TIME ZONE GMT – 4
LANGUAGE Spanish

CURRENCY Chilean Peso (Ch$)
NAVIGATIONAL DIFFICULTY ✪ ✪ ✪ ✪ ✪
FAMILY FRIENDLY 🍹 🍹 🍹
DIVING/SNORKELLING 🤿 🤿
SHORE-SIDE EATING 🍴 🍴 🍴
SIGHTSEEING 👕 👕 👕 👕 👕

Other than in large ports, the north of Chile offers little shelter for yachts but the southern half of the country, from Puerto Montt to Cape Horn, offers magnificent, wilderness cruising in largely sheltered waters.

POOR WEATHER, however, is not unusual, particularly in the high southern latitudes (far less temperate than the equivalent northern latitudes) where the risk of rain, snow and stormy weather is always present, even in high summer. Nevertheless, the incredible scenery – not least the Andes' snow-capped, volcanic peaks – easily makes up for the vagaries of the climate.

The part of the coast most accessible to yachts extends some 320 miles (515km) southwards from Puerto Montt to the Laguna San Rafael. Here, you will find almost limitless cruising possibilities on a coast studded with literally thousands of sheltered bays, coves and deep fjords. The surrounding landscape is beautiful and unspoilt and, apart from the area around Puerto Montt, and on Chiloé Island where there is a sizeable population, people are something of a rarity beyond the pretty,

isolated fishing villages – wildlife, however, is abundant. The region's absolute highlight is without doubt the glacier that terminates in the iceberg-strewn Laguna San Rafael. Here, at the head of a short, twisting, easily navigable river, the mile-wide glacier almost continually calves huge slabs of blue-tinged ice from its 150ft (46m) high wall. Booming, rumbling and cracking like a battery of artillery, it is truly awesome.

Torn by prevailing westerlies of redoubtable strength, Chile's south-western coastline was much feared by sailors in past times. Since sail was displaced by motor, merchant ships have used the "canals" – a maze of deep, inland waterways formed by the descent of the Andes foothills into the Pacific Ocean – to provide an almost continuously sheltered passage for the 750 miles (1,207km) from the Gulf of Penas to the Straits of Magellan, the Beagle Channel and Cape Horn. The main route is well charted and buoyed, but perhaps of more interest to yachtsmen are the many side canals that reach inland towards the Andes, often terminating in breathtaking sea glaciers. At the southern end of this stunning, sheltered passage yachts are able to approach the Wollaston Group, one of which is Cape Horn Island.

OSORNO VOLCANO

LAGUNA SAN RAFAEL

PUNTO ARENAS

THE SOUTHERNMOST city on earth, Punta Arenas overlooks the Straits of Magellan. The islands are a sanctuary for some extraordinary wildlife, including sea lions, condors, and Magellanic penguins.

The power and the glory of nature on an overwhelmingly grand scale. Volcanoes and lakes give way to a rugged, labyrinthine coast.

THE CALBUCO VOLCANO, here viewed over the Rio Blanco near Puerto Montt, is one of the most active volcanoes of the southern Chilean Andes.

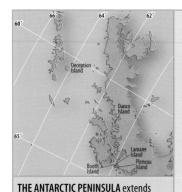

THE ANTARCTIC PENINSULA extends over 1,200 miles (1,930km).

Antarctica
Antarctic Peninsula

CHART 3205, 1774, 4009, 4907	**NAVIGATIONAL DIFFICULTY** ✹ ✹ ✹ ✹ ✹
BEST FOR CRUISING December – February	**FAMILY FRIENDLY** 🥤
AVERAGE TEMPERATURE 0°C 32°F	**DIVING/SNORKELLING** 🤿 🤿 🤿 🤿 🤿
PREVAILING WIND WNW	**SHORE-SIDE EATING**
TIME ZONE GMT – 4	**SIGHTSEEING** 👕 👕 👕 👕 👕
LANGUAGE N/A	
CURRENCY N/A	

Sailing in the Southern Ocean in a small boat has been compared to playing Russian roulette and yet, here I was doing it again, this time on my *Aventura III*, an aluminium Ovni 43 (13.1m), specially equipped for a voyage to the frozen continent. The unique scenery and abundant and extraordinary wildlife tempt a small number of sailors to take up the challenge of reaching Antarctica by sailing across the Drake Passage to the Antarctic Peninsula.

WE HAD MADE our last preparations at Puerto Williams, a sleepy Chilean military base set on the banks of the Beagle Channel that prides itself for being the southernmost settlement in the world. Less than 60 miles (96km) from Cape Horn, Puerto Williams is a good place to prepare for the crossing of the Drake Passage.

We were fortunate as a ridge of high pressure had given us a spell of unusually good weather for the 500-mile (805km) passage to Deception Island. We romped south in glorious weather and had no problem dodging the few icebergs that we encountered on the way. The weather broke just as we closed with Deception Island and we were blasted through the aptly-named Neptune's Bellows, a narrow opening that leads into the perfectly sheltered waters of the sunken crater of a dormant volcano.

Its location off the tip of the Antarctic Peninsula makes Deception Island a good starting point for a cruise along the peninsula, which is fronted by a jumble of islands of all shapes and sizes so that – in an area where sudden changes of weather are the rule – shelter is never too far away. The sheltered waters attract about 30 sailing yachts every year, although most of them

ICEBERG

ALBATROSS

WEATHER

THE BEST TIME to head south from Cape Horn is on the back of a depression, as the winds veer gradually from west to north-east, during the relatively safe season between December and early March.

Way down in the Southern Ocean across the Drake Passage lies a magnificent icy wilderness, a challenge for visiting yachts, home to humpback, leopard seal and penguin.

THE GLACIATED MOUNTAINS of the Antarctic Peninsula are truly awesome. The average altitude in Antarctica is over 7,500ft (2,286m).

PENGUINS IN THE ANTARCTIC show no fear of humans, and wander to and fro between land and water feeding their chicks.

CROSSING DRAKE PASSAGE is the price one has to pay for the privilege of visiting Antarctica.

are charter yachts that operate out of the Argentine port of Ushuaia as the difficulty of getting there means that very few cruising boats venture this far south. Charter yachts operating in the area are part of the International Association of Antarctica Tour Operators (www.iaato.org).

The scenery is breathtaking in its splendour, but there is another equally attractive dimension to the Antarctic experience and that is the abundant wildlife. Because they have absolutely no fear of man, it is possible to observe animals at close quarters without interfering with their day-to-day life. Words cannot describe the pleasure of spending hours in the midst of a busy penguin colony, totally ignored, observing the birds returning from a fishing trip to feed their chicks. That the parents manage to identify their young from amongst scores of identical-looking balls of fluff is nothing short of miraculous.

Before all whaling and fishing activities were banned south of the Antarctic Circle, this area had been frequently visited by whalers during the Antarctic summer and we found remains of their activities at almost every stop. On a small islet we came across the surprisingly well-preserved wooden hulls of small chase boats used by the whalers. On nearby Danco Island is an old cabin belonging to the British Antarctic Survey, the unoccupied wooden hut being maintained as an emergency shelter. Later, we came across several food depots, set in prominent places and marked by a perch, which provide survival rations to anyone lost in this wilderness. These principally serve the several research bases dotted about the Antarctic Peninsula although, compared to their predecessors, scientists these days rarely venture far from their bases.

One of the highlights of an Antarctic cruise is the Lemaire Channel, a five-mile (8km) long narrows between Booth Island and the Antarctic Peninsula. In a relatively small area are concentrated all the elements that make up the majestic grandeur of Antarctic scenery: soaring snow-clad peaks, massive glaciers, countless icebergs – large and small. Lemaire Channel is a favourite feeding ground for humpback whales that spend the summer in these waters gorging themselves on the nourishing

THE LEMAIRE CHANNEL is a spectacular 5-mile (8km) long narrows between Booth Island and the Antarctic Peninsula.

krill. We nearly bumped into a couple sleeping peacefully on the surface, their massive bodies undulating in the gentle swell. Photographic session over we anchored in the lee of nearby Peleneau Island.

To reach the sheltered anchorage we had to pass through a shallow area littered with grounded icebergs, described by my daughter Doina on our previous trip to Antarctica as the "iceberg cemetery". Rain, wind and sun work relentlessly on the stranded icebergs, moulding them into shapes undreamed of by even the most inspired sculptor. We took a dinghy trip through this ice gallery, competing with each other in identifying the multitude of shapes: a sphinx, a jumbo jet, a cathedral spire, even an amazing likeness of the Loch Ness monster.

After several days of sunny weather, the daily weather forecast of the Chilean meteorological office warned us of the impending arrival of a threatening low-pressure system. We quickly made our way to what I knew was the safe all-weather anchorage at Port Circumcision. The name was bestowed on it by a French explorer, Jean-Baptiste Charcot, who happened upon it on New Year's Day,

1909. The strengthening wind had almost blocked the entrance with ice but we managed to squeeze through and anchor in a shallow spot where we avoided even the smaller bergs. We always anchored with two anchors set in tandem and, for added security, took long lines ashore that were fixed with stainless steel strops to rocks or large boulders.

Soon the wind had reached 50 knots and the small bay was entirely closed in by ice, but we felt safe enough to take the dinghy ashore. We landed on the rocky beach right in the middle of a large penguin colony. As we stepped ashore a penguin followed us closely, covered in blood and badly wounded. It had obviously been mauled by a leopard seal but had, somehow, managed to escape and was now determinedly making its way to feed its chick.

Determined to be the yacht that reached furthest south that season, after the storm had petered out, we set off for the Pitt Islands. Once in open water, the ice started thickening and by the time we closed with the small island group we were ploughing through a lot of brash ice. The dull grey day made the bleak place even bleaker. There were hardly any animals about, except a large leopard seal that gave us a most hateful look for invading its territory.

BRASH ICE is the accumulations of floating ice made up of fragments of the wreckage of larger forms of ice.

ROUGH SEAS Sudden changes in weather are common in Antarctica, and storms blow up quickly in these icy seas.

RAIN, wind and sun mould stranded icebergs into shapes undreamed of by even the most inspired sculptor.

We had now reached 65°25′S, 65°29′W. This was as far south as we could go, as from here unbroken ice stretched to the horizon. I realized that this was going to be our turning point and the thought filled me with a deep sense of regret because none of us was ready to leave this wonderful and unique world.

The crossing of Drake Passage is the price one has to pay for the privilege of visiting Antarctica. The tactic for the northbound voyage is to leave from as far west as possible, and also to keep some westing in hand for the intended landfall at Cape Horn, where the prevailing winds are from the north-west and there is also an east-setting current. With no depressions showing close to the west on the daily weatherfax we left immediately and for the first two days our gamble paid off as we made excellent progress.

A few hours of calm signalled a change in the weather, and the returning winds veered to the north-west and blew ever harder. As by now we were less than 100 miles (161km) from Cape Horn and

had a good deal of westing in hand, we decided to heave to for the night with three reefs in the mainsail and the wheel lashed to windward. By morning we started sailing again and anchored off Horn Island almost exactly four days after leaving Antarctica.

LEOPARD SEALS prey on the penguins and can respond aggressively to the presence of humans.

TAHAA ISLAND and its larger neighbour Raiatea offer the experience of true unspoilt French Polynesia.

The Pacific

Fiji, Tonga, the Marquesas, Tahiti, the Galapagos: coral sands, waving coconut palms, smiling faces, exotic flora and fauna, when yachtsmen dream of sailing away from it all, they conjure visions of the fabled South Sea Islands. Paul Gauguin, Jacques Brel, Robert Louis Stevenson, circumnavigators from Joshua Slocum to Bernard Moitessier, artists and outcasts all have sought to escape from the cares of civilization to their own island, a personal Pacific fiefdom. Whether stranded for years, or on holiday for a week, enchantment is still to be found in places such as Vanuatu and among the reefs and coral heads of the Tuamotus. Keep a good lookout, navigate by the sun, and all will be revealed. Welcome to paradise (but watch your depth sounder).

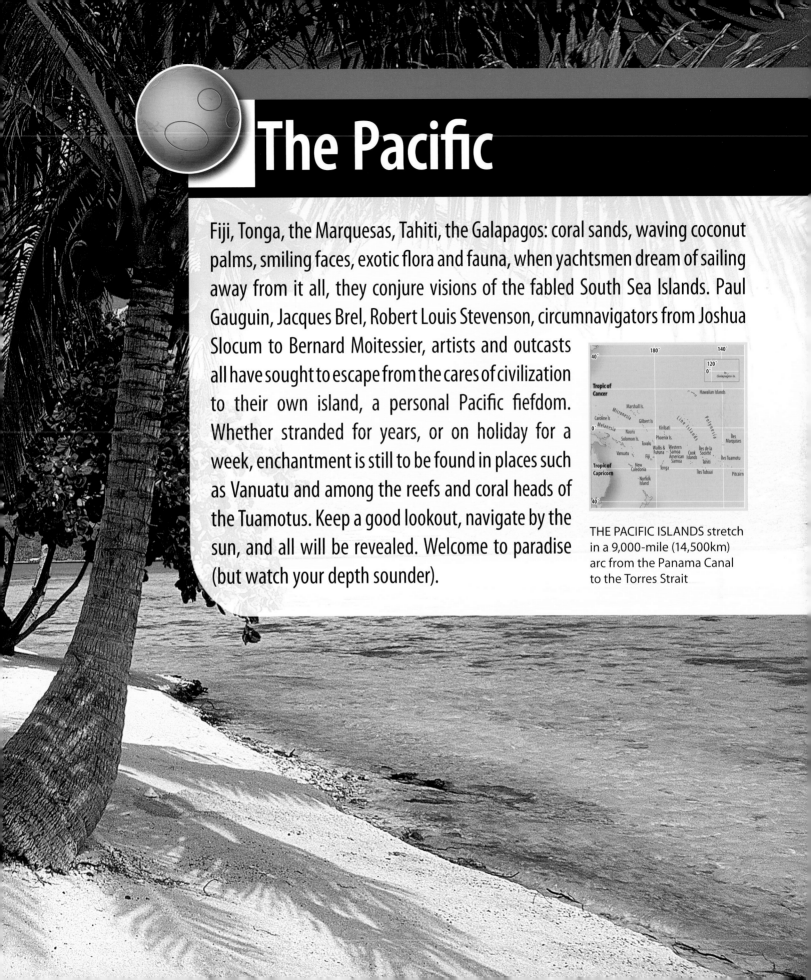

THE PACIFIC ISLANDS stretch in a 9,000-mile (14,500km) arc from the Panama Canal to the Torres Strait

HAWAII

GALAPAGOS ISLANDS

PACIFIC ISLANDS

The South Seas have been a tempting destination for sailors ever since the first European ships arrived on the scene in the 18th century. Stretching in a 9,000 mile-long (14,500km) arc from the Panama Canal to the Torres Strait are some of the most attractive islands anywhere in the world. These are the idyllic landfalls that many sailors dream of: palm-fringed lagoons with tiny islets dotted about turquoise waters and a warm welcome to those who arrive by sea. It is their very remoteness that puts most of those islands beyond the scope of the average voyage so in spite of the proliferation of yachts worldwide, the number of boats cruising the South Pacific is still relatively small and is counted in hundreds rather than thousands. Chartering, of course, is always an option for those who want to cruise these islands.

The region is under the influence of the south-east trade winds, which are stronger and more consistent from May to October. The best conditions are between June and August. Most of the South Pacific is affected by tropical cyclones whose season lasts from December until the end of March.

The best conditions are between June and August with exhilarating trade-wind sailing under unpolluted starry skies.

Because of the direction of the prevailing winds, routes must be planned carefully so as to take full advantage of them. The main route runs from east to west calling at all major island groups. Most yachts sail this classic route from Galapagos to Marquesas directly, but a few yachts make a detour to visit Easter Island and Pitcairn before reaching French Polynesia. West of Tahiti the options multiply but those with enough time can easily plan a route that zigzags between the most desirable destinations. Those short of time may try to sail the entire South Pacific in one season but the majority are happy to spend longer in the South Seas.

Most cruising yachts leave the tropics for the cyclone season by sailing to New Zealand or Australia. For those who decide to stay in the tropics, there are a number of marinas where boats may be left unattended during the critical period. Because of the general absence of sheltered harbours, cruising during the cyclone season is not recommended. The best repair centres are those that support their own yachting community, such as Tahiti and Suva. Thriving charter operations in Raiatea and Vava'u have resulted in a marked improvement in the standard of facilities.

THE SOCIETY ISLANDS

FIJI

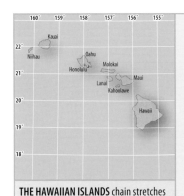

Hawaiian islands
Kauai to Hawaii

CHART 1510, 1308, 1309; NOAA 540
BEST FOR CRUISING Year-round
AVERAGE TEMPERATURE 26°C 78°F
PREVAILING WIND NE
TIME ZONE GMT – 10
LANGUAGE Hawaiian and English
CURRENCY US Dollar (US$)

NAVIGATIONAL DIFFICULTY
FAMILY FRIENDLY
DIVING/SNORKELLING
SHORE-SIDE EATING
SIGHTSEEING

THE HAWAIIAN ISLANDS chain stretches for 5,000 miles (8,050km).

The Hawaiian Islands, lying 2,000 miles (3,220km) south-west of California, have recently shifted from just a stop-off for yachts en route to the South Pacific to becoming a cruising destination in their own right.

THERE IS GOOD NEWS and bad news about Hawaii. It has miles of uninhabited coastlines, gorgeous scenery, empty beaches and secluded anchorages. On the other hand, it's in the middle of the Pacific with almost constant trade winds and ocean swells, so many anchorages are not for landlubbers. That said, there's a lot to see and enjoy in the Hawaiian Islands, and chartering is on the increase.

Rising from an ocean floor more than two-and-a-half miles (4km) deep, the eight main islands are just part of a chain of volcanic islands that stretch 5,000 miles (8,050km) and include Midway. But cruisers will probably only sample six of these, and you can spend a week on one island.

Oahu, with the international airport and Honolulu, draws cruisers to Waimea Bay but only in summer: in winter, surfers tackle 50ft (15m) waves here. Kaneohe Bay is a great anchorage and the most popular sailing area in the islands. You can't overnight there, but Pearl Harbor is worth a visit for the historical impact.

The Molokai Channel, funnelling wind and seas through the islands, can be daunting (it's the finish for the TransPac Race). Molokai has a good anchorage near Kalaupapa, but I'd spend my time exploring other islands.

Hanalei Bay on Kauai was the backdrop for the movie *South Pacific* and a beautiful anchorage, while the NaPali coast, made famous in *Jurassic Park*, is primal: take time for a swim at Kalalau waterfall.

Maui has the old whaling port of Lahaina, and is near the anchorage and fish preserve of Honolua Bay for snorkelling. Hawaii is the big island, and the Kona Coast is famed for sport fishing. If the volcano is active, it's spectacular from offshore.

The island climate is dominated by the North Pacific High, which provides steady trade winds, strongest in summer. The islands create huge lees and, aside from occasional fronts, rainfall is moderate. Besides, it's warm rain.

As well as the spectacular scenery, one of the attractions of the Hawaiian Islands is the sealife, including spinner dolphins and humpback whales. The sportfishing is superb as well, including blue marlin, wahoo and tuna.

On top of all this, you can learn to hula!

HONOLULU HARBOUR

HANALEI BAY, KAUAI

WILDLIFE

THROUGHOUT the islands, you'll encounter the spinner dolphin, named for its high spinning leaps. From autumn to spring, the humpback whales visit the islands, with more than 1,500 arriving each year.

A VERY LIVELY VOLCANO, hula, surf, Mai Tais, moonlight, rainbows and the Aloha spirit are principal ingredients in the Hawaii experience.

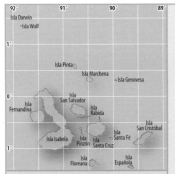

	92°	91°	90°	89°	

THE GALAPAGOS comprise 13 large islands and more than 100 islets.

Ecuador
Galapagos

CHART 1375
BEST FOR CRUISING February – May
AVERAGE TEMPERATURE 26°C 79°F
PREVAILING WIND Light SSE
TIME ZONE GMT – 6
LANGUAGE Spanish
CURRENCY US Dollar (US$)

NAVIGATIONAL DIFFICULTY
FAMILY FRIENDLY
DIVING/SNORKELLING
SHORE-SIDE EATING
SIGHTSEEING

Straddling the equator on the direct route from the Panama Canal to French Polynesia, the "Enchanted Islands" are a tempting landfall for cruising sailors on their way to the South Seas. Some 600 miles (965km) west of Ecuador, this archipelago of 13 large islands and more than 100 smaller ones is famed for its rich wildlife.

NOTHING HAS CONTRIBUTED more to the fame of the Galapagos than the consequences of the five-week visit in 1835 by the British naturalist and geologist Charles Darwin. It was in his role as the geologist aboard HMS *Beagle* that Darwin came to the islands, but it was the information he collected on the flora and fauna here that led him to develop his groundbreaking theory of evolution.

Administered by the Ecuadorian government, this natural sanctuary – which is now one of the most sought-after tourist destinations in the world – is protected by rigorous conservation laws. Strict regulations apply to all visitors, and in particular to those arriving by yacht. There are four official ports: Baquerizo Moreno on San Cristóbal Island, Puerto Ayora on Santa Cruz, Puerto Velasco Ibarra on Floreana and Puerto Villamil on Isabella. Visiting yachts are not allowed to stop anywhere outside those four ports, so the solution for those who wish to explore some of the islands that are off limits is to leave their boat in either Puerto Ayora or Baquerizo Moreno and join day excursions organized by local tour operators. For those seeking more serious and insightful exploration, excursions lasting several days are also available.

With some perseverance, anyone prepared to pay the high fees may obtain an individual cruising permit. The itinerary may

PUERTO AYORA

BARTOLOMÉ ISLAND

FUR SEALS

DARWIN described Galapagos fur seals during his epic voyage on the *Beagle*: "They appeared to be of a loving disposition, and lay huddled together, fast asleep…"

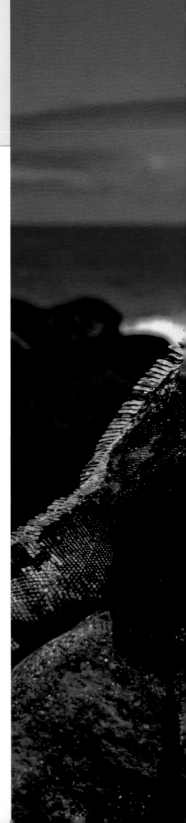

Animal magic in the "Islands of the Tortoises". Dive with sharks, snorkel with penguins, walk with tortoises and wonder about evolution.

THE EXTRAORDINARY marine iguana of the Galapagos Islands famously inspired Charles Darwin in his study of evolution.

include any island but the yacht must be accompanied by a licensed guide at all times. Charter boats operate on the same principle and a variety – both power and sail – operate out of Puerto Ayora. This is the largest and most developed of the islands' towns and here, in addition to its wide range of restaurants and shops, is the Charles Darwin Research Station, which provides an excellent overview of the islands.

The Galapagos land area is some 5,000 square miles (12,950km²), the Galapagos Marine Reserve covers around 50,000 square miles (129,450km²). On land, in the air and in the sea, both the abundance and the variety of wildlife is simply staggering. And, here, you really can walk with the animals; unperturbed by humans, they appear to accept us in their environment. Each island has its own resident species: penguins on San Salvador, sea iguanas on Santa Fé, land iguanas on Fernandina, frigate birds on Seymour, sea lions on San Cristóbal, giant tortoises on Isabella, white-tipped sharks at Bartolomé. Española has the islands' largest colony of blue-footed boobies – their gentle courtship dance is a sight to behold – and the island is also an important breeding ground for sea turtles who lay, then bury, their eggs on its sandy beaches.

It is also possible to arrange diving and snorkelling trips. While the Galapagos Marine Reserve is on the equator, the cold water currents from Antarctica and warm water from the tropics converge and this particular mix is ideal for both cold and warm

BLUE-FOOTED BOOBIES are particularly common on Española Island, where they perform their spectacular dives to catch fish.

VOLCANIC MOUNDS led Darwin to describe "the strange wildness of the view…such a place Vulcan might have worked".

water marine life. There are more than 500 species of fish plus rays, eels, sea turtles, sea lions… And, here, you can dive with sharks – hammerheads and white tips are common – and snorkel with penguins.

The dark grey cone-shaped islands of the Galapagos are a series of high volcanic peaks – and they are among the world's most active volcanoes today. Mangrove swamps on the wet coastal zone give way to arid lowland planes where prickly pear cactus thrive. Climb a little higher – where the air becomes increasingly humid – to find exotic trees and shrubs then, on islands where the peaks reach over 3,000ft (900m), the vegetation changes yet again and species such as the Galapagos tree fern and liverworts predominate.

SAN CRISTÓBAL (above) is the main administrative centre of the Galapagos and has an official port: Baquerizo Moreno.

THE FAMOUS GIANT TORTOISES (left) gave the archipelago its name; *Galapago* means "tortoise" in Spanish.

The islands' early human history features pirates, convicts, colonists and whalers. During the early 1500s, the Galapagos – Floreana in particular – became a hide-out for pirates raiding Spanish colonial ports. Towards the end of the 17th century, British whalers discovered the riches these waters held for them and, by 1844, not only had they hunted out the whales to near extinction, but they had also wiped out the tortoise population on three islands – because they could survive for many months without water or food, tortoises made ideal ship's stores.

Away from the bustle of Puerto Ayora on Santa Cruz, some yachts setting off on the long passage to the Marquesas make a last stop at Puerto Villamil, on Isabella. With its few very basic bars and restaurants, Puerto Villamil is a mellower version of Puerto Ayora. Although the largest island of the archipelago, Isabella is off the beaten track and one feels its wild interior has hardly changed since only the animals roamed these islands.

FLOREANA is the southernmost island of the Galapagos and was the first to be inhabited.

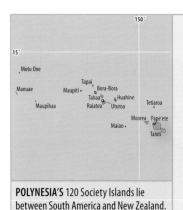

French Polynesia
The Society Islands

CHART 4607, 1382, 1436, 1107
BEST FOR CRUISING April – November (tropical storms November – May)
AVERAGE TEMPERATURE 26ºC 79ºF
PREVAILING WIND SE
TIME ZONE GMT – 10
LANGUAGE French and Polynesian

CURRENCY Cour de Franc Pacifique/Pacific Franc (CFP)
NAVIGATIONAL DIFFICULTY 🧭 🧭 🧭 🧭
FAMILY FRIENDLY 🍹 🍹 🍹 🍹
DIVING/SNORKELLING 🤿 🤿 🤿 🤿
SHORE-SIDE EATING 🍽 🍽 🍽
SIGHTSEEING ⛩ ⛩ ⛩ ⛩

POLYNESIA'S 120 Society Islands lie between South America and New Zealand.

No printer's ink can capture the iridescent shades of indigo and emerald that greet sailors in the palm-fringed lagoons of the South Pacific, one of the world's most exotic cruising grounds. We were sailing from Tahiti, Pearl of the Pacific, to the outer islands. On the horizon, 17 miles away, lay the jagged mountain spires of Moorea, where Hollywood filmed *Mutiny on the Bounty* and Captain Cook gave his name to one of the bays.

BLUE AND GREEN, the dominant colours of the South Seas, come in an unforgettable, seemingly impossible, variety of shades – from the lustrous turquoise of the lagoons, encircled by a deadly necklace of coral, to the deep ocean blue beyond.

A day or two later our 42ft (12.8m) catamaran *Kokiri* (Triggerfish) swung to her anchor in the mirror-calm, picture-postcard blue lagoon of Raiatea. Known as "Sacred Island", Raiatea is the cultural heart of the Tahiti Polynesian group and home to the main yachting base in French Polynesia. Here, the majority of yacht charter companies sailing these islands have their home bases and many offer charters with professional skippers. The rainy season lasts from December to April, the dry season – during which the evenings are cooler – is from July to October and the temperature year-round a comfortable 24–28ºC (75–82ºF).

Less than half a mile away from our anchorage the thunder of surf pounding on the reef was like an express train…but I'd long forgotten the commuter crush on the 0732 from Havant to Waterloo. The only reminders of civilization were two tiny triangles of white sail on the horizon and a tiny house nestling amongst the

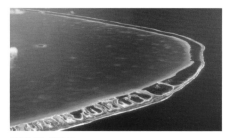
CORAL REEF

PALM-FRINGED LAGOON

TIARE TAHITI

THE TIARE TAHITI is the emblem of French Polynesia. A blossom is traditionally presented to travellers upon arrival in Tahiti and is worn behind the ear. How it is worn denotes a person's marital status.

Picture-perfect paradise amid the shimmering pearls of the Pacific. Fragrant flowers and heady vanilla scent the air. Smile and, here, the world smiles with you.

MOOREA, with its jagged peaks swathed in lush greenery and surrounded by crystalline lagoons, is everyone's dream of Polynesia.

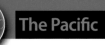

swaying coconut palms on the island astern. Above, fluffy white clouds were airbrushed powder blue by the reflected ocean beneath. This is what the brochures mean by "blue water sailing".

For more than 200 years, Tahiti and her islands have represented the tropical paradise myth for Europeans. They inspired Paul Gauguin to paint and the crew of Captain Bligh's ship, HMS *Bounty*, to mutiny and sell the ship's nails for native girls. Girls in grass skirts and coconut-shell bras are still swinging their hips to a drum beating out the provocative, rhythmic "tamare" dance, which has entranced visitors since Fletcher Christian first set eyes on the scene. It's a scene better witnessed on a beach in moonlight than at a five-star hotel floorshow. From the deck of a sailing yacht you can still discover the unadulterated romance of these islands.

Polynesia's 120 Society Islands lie 17 degrees south of the Equator, between South America and New Zealand. Captain Cook first sailed here in 1769 and in his wake followed writer-

TAHITIAN DANCERS, in their famous coconut-shell bras, are part of the South Sea legend.

TAHITI ISLAND, known as the Pearl of the Pacific, is where the artist Paul Gauguin spent the last few years of his life.

sailors as diverse as Jack London, Robert Louis Stevenson and Eric and Susan Hiscock.

Now that the globe has shrunk, paradise is yours for the price of two ten-hour flights from London, plus a four-hour stopover in Los Angeles – indeed, flights to Tahiti operate from most countries. Any excess baggage will be under your eyes as you are greeted at Tahiti's Faa Airport by a three-piece band serenading you with a ukulele and putting a flower, a Tahitian gardenia (Tiare Tahiti), behind your ear.

There's a "language of flowers" in the islands. If you wear the flower behind your right ear, it means you are single and available. Worn behind your left ear it denotes you are married, engaged or otherwise taken. Worn behind both ears you are married but still available. Worn backward behind your ear you are available immediately!

RANGIROA'S lagoon supports an astounding assortment of marine life, which makes it a prime spot for snorkelling.

THE SUN SETS in a blaze of colours over Tahitian houses on stilts, which are a common sight on the larger islands.

FAAROA RIVER (above), with its magnificent jungle-like setting, is the only navigable river in the French Polynesian Islands.

Pape'ete, the administrative capital of Tahiti and port of entry of French Polynesia, is vibrant and noisy. "By Pacific standards it's a humming metropolis," says the sailors' *Pacific Crossing Guide*. The island's coastal road is the closest Polynesia comes to a motorway. An international community of cruisers moor to the downtown quayside beside the four-lane highway, flags of the world fluttering from their rigging. Tahiti is a place to get things fixed. It's also the first place for crew changes on the coconut milk run from Panama.

Here, too, is the biggest supermarket between America and New Zealand for re-provisioning. But you would be wiser, and richer, if you were to arrive in Tahiti well stocked. For not only is French Polynesia one of the most exotic, beautiful places to cruise, it's also one of the most expensive. Rumour had it that the

MOOREA (below) is where Hollywood filmed *Mutiny on the Bounty* and Captain Cook gave his name to one of the bays.

HUAHINE, also referred to as the "Garden Island" for its rich and varied vegetation, is relatively unspoilt.

laundry charges by natives in the Marquesas were so expensive that one sailor left his washing behind because the clothes were cheaper than the laundry bill. Chartering in this region you should, anyway, make sure to take plenty of cash or travellers' cheques, and it's worth noting that cash machines don't accept MasterCard so take VISA.

Most charter sailors have an overnight stopover at Tahiti, before flying another 125 miles (200km) north-west to Raiatea, the largest of the Leeward Islands. Here you'll discover the unspoilt beauty of French Polynesia – a balmy scent of vanilla and frangipani instead of diesel fumes. Choose between Bora-Bora, Tahaa, Raiatea, Huahine and Moorea – island pearls of the Pacific.

From Raiatea's tiny airport we were driven to Apooiti Marina to board our charter yacht. After a quick sortie into Uturoa town for fresh provisions, we set sail for Isle Mahea, a motu – a small, flat island on the barrier reef – where we would anchor for the night. The tidal range in these waters is less than one foot (0.3m), but the currents running through the lagoon passes (gaps in the barrier reef) can be up to four knots or more. This may be a sailors' paradise, but treacherous, low-lying coral reefs can test the skills of the most experienced yachtsman.

Our first stop, 23 miles west, was the island of Huahine, also known as the "Garden Island" for its lush green jungle-like scenery.

Unspoilt by tourists or hotel chains, Huahine is quiet and peaceful. We anchored off Bali Hai for lunch and relaxed in the cockpit watching life pass by. Just as the British go jogging, or walk their dogs, the Tahitians paddle pirogues, the local outrigger canoes. Families were also out in boats, spear-fishing for their supper off the reef. We took the dinghy ashore and walked into Fare village. A young girl cycled past in the afternoon rain, her hair garlanded with flowers. She flashed a friendly smile and I wished my camera hadn't been in its case. Everyone on Huahine is friendly.

At night you can count the stars, invisible to big-city folk, and you'll find yourself talking in hushed tones, so you don't break the spell. We motor-sailed south next morning, inside the barrier reef, past a backdrop that hasn't changed in 500 years.

Later, we returned to Raiatea and Baie Faaroa, which has the only river in French Polynesia. We took the yacht's dinghy into the interior, like intrepid jungle explorers. You can safely walk barefoot in Polynesia's jungles. There are no poisonous snakes or spiders. At the navigable head of the river we found a native girl cutting banana stalks. We followed a footpath to the botanical gardens where you could pick oranges, bananas, breadfruit and the nono fruit.

The centrepiece of these islands, with their flat coastal strip, is the spectacular jagged peaks and spires of the volcanic

MARAE TAPUTAPUĀTEA on Raiatea, is the most famous of many religious sites scattered across the island.

TAHAA, close to the island of Raiatea, supports large populations of turtles in and around its lagoons.

mountains covered in luxuriant green vegetation. Later we sailed to Baie Opoa to visit the ancient sacred site of Taputapuātea's marae temple. A marae is a terrace paved with stones that served religious and ceremonial purposes; you will find marae sites on various of the French Polynesian islands.

Bora-Bora, apart from Tahiti, is the most developed of the Society islands, with lots of top-class hotels and

MOUNT OTEMANU creates a splendid backdrop to the lagoon at Bora Bora.

fabulous restaurant haunts of the rich and famous: places such as Bloody Mary's, where you might bump into a Hollywood A-lister, or the Lagoonarium where you can swim with sharks, turtles and manta rays. This is the ultimate French chic mixed with a good helping of South Pacific charm.

BORA-BORA, despite its popularity, retains its charm.

TAHAA LAGOON is a stunningly beautiful natural aquarium where you can find grey sharks, napoleons and shoals of barracuda.

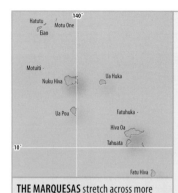

French Polynesia
Marquesas

CHART 1640
BEST FOR CRUISING April – September
AVERAGE TEMPERATURE 25ºC 77ºF
PREVAILING WIND SE
TIME ZONE GMT – 9
LANGUAGE Marquesan and French
CURRENCY Pacific Franc (CFP)

NAVIGATIONAL DIFFICULTY
FAMILY FRIENDLY
DIVING/SNORKELLING
SHORE-SIDE EATING
SIGHTSEEING

The spectacular scenery of the Marquesas, with their craggy soaring peaks and lush vegetation, elevates them to amongst the most beautiful islands in the world. Unfortunately their outstanding beauty is marred by a shortage of protected anchorages, as most bays are affected by the ever-present ocean swell as well as the painfully irritating nono flies.

HOWEVER, the Marquesas have a lot more to offer than natural beauty and the 100th anniversary in 2003 of Paul Gauguin's death on the island of Hiva Oa spurred its small community into a burst of activity. The artist's home in Atuona, Maison de Jouir (House of Pleasure), has been carefully restored to display reproductions of the famous canvases he painted during his sojourn on the island. Barely tolerated by the locals while he lived in their midst, today's inhabitants view Gauguin as an undisputed celebrity who put their remote island on the world map.

A bumpy ride along a rough track leads to the archaeological site at Puamau village on Hiva Oa's northern shore. The site is famous for an ancient stone tiki about 10ft (3m) high and the largest of its kind in the Marquesas. Known by their original name as Te Henua Enata, meaning Land of Men, the islands had a highly developed civilization by the time the first Europeans set foot here in 1595. The first to arrive was the Spanish navigator Alvaro de Mendaña, who named the islands Las Islas de la Marquesa, after the Marchioness of Mendoza, whose husband had sponsored his expedition.

Extensive ruins of dwellings and forts are still to be found on each island and are a sad reminder of the thriving community that once lived here. The local population was quickly decimated

TOHUA HIKOKUA, HATIHEU BAY

PAUL GAUGUIN

A STEEP ROAD leads up from Atuona to the small cemetery where Gauguin was buried in 1903. The tomb is beneath a gnarled tree whose white, fragrant flowers flutter down onto the simple stone grave.

Spectacularly beautiful, spectacularly far-flung and, for Paul Gauguin, Jacques Brel and Herman Melville, spectacularly inspirational.

HANAVAVE on Fatu Hiva, with its towering rock formations, is widely considered to be one of the most beautiful bays in the world.

by various diseases brought by those early visitors. Their tragic fate was later compounded by the forceful abduction of men to work on plantations, so that by the middle of the 19th century the population had been reduced from around 100,000 to a few thousand. The Marquesans never recovered from those traumatic years and today the total population of the islands is less than 9,000 – just six of the 12 islands are inhabited.

No sailor worth his salt will pass through the Marquesas without dropping anchor at Hanavave, on the island of Fatu Hiva, considered one of the most beautiful bays in the world. The surroundings are truly spectacular, with towering rock formations overlooking the tranquil bay. We had completed the 3,000-mile (4,830km) passage from the Galapagos Islands well ahead of any other yacht that season, and so *Aventura* had the picturesque anchorage all to herself. As we landed in front of the small village we were warmly welcomed by a young man who told us how much everyone was looking forward to the annual arrival of the yachts.

Visiting sailors, it seems, are extremely popular with the villagers because they have always been so helpful – repairing outboards, fixing television sets or playing soccer with the youngsters. About 250 yachts make landfall in the Marquesas

PUAMAU VILLAGE boasts some of the largest 'tikis' (ancient stone statues of Gods) found in Polynesia.

every year and the bumper arrival time is during April at the end of the cyclone season and the start of the safe winter sailing season. This is the best time to visit as the weather is pleasant and the islands are cooled by the balmy south-easterly trade winds. Very basic yachting facilities are available in the main port of Taiohae on Nuku Hiva. There is no locally based charter operation but, occasionally, crewed charter yachts brave the challenging 750-mile (1,205km) passage from Tahiti, usually stopping in the Tuamotus on the way.

HANAVAVE BAY, also known as the Bay of Virgins, is a must-see destination for any sailor visiting the Marquesas.

TIKI PARK IN NUKU HIVA contains a large collection of tikis in stunning surroundings backed by mountains.

While Hiva Oa thrives on its association with Paul Gauguin, Nuku Hiva's claim to fame is the setting of Herman Melville's book *Typee*. Hidden in the dense forest above the village is a well-preserved sacred site of massive stone terraces, large temples and impressive statues. Brooding statues stand guard over ancient graves, the oppressive atmosphere and sultry heat bringing to life Melville's gruesome tale.

UA HUKA, the smallest of the northern Marquesan group, is famous for its beautiful wood carvings.

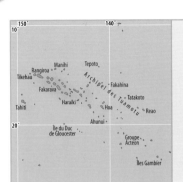

THE TUAMOTUS form the largest chain of atolls in the world.

French Polynesia
Tuamotus

CHART 3664
BEST FOR CRUISING April – November (tropical storms November – May)
AVERAGE TEMPERATURE 26ºC 79ºF
PREVAILING WIND SE
TIME ZONE GMT – 10
LANGUAGE French and Polynesian

CURRENCY Pacific Franc (CFP)
NAVIGATIONAL DIFFICULTY
FAMILY FRIENDLY
DIVING/SNORKELLING
SHORE-SIDE EATING
SIGHTSEEING

The Tuamotus, east of Tahiti, were dubbed the "Dangerous Archipelago" by French explorer Louis-Antoine de Bougainville as far back as 250 years ago. Some 78 coral reef atolls span an area approximately the size of Western Europe.

ATOLLS ARE low-lying islands, essentially high sand bars on coral reefs encircling volcanoes that sank into the oceans millions of years ago. It was here that Thor Heyerdahl's famous Kon-Tiki expedition came to grief when his balsa raft smashed into the reef at Raroia in 1947. The Tuamotus are littered with wrecks, the most recent stranding being that of Sir Francis Chichester's 53ft (16.1m) ketch, *Gipsy Moth IV*, in April 2006 on the reef at Rangiroa, the largest atoll in the Tuamotus, and the second largest in the world. Rangiroa, boasting some of the best dive sites in the world, means 'far sky'.

The Tuamotus is especially dangerous to yachts. Apart from submerged reefs and erratic winds, there are strong, shifting currents, which can sweep sailors off course. The passes into the lagoons have strong currents, depending on the phases of the moon or how much water is in the lagoon. In the 20th century some islands were used for French nuclear experiments.

The golden rule is never sail near the reefs at night or with the sun ahead of you. My first experience of entering a lagoon pass in the South Seas was unforgettable. First there was the distant sound – a constant roar – of the pounding of the deep-blue Pacific, self-destructing on the coral reef. On either side of the pass, hundreds of tons of water explode in shrapnel of white spray and foam. The reef sometimes rises almost vertically off the seabed. With barely enough time to marvel at such a graphic demonstration of nature's force and fury, the current speeds you onwards, with shades of iridescent blue, turquoise and emerald flashing under your keel. Suddenly you glide into the peaceful, protected, mirror-smooth waters of the lagoon. Here, if you are lucky, you are immediately enfolded in waters of such crystalline transparency that the yacht will seem suspended in a liquid mirage. Outside, the Pacific may rage and roar, but inside the lagoon you are safe – except, of course, for the shallow patches and outcrops of coral, known as "bommies".

MANTA RAY, RANGIROA

FAKARAVA

PEARL FARMING

PEARL BEACH RESORT, Tikehau, in the Tuamotus, is a tropical paradise for more experienced sailors.

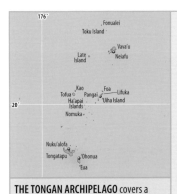

THE TONGAN ARCHIPELAGO covers a distance of about 500 miles (800km).

Melanesia
Tonga and Vava'u

CHART NZ82	
BEST FOR CRUISING May – October	
AVERAGE TEMPERATURE 24°C 75°F	
PREVAILING WIND SE	
TIME ZONE GMT + 13	
LANGUAGE Tongan	
CURRENCY Pa'anga/Tongan Dollar (PT/$T)	

NAVIGATIONAL DIFFICULTY	✦ ✦ ✦ ✦
FAMILY FRIENDLY	♟ ♟ ♟ ♟
DIVING/SNORKELLING	🤿 🤿 🤿 🤿 🤿
SHORE-SIDE EATING	🍽 🍽
SIGHTSEEING	♟ ♟ ♟

This Polynesian kingdom, situated in the heart of the South Pacific, consists of over 160 coral and volcanic islands, of which fewer than one quarter are inhabited. Best known among sailors is the northern group of Vava'u, whose maze of islets and reefs provides one of the best cruising grounds in the South Pacific.

TRILITHON

THE CAPITAL NUKU'ALOFA on the main island of Tongatapu is more advanced than the outer islands, but even there the atmosphere is slow and peaceful. A spacious harbour allows sailors to leave their yachts in safety while visiting this interesting island to see the mysterious trilithon (stone archway) at Ha'amonga 'a Maui, the blowholes at Houma, the flocks of flying foxes at Kolovai or the tombs of the Tu'i Tonga dynasty in the ancient capital of Mu'a.

Towards the end of June/beginning of July with the blooming of Tonga's national flower – the heilala – the kingdom's most important festival is staged in Nuku'alofa on Tongatapu. The vibrant and colourful celebrations continue for a week. The more northerly islands of Vava'u and Ha'apai stage their festivals earlier in the year.

The 88-year-old king Taufa'ahau Tupou IV died in 2006 and was succeeded by his son Siaosi Taufa'ahau Manumataongo Tuku'aho Tupou, who took the title of George Tupou V. The Tongan royal family is the oldest reigning dynasty in the Pacific and one of the oldest in the world. The small, predominantly Christian country is run along feudal lines and shortly before the late king's death there was widespread unrest among the 100,000 inhabitants who demanded that the ossified system be reformed. A few improvements were made and it is expected that the new king

BLOW HOLES

HEILALA FESTIVAL

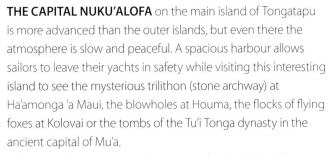

VIBRANT and colourful, Heilala's week-long celebrations feature a packed programme of traditional dance and music plus parties, parades and regattas.

A beautiful maze of lush islands with deserted beaches and coral reefs. Slow to a gentle tick-over on Tongan time and find peace, tranquillity and a warm welcome in the "Friendly Islands".

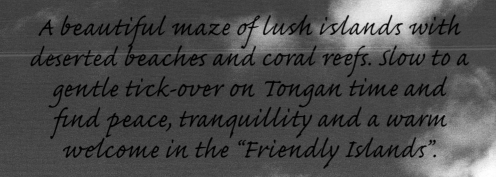

TONGA'S climate is tropical and oceanic, with warm weather and ample rainfall all year round. Typhoons occasionally occur.

will take further steps to modernize his country. Local customs and dress code are strict, and both locals and visitors are expected to respect Sunday observance.

The islands of Vava'u have been one of the favourite cruising destinations in the South Pacific for a long time. The unique potential of their sheltered waters was recognized in the early 1970s when South Pacific Yacht Charters opened the first charter operation in the South Pacific. The strategic location of Vava'u at the crossroads of several sailing routes, as well as the reputation of its main port, Neiafu, as a safe hurricane hole turned Vava'u into a busy yachting centre with a good range of repair and shore facilities. Several charter companies are based at Port Refuge and charter activity – both bareboat and crewed – is now a booming business that covers all of Tonga.

Vava'u is also the favourite destination of some travellers of a very different kind: scores of humpback whales that gather to breed between June and October. They can be seen frolicking with their young throughout the islands and their chatter can be heard reverberating through the hull of one's boat. Several local operators offer whale-watching tours and their boats sail to within feet of these benign giants. Snorkelling with them is the latest thrill, but when I tried it and managed to swim reasonably near a huge female and her newly born calf, the interest was

NEIAFU HARBOUR (above), Vava'u Island's main port, is a safe hurricane hole in the South Pacific.

CAPTAIN COOK stopped in the Tonga Islands (below) in 1773, and dubbed them the "Friendly Islands".

HUMPBACK WHALES gather around the islands to breed between June and October.

PORT REFUGE is used as a base by several charter companies, and charter activity is a growing industry.

disappointingly one-sided and they both sounded before I could get really close up. The last time I had seen whales at such close quarters had been in Antarctica, where those same humpbacks congregate in summer to gorge on the abundant krill before migrating back to the tropics for the winter. Their highly accurate navigation system allows them to return always to the same destination without fail.

Tonga's climate is warm and humid, although, thanks to fresh sea breezes, less so than other tropical islands. May to October is the dry season, while December to March, which is also the hurricane season, has more rain. From April to November the south-east trade winds predominate, although sudden squalls can occur from other directions.

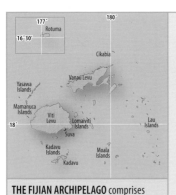

Melanesia
Fiji

CHART 2691
BEST FOR CRUISING May – October
AVERAGE TEMPERATURE 24°C 75°F
PREVAILING WIND SE
TIME ZONE GMT + 12
LANGUAGE Fijian, some English spoken
CURRENCY Fijian Dollar (F$)

NAVIGATIONAL DIFFICULTY
FAMILY FRIENDLY
DIVING/SNORKELLING
SHORE-SIDE EATING
SIGHTSEEING

THE FIJIAN ARCHIPELAGO comprises more than 300 islands.

Fiji has all the ingredients of a perfect cruising destination and few yachts that sail through the South Seas bypass this fascinating, picturesque country with its secluded anchorages and warm-hearted people. A traditional way of life is still thriving in the outer islands – and especially in the Lau Group. In order to preserve custom and convention in the local communities, the authorities do not allow yachts to visit the eastern islands except if in possession of a cruising permit.

IN ALL RURAL AREAS, local etiquette should be observed and one is expected to pay a courtesy visit to the chief or headman of the island or village bearing a gift. In the past this used to be a gift of kava roots, locally known as yagona, a mildly narcotic drink that looks and, to the uninitiated, tastes like muddy water. The ceremony that accompanies the drink is so colourful that the obligatory draining of half a coconut shell offered by the host is a small price to pay for the instantaneous welcome that results from it.

Even in these days of GPS and radar, navigation in Fiji's reef-infested waters is not easy. The problem is exacerbated by the insistence of the authorities that any yacht arriving from abroad must not stop anywhere before clearing in at an official port of entry. The most convenient port for those intending to cruise eastern Fiji is Savusavu, on the south coast of Vanua Levu, Fiji's second-largest island. Its two marinas are very popular with foreign sailors many of whom have made their semi-permanent home there. The narrow harbour is well sheltered and has survived a couple of recent tropical cyclones unscathed.

FIJIAN TAXI

DUNRAVEN WRECK

TRADITIONAL FISHING

ALTHOUGH net-fishing was often practised by women, men have practically taken over the activity with the introduction of large gillnets. Traditional nets were made from vines.

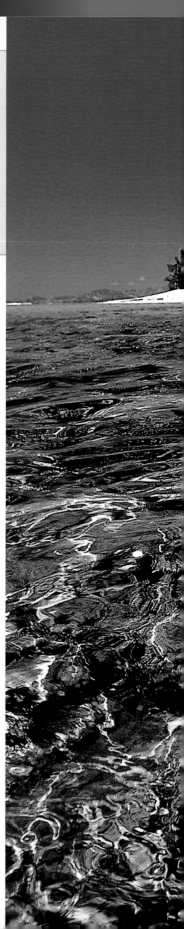

Fiji's diverse blend of custom and convention, coral reefs and sheltered anchorages make it a must-see for any yacht passing through. But navigation is not for the faint-hearted.

THE FIJIAN ARCHIPELAGO, at the crossroads of Melanesia and Polynesia, ranges from small coral atolls to large volcanic islands.

The capital Suva – on Viti Levu – is another well-protected harbour and the welcoming Royal Suva Yacht Club is one of the most popular watering holes on the South Pacific cruising circuit. Nowhere in Fiji is the ethnic mix of the native Fijians and the later-arrived Indians more visible than in Suva's vibrant market, dominated by piles of exotic fruit, sacks of fragrant spices and tablefuls of wooden carvings.

South of Suva lie the islands of Kadavu, a small archipelago where traditions are still very much alive but where visiting yachts are more than welcome. An interesting stop is at the village of Daku, where the villagers have embarked on an ambitious programme of organic farming coupled with strict rules for the protection of their environment.

In recent years a number of marinas have been built on the west coast of the main island of Viti Levu and as they are close to Nadi international airport. Denaru Marina has the best facilities and is the most important charter base in the area. Bareboat charter is not available in Fiji but there are various operators offering a range of crewed yachts for charter.

Close by Viti Levu lie two island groups that are most popular with both charter and cruising yachts: the Mamanucas and

VITI LEVU'S Yanuca Island is a tropical paradise surrounded by pristine white beaches, turquoise lagoons, swaying palm trees and well-protected harbours, offering a truly magical escape destination.

THE ISLAND OF MALOLOLAILAI has lush tropical gardens and extensive coconut plantations. Most importantly it is home to the Musket Cove Yacht Club, a place close to the hearts of long-distance cruising sailors.

Yasawas. The latter is a string of largely unspoilt islands with clear waters and scenic anchorages. The Mamanucas are just as attractive but more developed, with several resorts among which the best known is Malololailai Island. This is home to the Musket Cove Yacht Club, a place held in great affection by long-distance cruising sailors. One of their number, the Australian Dick Smith, who roamed these waters in the 1960s, fell in love with Fiji and settled down here. He founded what is surely the most informal yacht club in the world, where those arriving on their own boat become life members on payment of one Fiji dollar and their name and that of their yacht is carved into an overhead beam. A small marina was inaugurated recently and sailors may use all of the resort's facilities. It is in every sense of the word a home away from home.

MALOLOLAILAI ISLAND has 12
wonderful palm-fringed beaches.

Fiji's tropical climate is best enjoyed during
the winter season (April to October) when
the islands are cooled by the south-east
trade winds. The cyclone season lasts from
late November to March and while many
cruising boats leave the tropics during the
critical period to sail to New Zealand or
Australia, there are now a few places in Fiji
where boats can be left unattended during
summer, best among them the marinas on
Viti Levu's west coast.

THE LAU ISLANDS are a jumble of small
islands straddling the eastern approaches.

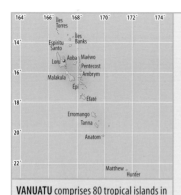

VANUATU comprises 80 tropical islands in a Y-shaped archipelago.

Melanesia
Vanuatu

CHART 1577, 1581, 1638
BEST FOR CRUISING May – October
AVERAGE TEMPERATURE 23ºC 73ºF
PREVAILING WIND SE
TIME ZONE GMT + 11
LANGUAGE Bislama, French and English
CURRENCY Vatu (VT)

NAVIGATIONAL DIFFICULTY
FAMILY FRIENDLY
DIVING/SNORKELLING
SHORE-SIDE EATING
SIGHTSEEING

Sailors often look back nostalgically to a golden past when there were still plenty of unspoilt places to explore and you could sail around the world on a shoestring. Things have undoubtedly changed but there are still a few notable exceptions. Such a place is Vanuatu, formerly known as the Condominium of the New Hebrides once administered jointly by Britain and France.

YASUR VOLCANO, TANNA

WHEN WE ARRIVED there shortly before independence in 1979, we came across some of the most isolated and undeveloped communities that we had seen anywhere on our travels. Nearly 30 years later life in the outer islands has changed very little and cruising sailors can still find there much of what has disappeared elsewhere. With a population of around 220,000, the islands have survived the attempts of missionaries to subvert its culture, and its landscape the depredations of ruthless traders, for whom sandalwood was the main attraction, and also slavery.

WALA ISLAND

Stretching in a long chain from south to north the islands have everything one could wish for: calm anchorages, welcoming villagers and some of the most interesting sights in the Pacific. There are two highlights: Yasur volcano on Tanna and the land-divers of Pentecost Island. The volcano has been reclaimed by the villagers who live on its slopes and they guide visitors to the rim of the mighty crater. This is as close as anyone would want to come to a live volcano, as even from a safe distance the spewing lava inspires an acute sense of the dangerous power within.

One can see live volcanoes in other places, too, but Vanuatu offers a unique – and thrilling – volcano-related attraction in the

TANNESE VILLAGERS

ESPIRITU SANTO, VANUATU, has soft, white sand beaches; crystal clear water, jungle walks; friendly villages; and good food.

THE VANUATU famously enjoy life's simpler pleasures in a country of unique and diverse customs and culture.

LAND DIVING performances by men from a handful of villages take place at Pentecost Island in late April and early May.

Nagol, an ancient ceremony held on the island of Pentecost to celebrate the yam harvest. Every year, men from the south side of Pentecost put on a land-diving performance that inspired the bungee-jumping craze. Words cannot describe the intensity of excitement that you feel as diver after diver hurtles up to 100ft (30m) towards the ground, with only a length of vine tied to his ankles. The adrenaline courses through your veins as if you, yourself had taken that awesome death-defying leap.

While Tanna and Pentecost attract a number of tourists, the outer islands are visited only by cruising boats. Here, people continue to live as they always have done: gardening, fishing, hunting, and having very little contact with the outside world…just as in days gone by. Indeed, many of the islands in the archipelago have been inhabited for many thousands of years and ancient tribal customs and traditions remain very much in evidence.

The climate is tropical with two distinct seasons. May to October is relatively cool and dry, while November to April is hot and humid. January to March are the rainy months. The cyclone season lasts from December until early April. While a good number of unmarked rocks lurk in the Vanuatu waters, a skippered charter will make for angst-free sailing. Your skipper's local knowledge should also ensure that your itinerary includes snorkelling and diving, beach picnics and sightseeing, or you might include a day's game-fishing charter – there are rich pickings on the reefs and in deep water.

VANUATU sealife includes sea fans, soft corals and thousands of curious fish. You might also see the extraordinary dugong.

Diving in Vanuatu is not challenging, but rewarding. Most reefs begin in 35ft (10m) or less and drop away to varying depths. The submarine landscape mirrors that found above: mountainous terrain with plunging cliffs, grottoes and overhangs, huge caves and intricate interconnecting underwater tunnels formed by frozen lava. There you'll find sea fans, soft corals and acropora gardens, plate corals and sponges and thousands of curious fish, besides the remains of man's handiwork: planes, an old square rigger, a destroyer and the wreck of the 22,000-ton SS *President Coolidge*, a converted troop ship that sank during World War II close off the beach, and is perhaps the most famous. The forward holds are jammed with guns, helmets and gas masks, while personal effects are scattered across the promenade deck and bow. A number of scuba operations cater for reef and wreck divers, based in Espiritu Santo.

Vanuatu is certainly remote, still unspoilt, compared to so many islands, and yet only two to three hours by plane from Brisbane, Sydney and Auckland. That it holds its own golf open suggests that any over-romantic image of pristine paradise can be taken with a pinch of salt. For any golf-aficionados sailing its waters, however, a round in such surroundings may rank as high as any of its many natural attractions.

ESPIRITU SANTO is the base for a number of scuba operations that cater for reef and wreck dives.

THE GOLD COAST area of Queensland, Australia, includes the excellent marina facilities of Southport.

Australasia and the Far East

Once upon a time, Australia, South America, Africa, India and the Antarctic were joined in one vast land mass. Fortunately for present-day yachtsmen the break-up all those millions of years ago created sailing waters of incomparable diversity; islands with fascinating cultures; fjords to rival Norway; and one mighty coral reef stretching half the length of a continent, aptly named the Great Barrier. Throw Australia's great city, Sydney, and its huge natural harbour into the mix; include its New Zealand rival, Auckland, the aptly named City of Sails, surrounded by its Bay of Islands; add a dash of French-influenced spice islands, and a pinch of the Far East and you have more than enough variety to tempt the most jaded of cruising palates.

AUSTRALASIA and the Indian Ocean contain thousands of stunning tropical islands and the world's largest coral reef.

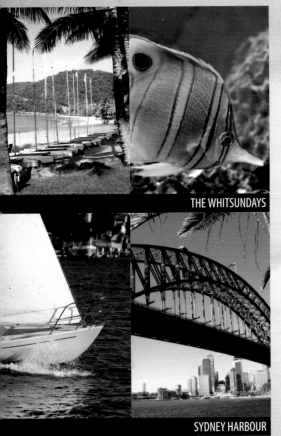

THE WHITSUNDAYS

SYDNEY HARBOUR

AUSTRALASIA AND THE FAR EAST

About 120 million years ago the super-continent of Godwana, which was made up of present-day Australia, South America, Africa, India and Antarctica, began to break up and the current continents, subcontinents and islands were formed. From Antarctica to Thailand, sailing yachts criss-cross the oceans that now separate those lands and include some of the most attractive cruising destinations in the world. Foremost amongst them are Australia and New Zealand: both countries have large yachting communities of their own, and both have won the coveted America's Cup.

Australia's Great Barrier Reef is one of the natural wonders of the world and provides sailors and divers with the opportunity to enjoy the beauty of this vast area both above and under water. Tropical Australia is affected by tropical storms whose seasons coincide with the summer months in both the South Pacific and Indian Oceans. In contrast, New Zealand and sub-tropical Australia lie south of the cyclone belt and are considered relatively safe cruising grounds all year round.

New Zealand and sub-tropical Australia are considered safe cruising grounds all year round.

Yachting has made great strides in the North Indian Ocean in recent years with well-endowed centres along the west coast of the Malay Peninsula, from Phuket to Singapore. One area that is rapidly catching up is the United Arab Emirates, where man is busily making up for what nature failed to provide and harbours, beaches and even entire islands are being created from scratch.

The weather throughout the North Indian Ocean is dominated by the north-east monsoon of winter and spring, and the south-west monsoon of summer and autumn. The former provides benign weather conditions when yachts undertake the passage from South-east Asia to the Red Sea and Mediterranean.

South of the equator, the island groups scattered across the South Indian Ocean make convenient stepping stones from the South Pacific to South Africa. The best sailing conditions are from June to October, with steady south-east trade winds. Mauritius, Madagascar and Réunion are the most popular cruising destinations. The tropical storm season lasts from late November to early April and affects all tropical areas with the notable exception of the Seychelles and Chagos.

MALDIVES

SEYCHELLES

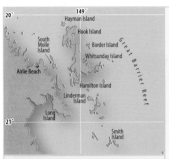

THE WHITSUNDAY ISLANDS comprise 73 continental islands right at the heart of Queensland's Great Barrier Reef.

Australia
The Whitsundays

CHART AUS252
BEST FOR CRUISING June – October
AVERAGE TEMPERATURE 23°C 74°F
PREVAILING WIND SE
TIME ZONE GMT + 10
LANGUAGE English
CURRENCY Australian Dollar (AU$)

NAVIGATIONAL DIFFICULTY
FAMILY FRIENDLY
DIVING/SNORKELLING
SHORE-SIDE EATING
SIGHTSEEING

As our cook on board the 50-footer (15.2m) laced up her heavy walking boots it seemed somewhat eccentric. We were going ashore on Border Island, one of the northernmost Whitsunday Islands, and in the near-tropical heat the rest of us wore flip-flops or deckies. A local Queenslander, she knew the area intimately and had promised to show us one of its best views – from the ridge at the top of the island looking east over the Coral Sea towards the Great Barrier Reef.

IT SEEMED even more eccentric when she picked up a stout piece of driftwood and drummed it on the ground at regular intervals as we climbed up through calf-high undergrowth. Until she explained, when it all became terrifyingly logical. "It's the taipans," she told us, "the vibration frightens them away so bang your feet as you walk and make sure you don't tread on one." The taipan is reputedly the world's most deadly snake. One bite delivers enough venom to kill 100 people. So it was a rather nervous sort of ragtag Dad's Army that marched, stamping, up the hill to the ridge. The view was spectacular but my mind was elsewhere.

For the Northern European, Queensland is a hell of a long way to go for a yacht charter but believe me it's worth it, especially if, say, a two-week charter is combined with a couple of weeks touring Australia. There are some 74 islands in the Whitsunday group, discovered by Captain Cook in 1770, scattered between 20° and 21° S, although the main area for charters is centred on Hamilton Island or nearby Airlie Beach.

TAIPAN

HAMILTON ISLAND MARINA

SULPHUR-CRESTED COCKATOOS

*More than seventy tall, green islands
shelter inside the Great Barrier Reef.
A national park afloat in the Coral Sea
where the sand between your toes is
as soft as silk.*

HILL INLET, Whitehaven Beach, on Whitsunday
Island is a stunning inlet where the tide shifts
the sand to create a beautiful fusion of colours.

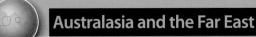

AZURE WATERS, glorious weather, great beaches, fascinating flora and fauna – Hamilton Island is the complete package.

After some 30 hours in the air on three different flights jet lag takes on a new meaning, and that feeling of detachment is further highlighted by what greets you as you arrive in Hamilton. Two tall towers of Hamilton Towers Hotel thrust up from the luxuriant tropical foliage whilst flights of screeching, sulphur-crested cockatoos circle overhead, to be replaced at dusk by enormous, rank-smelling fruit bats. And in a scene reminiscent of the British TV series *The Prisoner*, local transport is entirely by golf buggy.

   The islands are a national park and there are pretty strict cruising regulations and – quite rightly – draconian laws over dumping rubbish at sea, anchoring on coral, fishing and collecting coral. The result is clear water, clean beaches and unspoilt islands. The vast majority of the islands are also uninhabited and anyone cruising this area is likely to find

HAMILTON ISLAND and the nearby Airlie Beach are the main area for charters in the Whitsundays.

themselves as one of only two or three yachts in a near-perfect anchorage. There are some 128 of these, but not all are tenable depending on wind direction. Between June and October, the best months to visit, the wind is predominantly south-easterly.

But the most memorable feature of the Whitsundays is the quality and clarity of the air, as unpolluted as you'll find anywhere on the planet and it creates a very special, almost ethereal, light. The islands are tall, green and heavily wooded with mangroves, grass trees, eucalyptus, hoop pines, pandanns, she-oaks and in the spring, coastal orchids. "A bit like the BVI crossed with the West Coast of Scotland," we were informed – although you don't get many taipans, fruit bats and cockatoos in Scotland. And, of course, the snorkelling and scuba-diving are spectacular.

Self-sufficiency is the order of the day here because, although there are restaurants at the resorts on some of the islands, if one is to make the most of cruising the area these will be low on your list of priorities. Provisioning – ours was so complete that it was divided into day packs, right down to supplies of salt, pepper, soap and loo paper – and filling tanks can only be done at Hamilton or Airlie Beach where there are a number of companies specializing in victualling for charter boats. This dictates that the

SHUTE HARBOUR, Queensland, is a large sheltered inlet, and a busy boarding point for charter boats.

logical charter cruise will either head north or south from one of these bases for a few days, dropping in again in mid-cruise to re-provision and top up before heading off the other way. In our case, we started in the south.

The sailing is relatively straightforward, navigating by eyeball, although it is easy to get the islands mixed up. There are also a number of unmarked reefs and hazards. The tidal range is around 10ft (3m) and the resulting streams can kick up small but nasty seas in some of the narrow inter-island passages in wind against tide conditions. But for the most part seas are smooth, sheltered

NARA INLET, HOOK ISLAND, offers a number of anchorage options and is a popular first or last night stopover destination.

LINDEMAN ISLAND is the most southerly island of the Whitsundays, 20 miles (32km) from the coast.

WHITSUNDAYS' beaches are truly breathtaking, with brilliant silica sand that is among the purest in the world.

by the Great Barrier Reef 35 miles (56km) to the east.

On the southerly leg of our cruise, we visited Shaw, Thomas and Goldsmith Islands before returning to Hamilton via Anchor and Lindeman Islands. These islands are all beautiful but the second half of our cruise – to Hook, Hayman, Border and Whitsunday Islands – was the highlight of the trip. First of all it was the Nara Inlet on Hook, a tall-sided fjord-like inlet that boasts early Aboriginal cave paintings and a spectacular waterfall after

HAYMAN ISLAND'S world-class resort facilities are in marked contrast to the more untouched islands.

THE GREAT BARRIER REEF is the world's largest reef system and one of the natural wonders of the world.

rain, although the effect of the former is spoilt with rather more modern graffiti. Hayman is a world-class resort and worth a visit just as a contrast to the wildness of the other islands, but then it's back to the empty islands. At Butterfly and Manta Ray Bays in the

north of Hook coral heads, or bommies – not to mention the coral itself – pose a hazard to yachts and their anchor cables but fortunately the water is clear enough for a lookout in the bow to warn the helmsman in plenty of time.

Border Island, taipans apart, had easily the best snorkelling we experienced. I found myself here, swimming along in the clear water, wondering where all the fish were only to look back to see

WHITEHAVEN BEACH is a pristine beach on Whitsunday Island that stretches for over three miles (5km). Most people moor their boats in Tongue Bay and enjoy the breathtaking views over Hill Inlet.

100 or so following in my wake, obviously curious about this strange pink-and-white sea creature.

The last experience, however, outshone everything we had seen before. After anchoring in Tongue Bay, on the west side of Whitsunday Island, we landed and trekked across the narrow isthmus to the north bank of the wide, shallow Hill Inlet. This is Australian *Robinson Crusoe* territory. The silica sand is talcum powder fine and nearly as white. Looking across the inlet a half-mile (0.8km) or so away is the famous Whitehaven Beach, Australia's finest they claim, a swathe, a strand of white, sandy beach more than four miles (7km) long disappearing into the distance. Although busy during the holiday season in the daytime, in the evening the beach is almost deserted.

A final treat is to take a seaplane flight out to the Great Barrier Reef. As you fly over the islands you have a view to die for. The great spread of the spectacular Hill Inlet, the corals on Border and the sight of the Barrier Reef in the distance is an experience to make the spirit soar. The landing on the Reef and snorkelling in amongst the huge tree-like and brightly coloured corals are a must-do for anyone sailing these waters.

FROM MAY through to August, humpback whales are a familiar sight around the Whitsundays, and the crystal clear waters surrounding the islands are also home to a kaleidoscope of coloured coral and tropical fish.

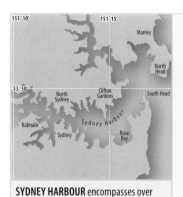

SYDNEY HARBOUR encompasses over 150 miles (240km) of shoreline.

Australia
Sydney Harbour

CHART AUS202
BEST FOR CRUISING September – April
AVERAGE TEMPERATURE 24ºC 75ºF
PREVAILING WIND Seabreeze in summer
TIME ZONE GMT + 10
LANGUAGE English
CURRENCY Australian Dollar (A$)

NAVIGATIONAL DIFFICULTY
FAMILY FRIENDLY
DIVING/SNORKELLING
SHORE-SIDE EATING
SIGHTSEEING

Inbound from the Tasman and Wellington, New Zealand, the sky was sodium-orange bright despite the rain as the city lighting reflected off the clouds. Despite being Australia's major city, parts of the shore are still dark because they are a national park, the towering North Head and lower, spit-like South Head amongst them.

SHAPING TO round Bradley's Head is when you see Sydney in all its magnificence. At any time the vista is wonderful. At night, after a 1,000-mile (1,610km) passage, it is enticing and exciting. It's hard to imagine the Sydney waterfront can be dull at any time.

But that night, the sheer beauty that European hands created in shaping one of world's best natural habours was breathtaking. Danish architect Jørn Utzon's Sydney Opera House is outrageously beautiful, its boldness necessary simply because of the Harbour Bridge. This had a mixed parentage, but 80 per cent of its steel was produced in the UK.

The best view of all, despite some very fancy waterfront houses, belongs to Admiralty House, the Governor General's official residence – the prime minister's is next door – on the opposing Kirribilli Point.

The bridge's "coathanger" double span now provides the ideal platform for the stunning fireworks habitually seen on New Year's Eve, but also – and most impressively – when the 2000 Olympics were opened. In a neat illusion, a Royal Australia Air Force F111 flew over the stadia at Homestead, went to full afterburner as it skimmed the bridge and "ignited" the fireworks.

Today, Sydney Harbour is a melée of traffic. Though Captain James Cook started the European settlement of Australia one harbour south at Botany Bay, which is the modern home to the

SYDNEY OPERA HOUSE

FIREWORKS OVER HARBOUR BRIDGE

YACHT MARINA

AT NIGHT, the beauty of Sydney Harbour comes into its own, with the stunningly illuminated opera house and bridge.

NAVIGATION IN the crowded waters of Sydney Habour requires constant vigilance.

THE SPIT-LIKE SOUTH HEAD forms a natural breakwater at the mouth of Sydney Harbour and is part of the national park.

THE SYDNEY-HOBART YACHT RACE is an icon of Australia's summer sport attracting huge media coverage.

airport and oil terminal, Sydney remains a working harbour. The Royal Australian Navy, container ships and liners all use ports close to the city's bohemian downtown.

The ferry traffic is continual, leaving yachts and dinghies to compete for space. The Royal Sydney Yacht Squadron at Kirribilli has a prime location. Visitors need reciprocal rights from their own club to enter. On the same side is the Sydney Amateur Sailing Club, an ideal place to capture the feel of the beer-and-pie 18ft-Skiff culture before watching these amazing boats hurtle out in the harbour, with a tennis ball mounted optimistically on the tip of the bowsprit to minimize collision damage. On the north side of the harbour is the equally welcoming Cruising Yacht Club of Australia, home of the famous Sydney–Hobart race.

Charter yachts – bareboat and skippered – solve the problem of how to sail in Sydney Harbour, unless you are lucky enough to be voyaging aboard your own yacht.

SYDNEY OPERA HOUSE is an architectural gem, and easily holds its own against the impressive span of Harbour Bridge.

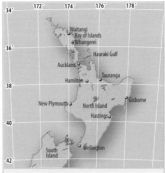

THE NORTH ISLAND covers 71,5000 sq miles (115,000km²).

New Zealand
North Island

CHART NZ522, NZ531
BEST FOR CRUISING November - April
AVERAGE TEMPERATURE 24ºC 75ºF
PREVAILING WIND NW
TIME ZONE GMT + 12
LANGUAGE English and Maori
CURRENCY New Zealand Dollar (NZ$)

NAVIGATIONAL DIFFICULTY 🧭 🧭 🧭
FAMILY FRIENDLY 👙 👙 👙
DIVING/SNORKELLING 🤿 🤿 🤿
SHORE-SIDE EATING 🍽 🍽 🍽 🍽
SIGHTSEEING 🏰 🏰 🏰 🏰

At some time, almost everyone will have met a bumptious New Zealander who just has to tell everyone in earshot that his beautiful homeland is "God's own country". Kiwis are known for their bragging, especially where sport is concerned, but visitors – and everyone should visit at least once in their lifetime – will suddenly realize that the Kiwi's real vice was understatement. The country's two fabulous islands not only offer scenic beauty on a grand scale but also some excellent cruising grounds and great weather.

IN VERY BROAD TERMS, the western shores of both North and South Islands are lee shores and relatively inhospitable to yachts and the eastern shores provide shelter and interesting cruising grounds, while the division between the islands, Cook Strait, is renowned for its strong winds – hence the nickname "Windy Wellington" given to New Zealand's capital.

Most visitors arrive in Auckland, which, housing more than a quarter of the country's inhabitants, is by far the largest city. With its Mediterranean climate, a fabulous waterside location looking out over the Hauraki Gulf and a boating-crazy population it is no wonder that Auckland is known as the "City of Sails". No other city in the world has such high per capita boat ownership, and this is reflected in its astoundingly large range of yachting facilities. In global terms, of course, Auckland ranks as a small city, and it's not exactly a magnet for fashion shopping. It will, however, ably satisfy any provisioning or boating demand, from every conceivable repair and maintenance task to shops selling the whole gamut of marine spare parts, while offering two superb

AUCKLAND

WAIHEKE ISLAND, AUCKLAND

BAY OF PLENTY, NORTH ISLAND

FROM THE CITY OF SAILS to the Bay of Islands, boat-crazy Kiwis have plenty to brag about: great cruising grounds and spectacular scenery.

AMONG THE ISLANDS of the Hauraki Gulf, the Chinese hat-shaped Rangitoto is a clue to the region's volcanic roots.

city-centre marinas edged by world-class waterside dining in a sub-tropical environ.

Step aboard a yacht, sail out between the skyscrapers of Auckland to starboard and the satellite town of Devonport to port and you are immediately among the islands of the Hauraki Gulf, where the Chinese hat-shaped Rangitoto is swift to remind that this is volcano country. Beyond, the sheltered waters of the Gulf offer five large islands and a myriad of smaller ones, all with safe anchorages.

Whether you have a day or a week at your disposal, there is plenty to do when not actually sailing these scenic waters. Walking is one of the major pastimes in New Zealand and there are well signposted trails on the "wilderness" islands of Rangitoto and Mototapu that form part of the Gulf's Maritime Park, as well as on the rugged little Rakino Island. Rakino is one of the Gulf's

WAIHEKE ISLAND'S breathtaking beaches and award-winning wineries and olive groves are a potent attraction.

most sparsely populated islands, its 40 or so inhabitants are served by just one shop and, environmentally friendly by nature, they willingly go without mains electricity, water or sealed roads. The largest island, Waiheke, on the other hand, is well colonized – particularly at its western end – and offers an abundance of superb beaches as well as visitor-friendly, award-winning wineries and olive groves, often with excellent restaurants. Thirty nautical miles to the east of Auckland and forming the Gulf's eastern boundary, the practically uninhabited Coromandel Peninsula is a real wilderness, its rolling green hills clad in grasslands and sub-tropical rainforest while the springtime shoreline is enlivened with the flame-red flowers of the native pohutukawa trees.

Forming the north-eastern wave break of the Hauraki Gulf, Great Barrier Island together with Little Barrier Island, a nature reserve where landing is prohibited, lie some 50 miles from Auckland. Getting there is more testing than merely sailing among the Gulf's islands, but it is a seriously rewarding trip. Great Barrier, 23 miles by five miles (37 by 8km) in size, is mainly forested and mountainous, rising to the 2,037ft (621m) high peak of Mount Hobson. With eco-tourism on the rise, hiking – or "tramping" in NZ terminology – is an ever more popular and major activity and more than 62 miles (100km) of well-kept tracks

COROMANDEL PENINSULA offers visitors a taste of true wilderness, from rolling grasslands to sub-tropical rainforest.

criss-cross the island and ascend to the peak of Hobson – stunning forest walks with spectacular views at their end. One word of warning: beware the athleticism of New Zealanders – what local guides might describe as an "easy walk" can mean a serious trek with many steep gradients. The island itself follows the general pattern of New Zealand with its east coast offering several large white sand bays and its west coast rugged and inhospitable. The only exceptions to this rule are Tryphena Harbour in the south, Whangaparapara Inlet and Fitzroy Harbour, protected by Kaikoura Island, in the north.

Fitzroy is one of New Zealand's great anchorages; protected from every wind direction it is large enough for anyone who wants solitude to find his own quiet corner, while provisions can be bought from a shop in the village of Fitzroy. Legend tells that a few years back, when sailing through the narrow passage between Kaikoura Island and the southern shore of Fitzroy, one visiting North American yachtsman saw a magnificent stag roaming wild among the island's trees. The yacht's owner, a frustrated huntsman who carried a rifle aboard, anchored his

THE BAY OF ISLANDS in the north-east of North Island is perhaps the most famous of all New Zealand's cruising areas.

yacht, returned to the island by dinghy, stalked the stag and shot it. Dragging the beast back to his dinghy he passed a sign that he had not previously noticed – it proclaimed "Deer Farm, Keep Out". He had killed the farm's prize stud animal!

To the south, Tryphena is less well protected from south-westerlies and less isolated, being served by the ferry from Auckland, while in suitably settled weather the open bays and beaches of the east coast provide great opportunities for safe swimming, diving and snorkelling for all ages. Although the roads are narrow and tortuous, a tour of this spectacular island is a must, and while there is no public transport taxis are available, as are hire cars. Basking in the Kaitoke natural hot springs is one of the more unusual activities, but golf, tennis and sportfishing are all on offer.

Perhaps the most renowned of all New Zealand's cruising areas, the Bay of Islands lies in the north-east of North Island

where this island-studded sunken valley twists inland to the small towns of Russell, Pahia and Opua. In size it is small – just 10 miles (16km) from one side to the other and 15 miles (24km) out to the outer reaches where the rugged Piercey Island is pierced by a navigable cave. Captain Cook is not generally known for

FITZROY ISLAND is one of New Zealand's great anchorages, protected from every wind direction.

CRUISE AROUND the magnificent Bay of Islands and make time for frequent trips ashore to explore.

humour in naming his discoveries, but in a rare burst he named the headland Cape Brett after Admiral Sir Piercey Brett, at that time a Lord of the Admiralty, because "Piercey seem'd very proper for that of the Island".

The main cruising interest is focused in the southern side of the Bay where a cluster of close-set, heavily indented and undeveloped islands – part wooded and part grassy – offer numerous beaches and safe anchorages. On shore, well-marked nature trails wind through trees and slopes, dotted with frequent explanatory notice boards, while some beaches offer barbeque areas. This is the ultimate family cruising ground where short sails can be interspersed with time ashore. But it was not always so…

In 1772, three years after Captain Cook's visit, the French explorer Marion du Fresne was killed and eaten here by the local Maori, after having broken a "tapu" law. Deeper into the estuary the town of Russell, a onetime capital of New Zealand, was once famous as the "hellhole of the Pacific", its brothels filled with roistering whalers, but today it is a pleasant waterside resort offering tourists a good selection of restaurants, a pub and a few shops. On the other side of the estuary, Opua has a dock for the occasional cruise ship, a large marina, a post office stores and a selection of marine-oriented businesses including a yacht charter company.

Should one wish to explore further, the town of Kerikeri lies at the head of another of the Bay's estuaries while some 35 miles (56km) away to the north-west is Whangaroa Harbour, a remote but incredibly scenic inlet that is well worth a visit. At the height of their fame the Spice Girls pop group stayed here in Kingfish Lodge, a luxurious fishing hotel at the inlet's entrance with its only access from the sea – no one knew who they were. No change today, then!

WHANGAROA HARBOUR'S remoteness is part of its attraction, as is the stunning scenery.

New Zealand
Marlborough Sounds

CHART NZ6153

BEST FOR CRUISING Late September – early March

AVERAGE TEMPERATURE 20°C 68°F

PREVAILING WIND NW

TIME ZONE GMT + 13

LANGUAGE English

CURRENCY New Zealand Dollar (NZ$)

NAVIGATIONAL DIFFICULTY

FAMILY FRIENDLY

DIVING/SNORKELLING

SHORE-SIDE EATING

SIGHTSEEING

Marlborough Sounds are located on the southern side of the Cook Strait, separated from Wellington by a ferry crossing. Here, the very northernmost tip of New Zealand's mountainous South Island tilts downwards into the sea to leave a labyrinthine maze of waterways that twist and turn deep inland between low hills clad in native forest. Around 20 per cent of the country's coastline is hemmed into this area bounded by Tasman Bay in the west and Cloudy Bay in the east.

WITH FIERCE WINDS whistling between the North and South Islands, and water sluicing with equal ferocity between the Tasman and Pacific, the strait's reputation for fearsome conditions is well founded. By contrast, the Marlborough Sounds are protected and sheltered with more than a 1,000 miles (1,610km) of bays, beaches and virgin scrub. Here, too, you'll find the big ferns that, when they reflect the hard sun of this country's gin-clear air, reveal the origin of New Zealand's "silver fern" national emblem.

In essence, there are two long, tortuous and magnificently scenic inlets: Queen Charlotte Sound, with the little town of Picton at its head, and Pelorus Sound, which winds inland to Havelock. Each is around 30 miles (48km) long. The outer limits of this largely undiscovered area are flanked by two islands, D'Urville to the north-west and Arapawa to the east. Separated from the mainland by the narrowest of channels, these islands might be a thousand miles away in terms of the feeling of isolation they engender.

This area was Captain James Cook's main base on his three voyages to New Zealand, in 1769 on the *Endeavour* and in 1773

FERNS

QUEEN CHARLOTTE SOUND

NELSON

In the wake of Captain Cook discover intricate waterways, bays and beaches within these magnificent, sea-drowned valleys.

FISH, DIVE OR SWIM, hike through ancient forest, dine out on local produce from game to oysters washed down with the finest Sauvignon Blanc.

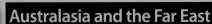

and 1777 on the *Resolution*. Here, links with the British explorer are much in evidence, from Ship Cove – his shore base – and Cook's Lookout on Arapawa Island to Endeavour Inlet off Queen Charlotte Sound, which he named after the wife of King George III. There's a quirkier link, too, in a species of pig that Cook is said to have put ashore to breed so that future navigators would have supplies of meat. The species survived and these, now feral, pigs are referred to by the locals (who have a way with words) as "Captain Cookers".

The whole Sounds region is not only a magnet for sailors but also for walkers exploring the 45-mile (72km) Queen Charlotte Track from Ship Cove to Anakiwa, either camping out or staying in isolated lodges that are often only accessible on foot or by boat. This means that many of the more popular overnight anchorages have a convenient restaurant serving excellent food and world-famous local wines.

Alternatively, fish are in such abundance that locals will be happy to tell visitors exactly where to find the best catches. On one occasion, such a spot was pointed out to us, along with a dry warning that, "You can only fish for ten minutes". The New Zealand government is strong on conservation, and where and

EDGED by myriad safe anchorages in sheltered coves and bays, the Sounds will warm the heart of any cruising yachtsman.

VINEYARDS IN HAVELOCK NORTH. The Marlborough area is renowned throughout the world for its fine wines.

what you can fish for is strictly controlled, so we did not question this advice. We went to the spot, dipped our hooks and were immediately successful, pulling in the most glorious four-pound blue cod, one after another. Nine-and-a-half minutes later we caught half a fish, and all the fish that followed were the same. A bizarre approach to conservation, perhaps? Then it dawned…as we reeled in our fish, they were being attacked by barracuda, which took under ten minutes to arrive on the scene.

Marlborough Sounds is a cruising destination without comparison and my best recommendation to cap a cruise here has to be a ride through French Pass, between D'Urville Island and the mainland. Named after French explorer Captain Dumont d'Urville who visited the area in 1827 with his frigate *Astrolabe*, the pass is a spectacular tidal gate; currents of up to seven knots rush through this narrow, rock-strewn passage edged by whirlpools and swirling water. Exciting today, in d'Urville's time passing through it, as he did, must have required not only great skill but also great courage. And even today it's not for the faint hearted.

CLOSE TO PICTON there are many scenic walks through the lush sub-tropical vegetation.

PICTON HARBOUR is the terminal for inter-island ferries and the self-proclaimed "Gateway to the Mainland".

THE SOUNDS region tempts sailors and walkers alike with its intricate inlets afloat and scenic tracks ashore.

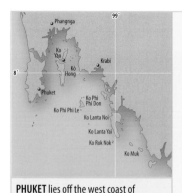

PHUKET lies off the west coast of southern Thailand in the Andaman Sea.

Thailand
Phuket

CHART 3941; plus Royal Thai Navy charts
BEST FOR CRUISING Year-round
AVERAGE TEMPERATURE 30ºC 86ºF
PREVAILING WIND November – May light to moderate NE; May – October SW
TIME ZONE GMT + 7
LANGUAGE Thai; English widely spoken in resorts

CURRENCY Thai Baht (THB)
NAVIGATIONAL DIFFICULTY
FAMILY FRIENDLY
DIVING/SNORKELLING
SHORE-SIDE EATING
SIGHTSEEING

It takes about three days sailing around the Andaman Sea under a tropical sun, lapped by warm waters, cooled by sea breezes to lose your clothes: sarongs are in, you'll be looking like sea gypsies and the boat will be festooned rather un-nautically with beach towels.

A SHALLOW-DRAUGHT catamaran is the best means of transport in these waters. Drop anchor off classic coral-sand beaches under palm trees, and sail – with just inches under your keel – up claustrophobic mangrove rivers overlooked by limestone karst cliffs that appear like spooky, dripping church candles, and into lagoons where monkeys play on the shore and lianas drip from the lips of craters.

In villages that seldom see a yacht, shop in Thai markets where a bag of fresh vegetables, a handful of chillies, two pineapples, a dozen eggs and a brace of mangoes cost pennies – don't barter here, it's not necessary and it's not polite. In a 10-day cruise around the Gulf of Phuket, eating authentic Thai food, drinking chilled fruit juice and Chang beer from a well-stocked fridge, swimming, lying in the sun, and making no more than 20 miles a day, time slows.

By leaving an anchorage before the crowds arrive, and arriving at the next island after they have left you have Thailand to yourself. Only at Ko Muk, where there is an 800ft (244m) swim through a tunnel in the side of a cliff to reach a hong (inland lagoon), do you risk getting your timing wrong. But then the terror of a pitch-black subterranean channel is easier to swallow when a horde of dog-paddling Korean kids in Day-Glo lifejackets are following in your wake, screaming, flashlights flashing. Strangely, rather than detracting from the

FISHING BOATS

EXOTIC FRUITS

TEMPLES AT PHUKET

PHUKET has several fabulous temples, perhaps the most spectacular being the Chalong Temple. If you visit a Thai temple be sure not to wear shorts or skimpy clothing or you won't be admitted.

RUN YOUR BOAT up the beach and relax under jungly palms, snorkel the reefs, and meander amid the mangroves on languid rivers.

surreality of the sunlit lagoon into which we miraculously burst, it added to it.

From Phuket Island head for Maya Bay on Phi Phi Le where Leo di Caprio cavorted in *The Beach*. At five o'clock in the evening it will be deserted. Then set sail for Ko Rok Nok, a Thai national park. There you can beach a catamaran on coral sand, swim and beach-comb, surprise a monitor lizard in the bushes, or surprise yourselves at the sight of a very phallic shrine.

From the hongs and beaches, snorkelling and reefs, and islands and naughty shrines in the south of the Gulf, those with a mind for adventure can head north towards the jungly delta in Ao Phang Nga. Mangrove rivers slide muddily down from the hinterland, the water becomes shallow and silty, and resort beaches are replaced by fishing villages set on stilts.

Armed with Royal Thai Navy chart Phuket to Kantang you can sneak into places that most charter companies tell you to avoid. Behind Laem Teng, a peninsula of sheer limestone, we discovered a mysterious river. Think *Apocalypse Now*. The sultry heat adds to the atmosphere.

Our next river appears to go nowhere, past fishing huts and small settlements, when a scene of pure delight opens up. On the left bank stands a wooden restaurant, on stilts, bedecked in flowers. We tie up the boat, step ashore and spend a lazy hour over the second best Thai meal of the trip. Shrimp tempura follows fiery sea bass in chilli and lemon, and noodles and Chang beer.

Everywhere you will see the longtail, a uniquely Thai craft. We saw 12ft (3.7m) longtails powered by little petrol lawnmower

THE UBIQUITOUS "longtail" boats have an engine mounted on a swivel attached to a propeller at the end of a steel tube.

engines and 50ft (15m) longtails with mighty bus engines balanced on the stern. All have one thing in common: no silencers. The Thais believe noise equals power.

A highlight of any cruise is the stilted village of Ko Pan Yi. Built entirely on wood and concrete pilings over the water, it is home to a thriving community of fishermen and tourist vendors. The narrow covered walkways are lined with stalls. Everyone lives cheek by jowl in ramshackle houses. Gold leaf railings and marble floors mark those of wealthy merchants. By four o'clock the day boats have taken the tourists home, and life as a Muslim fishing village is settling back to normal.

The place is placid, no-one shouts. We ask for beers and the young Muslim waitress giggles. Maybe it's the total lack of alcohol that gives the village such a sweet calmness?

At seven next morning we have the walkways to ourselves. Sarongs at 180 baht (£2.50), wooden elephants, spices, exotic tat,

PHANG NGA BAY has sheer limestone cliffs that jut vertically out of the emerald green water.

IN AO PHANG NGA muddy mangrove rivers wend their way to the coast.

scents, sounds and colour. By lunch time we are at anchor in a lagoon off Ko Hong. Ashore a big, grey-whiskered monkey with a long tail is picking over the rock pools with bony fingers for shellfish.

We dinghy into another liana-dripping hong. A National Guard dinghy bumps alongside. They require 200 baht and could they cadge a cigarette or two off us? We hand over the baht and cigarettes, they hand over our national park admission tickets and smile.

CHALONG is the centre of boating activity on the island and the home of the Royal Phuket Marina.

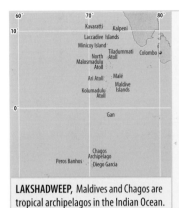

LAKSHADWEEP, Maldives and Chagos are tropical archipelagos in the Indian Ocean.

Indian Ocean
Lakshadweep, Maldives and Chagos

CHART Lakshadweeps 705; Maldives 2068; Chagos 4702, 3, 725

BEST FOR CRUISING December – March (NE monsoon)

AVERAGE TEMPERATURE 24–30ºC 75–86ºF

PREVAILING WIND NE

TIME ZONE Lakshadweeps GMT + 5:30; Maldives GMT + 5; Chagos GMT + 5

LANGUAGE Lakshadweeps Malayalam and Mahl; Maldives Divehi; Chagos N/A

CURRENCY Lakshadweeps Indian Rupee (Rs); Maldives Rufiyaa (Rf); Chagos N/A

NAVIGATIONAL DIFFICULTY 🧭 🧭 🧭

FAMILY FRIENDLY 👙 👙 👙 👙

DIVING/SNORKELLING 🤿 🤿 🤿 🤿

SHORE-SIDE EATING 🍴 🍴 🍴 (Lakshadweep 3; Maldives 4; Chagos 2)

SIGHTSEEING 🏰 🏰 🏰 🏰

Supporting just small populations or uninhabited, the atolls of these three tropical archipelagos rise from the 1,000-mile long (1,610km) Laccadive–Chagos Ridge that extends southwards in the Indian Ocean from 12ºN to 7ºS, carrying the Lakshadweep, Maldive and Chagos archipelagos.

THESE CORAL ISLANDS are the dream of every charter yacht, offering classic palm-fringed white sand beaches washed by warm, crystal-clear waters. But, to realize this dream at its best, visits must be made during the dry north-east monsoon season from December to March. By April the risk of strong tropical cyclones is high, while October to December is a season of strong winds and heavy monsoon rains. Throughout the year, temperatures usually remain between 24ºC and 30ºC (75–86ºF).

India does not usually feature on a list of the world's best cruising areas but 225 miles (362km) to the west of the town of Kozhikode (Calicut) on the Kerala coast is the Lakshadweep archipelago, owned by India and formerly known as the Laccadive Islands. Among these 36 coral islands and atolls lies the group's main cluster of 12 tiny atolls, nine of which are inhabited. The largest atoll is Andrott, 1.85 square miles (4.8km²), and the smallest Suheli Par, with just 141 acres (57ha). Thinly spread over 7,722 square miles (20,000km²) of the Indian Ocean, these islands have yet to experience the touch of the modern world and their charm lies in their unspoilt nature, superb white sand beaches, and world-class diving in the encircling reefs.

DESERTED BEACHES

BEACH HUTS

CORAL REEFS

SAIL AWAY to the coral islands of every sailor's dream: the palm-fringed pristine beaches of the Lakshadweep, Maldives and Chagos archipelagos.

MALDIVE RESORTS are largely sited on uninhabited islands, as a policy of the strictly Muslim government.

MARINE LIFE in the Maldive reefs includes the extraordinary giant moray eel, which grows up to 10ft (3m) long.

The Maldives is an independent nation whose 26 major atolls contain 1,196 islands, 200 of which are inhabited, forming a land area of 116 square miles (300km²), administered from the capital, Malé, that is situated on a motu (a coral island in the lagoon of an atoll) of North Malé Atoll. It is the policy of the Maldives' strictly Muslim government that tourism should be separated from traditional Maldivian life and, apart from in the capital, this is strictly observed. The many resort hotels have therefore been

FISHING is a an important traditional occupation off these islands that are so rich in sealife.

sited on uninhabited islands and draw their local labour from nearby islands that are in theory "off limits" to tourism. Maldivian atolls, which rarely rise more than about six feet (2m) above sea level, are of particular interest to cruising yachtsmen as many offer shelter within their fringing reef, as well as the possibility of some relaxation ashore and a European-style meal in a holiday resort. Again, the quality of the diving and suitability for water sports is unrivalled.

The most southerly archipelago, Chagos, is part of the British Indian Ocean Territory and comprises seven atolls and 60 tropical islands totalling some 24 square miles (63km^2). The archipelago has the largest expanse of undisturbed coral reefs in the Indian Ocean and fabulous wildlife, so strict conservation rules must be observed. In the 1960s and 1970s, these islands were forcibly depopulated, except for Diego Garcia on which – leased to the US as an airbase – landing is forbidden. The remaining atolls, particularly Egmont, Peros Banhos and Salomon, are visited regularly by many world-cruising yachts.

THESE BEAUTIFUL ISLANDS have yet to experience the touch of the modern world.

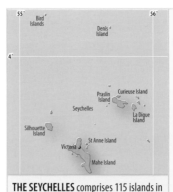

Indian Ocean
Seychelles

CHART 740, 742, 724
BEST FOR CRUISING March, April, October, November, but year-round
AVERAGE TEMPERATURE 30ºC 86ºF
PREVAILING WIND May – October SE; November – April NW
TIME ZONE GMT + 4
LANGUAGE English, French, Creole

CURRENCY Seychelloise Rupee (SR); US$ and € widely accepted
NAVIGATIONAL DIFFICULTY ⊛ ⊛ ⊛
FAMILY FRIENDLY ♟ ♟ ♟ ♟
DIVING/SNORKELLING 🤿 🤿 🤿 🤿 🤿
SHORE-SIDE EATING 🍽 🍽
SIGHTSEEING ♟ ♟

The sign just inside the main supermarket in Victoria, an emporium stocking everything from fish hooks and paraffin lamps to clothes pegs and frozen food, reads "Fish left at own risk", meaningless by itself but wholly relevant when a few yards away is a large, bustling fish, fruit and vegetable market, where Spanish mackerel are delivered by the truckful. It's also indicative of the richness of the seas around the islands, with fishing second only to tourism in importance to the economy.

THE SEYCHELLOISE boast that Victoria – capital of the islands and on the main island of Mahe – is the smallest capital city in the world. It does, however, seem to manage to cram in a bit of everything that you would expect to find in a capital, albeit on a small scale and in small numbers. The main island group, some 1,000 miles (1,610km) east of mainland Africa, consists of three islands, although there are many other smaller islands on the Seychelles plateau, many inhabited or with tourist resorts, scattered over a large area in the Indian Ocean. There are also many unmarked and extremely hard rocks so it pays for the navigator to be vigilant.

With a ten-hour direct flight from many European airports and a time difference of just four hours, many natural harbours and a year-round season it is easy to see why the Seychelles has become a popular yacht charter destination as an alternative to the Caribbean. It's also less crowded than the Caribbean. The islands owe their nearly year-round season to being in the

LA DIGUE

SPANISH MACKEREL

ROCK FORMATIONS

THE DISTINCTIVE fluted granite rock formations in the Seychelles are world renowned, whether in the grey shades of Mahe or the pinkish-red hues of Praslin and Curieuse.

Picture-perfect paradise islands where you'll find the world's most photographed beach, first-class snorkelling and the only place on earth where the exotic coco-de-mer grows.

DISTANCES between islands in the Seychelles are not great, with about 25 miles (40km) separating Mahe from the smaller Praslin.

monsoon belt and out of the cyclone belt. The two seasons run from May to October (south-easterly monsoon) and November to April (north-westerly monsoon), which has the strange effect of making one season's lee shore a secure anchorage and vice versa. Which is probably why, for our first night, we were advised to anchor off the west-facing Beauvallon beach when a 20-knot north-westerly was blowing. We chose a more sheltered bay to the east of St Anne island.

Anyone wanting to cruise just this main trio of islands, Mahe, Praslin and La Digue, will find enough to keep them occupied for ten days or two weeks, with fairly undemanding sailing in winds normally less than 20 knots. Long-term cruisers might choose to visit other islands in the group and, above all, enjoy the spectacular snorkelling for a month or more. "It's like swimming in an aquarium," commented one of our crew.

These islands are recognized the world over for their white sand beaches and distinctive fluted granite rocks and boulders, grey on Mahe and pinkish-red on Praslin and Curieuse. Their fauna and flora are also distinctive, from the giant and erotic coco-de-mer trees and nuts on Praslin, to the giant tortoises, giant crabs and giant spiders on nearby Curieuse but nothing,

COCO-DE-MER grows naturally only on its indigenous Praslin Island; a handful are on Fregate and Curieuse.

LA DIGUE has a tiny, shallow harbour where you can anchor with lines ashore and explore this car-free island on foot or by bicycle

apparently, that bites. The coco-de-mer nut is the islands' national symbol (and it makes for an unusual passport stamp); highly prized and extrememly expensive it grows only on Praslin and there, only in the Vallee de Mai, a UNESCO world heritage site.

Distances between islands are not great, with about 25 miles (40km) from Mahe to Praslin and typically there will be only four or five yachts, mainly charter boats, in anchorages. Outside Victoria, provisioning and eating out is possible in only two or three places. We enjoyed hiking across Curieuse, once a leper colony, from the anchorage at the eastern end to the restored house of Dr MacIntosh, who had been the leper colony's doctor. The walking, however, was hard work in the heat and should anyone choose to do the same, they would be advised to take their own water as no refreshment is available

WILDLIFE COMES SUPERSIZED on Curieuse: giant tortoises, giant crabs and even giant spiders!

IT'S EASY TO SEE why La Digue's atmospheric western coast is so popular with photographers.

before the long, hot trek back.

At Baie St Anne on Praslin it is possible to go alongside and likewise at La Digue there is a tiny harbour where you can anchor with lines ashore, though deeper-draught yachts might have to anchor off or pick up a mooring as it is quite shallow. No cars are permitted on La Digue, which leaves travel by foot or bicycle, with plenty available for hire. It's worth a visit down the western coast of La Digue to what is claimed to be the most photographed beach in the world. Good enough anyway for Bacardi and Bounty advertisements to be filmed here and tropical perfect with white sand, red rocks and, yes, swaying palm trees.

MAURITIUS lies about 500 miles (800km) east of Madagascar.

Indian Ocean
Mauritius to Madagascar

ADMIRALTY CHART Mauritius 711; Réunion 1495, 1497; Madagascar 2871, 706

BEST FOR CRUISING June – September

AVERAGE TEMPERATURE 25ºC 77ºF; Réunion 28ºC 82ºF

PREVAILING WIND SE (can be very strong off Madagascar)

TIME ZONE GMT + 4; Madagascar GMT + 3

LANGUAGE Mauritius English, Creole, French; Réunion French and Creole; Madagascar Malagasy and French

CURRENCY Mauritian Rupee (MRS); Réunion, Euro (€); Madagascar, Malagsy Franc (MFr)

NAVIGATIONAL DIFFICULTY 🕐 🕐 🕐

FAMILY FRIENDLY 🍹 🍹 🍹 🍹

DIVING/SNORKELLING 🤿 🤿 🤿 🤿

SHORE-SIDE EATING 🍽 🍽 🍽 🍽 (Mauritius 4; Réunion 4; Madagascar 2)

SIGHTSEEING 🏰 🏰 🏰

Rising from the depths of the Indian Ocean to the east of Madagascar, the reef-fringed, tropical isles of Mauritius and Réunion are a tourist heaven. They are a destination for two distinct groups of yachtsmen: circumnavigators and those who charter on arrival.

AN ISLAND REPUBLIC with a 200-mile (322km) long coral-fringed coastline dotted with white sand beaches, Mauritius is a haven for sun-worshippers, divers and big game fishermen. But leave your yacht in Port St Louis and head for the interior to discover spectacular mountain scenery and rare treats for botanists – a third of the flora here is unique to the island. Plan your visit between June and September; beware November to April, the rainy season, when there is a possibility of cyclones.

The slightly larger island of Réunion is a French Overseas Department (DOM) with strong cultural and commercial links to France. While there are some excellent white sand beaches in the Saint Gilles les Bains area, the island's interior is

staggeringly beautiful. In the cool of the hills, hiking is popular. There's an active volcano, some amazing waterfalls and the three dramatic mountain "cirques" (huge, sheer-walled amphitheatres) of Salazie, Cilaos and Mafate. Visiting sailors usually stay at the well-sheltered Pointe des Galets marina, but St Pierre, in the south of the island, also has a marina. Positioned within the south-east trades, the weather is much the same as it is on Mauritius.

It makes sense to pay a visit to Madagascar, but takes a serious sense of adventure to stray beyond areas regularly visited by tourists. Perhaps the best place to get a taste of this island republic is Nosy-be – "big island" in Malagsy – in Madagascar's north-west. Here, one clears in at the appropriately named port of Hell-ville, locally known as Andoany. While the colonial-style buildings in this charming but dilapidated town seem to have received no maintenance since the French left in 1960 (the lighthouses shown on the charts are not functional) the inhabitants of Nosy-be's attractive interior and off-lying islands live in well-organized village communities. Madagascar's highlights? Lemurs and chameleons, the beautiful landscape and meeting the friendly, welcoming locals.

RÉUNION ISLAND

LEMUR

NOSY-BE ISLAND

SANDY BEACHES, coral and clear waters, but
the real fascination lies in these islands' interiors:
volcanic mountains, hot springs, cool waterfalls.

Useful websites

www.noonsite.com

Jimmy Cornell's website is the first (and possibly only) port of call for those planning a world cruise. News, advice, books, charts and knowledge gained from three circumnavigations: an internet extension of his peerless *World Cruising Routes*.

www.cruising.org

Dedicated to yacht cruising, The Cruising Association's HQ in London contains a vast library of books and charts covering every area in the world. Membership is a must for anyone thinking of "living the dream".

www.ybw.org

Another one-stop website from the publishers of *Yachting World*, *Yachting Monthly*, *PBO*, *Classic Boat* and motor boat titles, with blogs, news, forums and information.

www.sailmag.com

US Sail magazine's website.

For sailing schools, visit your national association:

www.rya.org.uk

www.american-sailing.com

www.ussailing.org

There are quite literally thousands of charter companies operating all over the world, offering bareboat, flotilla, or skippered and crewed charters for sailing yachts, motor yachts and multihulls. Some are multinational companies with thousands of boats around the world, such as the ubiquitous Moorings and Sunsail, and some are individual boat owners who offer an intimacy with a single charter destination, such as Lynda Childress and her husband Kostas who sail their Atlantic 70 *Stressbuster* amidst the fabulous Greek Islands.

www.greecesailingcharters.com

Here are just a handful of recommendations:

www.moorings.co.uk

www.sunsail.co.uk

www.nautilus-yachting.com

www.top-yacht.com

www.horizonyachtcharters.com

www.sailing-charter-thailand.com

Bibliography

There are any number of books on sailing and the sea, including dedicated pilot books for most areas. These contain not only vital navigational information, but the best of them will throw light on culture, customs, etiquette and climate. For example, Tom Cunliffe's *Shell Channel Pilot* is the definitive word on cruising the English Channel. As well as giving comprehensive information, it remains one of the best reads on the subject. Colin Jarman's *East Coast Pilot* evokes the atmosphere of England's beautiful but tricky East Coast, while also capturing its essential flavour.

Tom also recommends any of the excellent *RCC Pilotage Foundation* guides, specifically Judy Lomax's on his favourite Norway, and Imray's pilot guides also come highly recommended, for example *Greek Waters Pilot* by Rod Heikell. For the Caribbean look for the name Don Street.

Advice for would-be charterers comes no better than Chris Caswell's *Chartering A Boat, Sail and Power*; and those tempted to spend a gap year hitch hiking round the world on a yacht should at least thumb through *The Hitch-hiker's Guide to the Oceans:*

Crewing Around the World by Alison Muir Bennett. And for a wealth of weather lore and ocean pilotage, James Clarke's *The Atlantic Pilot Atlas* is required reading for all ocean cruisers – his latest book is a complete manual for training of yacht crews, *Reeds Superyacht Manual*.

For bunkside reading, ship aboard Paul Gelder's *The Loneliest Race* (the 1994-95 BOC Around Alone solo race); or *Gipsy Moth IV: A Legend Sails Again*. He is also the editor of the more salutory *Total Loss*, an anthology of true-life stories of yachts lost at sea. Tom Cunliffe's *Hand Reef & Steer*, on the triple skills needed by proper seamen, and *Topsail & Battleaxe*, which recalls his voyage in the wake of the vikings, are both fascinating. For lighter hearted reading anything by Des Sleightholme will evoke a chuckle and there is always Patrick O'Brian and CS Forester's peerless *Hornblower* for the days when the wind howls and the rain falls in stair rods (it can even happen in paradise).

A number of our authors' books are listed below, along with a general bibliography comprising some of the best sea literature from Joshua Slocum to Robin Knox-Johnston. Last but not least this classic account of his solo circumnavigation in the wooden ketch *Suhaili*, the first such non-stop round the world voyage, *A World of My Own*, will either inspire, or put you off sailing for ever...

For lighter hearted reading anything by JD Sleightholme will evoke a chuckle and the Editor-in-chief also humbly recommends his own modest tome, *The Trouble with Old Boats*, inspired in part by the time he spent as JDS' assistant editor on Yachting Monthly. Finally there is always Patrick O'Brian and CS Forester's peerless Hornblower for the days when the wind howl ...

A Passion for the Sea, Reflections on Three Circumnavigations
  Jimmy Cornell
After 50,000 Miles Hal Roth
Chartering A Boat, Sail and Power Chris Caswell
Cruising Ports: the Central American Route Capt. Pat Rains
Cruising Under Sail Eric Hiscock
Handbook of Offshore Cruising Jim Howard
Mexico Boating Guide Capt. Pat Rains
MexWX: Mexico Weather for Boaters Capt. Pat Rains
Ocean Cruising Countdown Geoff Pack
Self Sufficient Sailor Lin and Larry Pardey
Sell Up and Sail Bill and Laurel Cooper
Sensible Cruising: the Thoreau Approach Don Casey
Sensible Cruising Don Casey and Lew Hackler
The Atlantic Crossing Guide Anne Hammick
The Capable Cruiser Lin and Larry Pardey
The Circumnavigator's Handbook Steve and Linda Dashew
The Circumnavigators Donald Holm
Two Years Before the Mast Richard Dana
Voyaging on a Small Income Annie Hill
Wandering Under Sail Eric Hiscock
World Cruising Handbook Jimmy Cornell
World Cruising Routes Jimmy Cornell

CLASSIC BOOKS

A Gipsy of the Horn Rex Clements
A Gypsy Life Clare Allcard
Adventures Under Sail H. W. Tilman
At Any Cost: Love, Life and Death at Sea Peter Tangveld
Cape Horn, The Logical Route Bernard Moitessier
Dove Robin Lee Graham
Eight Sailing/Mountain-Exploration Books H. W. Tilman
Maiden Voyage Tanya Aebi
Once is Enough Miles Smeeton
Sailing Alone Around the World Joshua Slocum

The Cruise of the Amaryllis GHP Muhlhauser
The Cruise of the Islander Harry Pidgeon
The Cruise of the Teddy Erling Tambs
The Magic of the Swatchways Maurice Griffiths
The Sea is for Sailing Peter Pye
Trekka Round the World John Guzzwell

CRUISING STORIES

100 Magic Miles of the Great Barrier Reef: the Whitsunday Islands
  David Colfelt
Gipsy Moth Circles the World Sir Francis Chichester
Honey, Lets Get a Boat Ron and Eva Stob
Kawabunga's South Seas Adventure Charles Dewell
Living a Dream Suzanne Giesemann
Oyster River George Millar
Rough Passage R.D. Graham
Sailing Promise Alayne Main
The Hawaiian Voyages of the Ono Jimmy Steve Dixon
The Thousand Dollar Yacht Anthony Bailey
Two Girls, Two Catamarans James Wharram

NAVIGATION AND SEAMANSHIP

Aground: Coping with Emergency Groundings James Minnoch
Basic Astro Navigation Conrad Dixon
Boater's Bowditch Richard Hubbard
Celestial Navigation for Yachtsmen Mary Blewitt
Chapman Piloting Elbert Maloney
Hand, Reef and Steer Tom Cunliffe
Heavy Weather Sailing Adlard Coles
Mariner's Weather Handbook Steve & Linda Dashew
Practical Seamanship Steve Dashew
Storm Tactics Lin and Larry Pardey
Surviving the Storm Steve Dashew
The Ashley Book of Knots Clifford Ashley
The Complete Book of Anchoring and Mooring Earl Hinz
The Complete Yachtmaster Tom Cunliffe
The Onboard Medical Guide Dr. Paul Gill

MAINTENANCE

Boatowner's Handbook John Vigor
Boatowner's Mechanical & Electrical Manual Nigel Calder
Marine Diesel Engines Nigel Calder
Seaworthy Offshore Sailboat John Vigor
The Care and Feeding of Sailing Crew Lin Pardey
The Complete Riggers Apprentice Brion Toss
Understanding Rigs and Rigging Richard Henderson

Index

Author Acknowledgements

A book with as wide a scope as this relies on the expert input of many, and the editing skills of a few. Tom Cunliffe passed me the baton, and Jimmy Cornell defined the book's parameters, while contributing hugely from his experience of three circumnavigations. Fourteen other journalists, editors, skippers and authors wrote of their favourite charter destinations. And all benefited from the design and editorial skills of Rona Johnson, Jennifer Close and the team at Studio Cactus. It is a wonderful project that, nevertheless, merely scratches the surface of the sailing possibilities the world has to offer.

Studio Cactus would like to thank Adrian and Rona for their unerring professionalism and indomitable good humour. Special thanks to all of the authors, especially the remarkable Mssrs Cunliffe and Cornell who helped get this project afloat in the first place. Thanks to Sharon Cluett and Sharon Rudd for their styling and design expertise and to Jennifer Close for her editorial skills. Thanks also to the very lovely team at the AA, and especially the very, very nice Mic Cady, Paul Mitchell, Geoff Chapmann and Susan Lambert. Many thanks to Kathryn Rudd and Ernie Ip for help with picture credits, Lorel Ward from Photolibrary Group Ltd, Penelope Kent for the index and, finally, special thanks to Sarah Norbury for her wonderful introductory material and her expert proofreading.

Picture credits

Studio Cactus would like to thank the following photographers, companies and picture libraries for their assistance in the preparation of this book.

Abbreviations for the picture credits are as follows: (t) top; (b) bottom; (l) left; (r) right; (c) centre.

Note: All images © Photolibrary Group Ltd unless otherwise listed below.
1 Graham Prentice, 4/5c Cheryl Casey, 5bl Goga, 5br Christian Musat, 8/9 Chris Sargent, 12tr Radovan, 12bl Sebastien Windal, 13tl Paul Merrett, 13tr Dennis Sabo, 13bl MaxPhoto, 14/15 Photo Shot, 16tr Linux Patrol, 22tl Perov Stanislav, 22tr Taolmor, 22cl Andrew Buckin, 22cr Camilo Torres, 22/23 Photoshot.com, 23tl runamock, 23tr Agata Dorobek, 23cl Arman Zender, 23cr Roman Nikulenkov, 24cr Christian Musat, 24br Philip Lange, 25 Ulrike Hammerich, 26bl Elena Aliaga, 26tr dubassy, 27tl Castka, 27b dubassy, 28t Christian Musat, 29t David Hughes, 29b Daniel Radicevic, 30/31 Andreas G. Karelias, 32bl Carsten Medom Madsen, 32tr Modestas Gedrimas, 33 Cornel Achirei, 34tr Luciano Mortula, 35 Patricia Hofmeester, 36tr Luciano Mortula, 36b Angelo Gilardelli, 37tl claudio zaccherin, 38bl Iuri, 38cr R.J Lerich, 39 Danin Tulic, 40bl Alexey Arkhipov, 40br Regien Paassen, 41 Alexey Arkhipov, 42l Goga, 43 Michail Kabakovitch, 44tr rj lerich, 44cr Agata Dorobek, 44br Pierdelune, 46br Florin Cirstoc, 48bl Marek Chalupnik, 49t Caroline Moore, 49bc Dumitrescu Ciprian-Florin, 49br Ladislav Bihari, 50 newweird, 51tr Pierdelune, 51cr Ivo Vitanov Velinov, 51bl dim0n, 51br easyshoot, 52 bl R.J Lerich, 52br runamock, 53 R.J Lerich, 55 R.J Lerich, 56tr Styve Reineck, 56cr Styve Reineck, 56br Styve Reineck, 57 runamock, 58 Pixage Photography, 60tr Elen, 60cr Can Balcioglu, 60br Marc van Vuren, 61 Bill McKelvie, 62b Efremova Irina, 63tr Bill McKelvie, 63b Bill McKelvie, 64cr Karel Slavík, 65 Marc C. Johnson, 66/67 Rui Vale de Sousa, 68tl Stephen Aaron Rees, 68cl Bill McKelvie, 68cr Christian Noval, 68/69 Stephen Finn, 69tl Clara Natoli, 69tr TTphoto, 69cl Elena Elisseeva, 69cr Ales Liska, 70tr Kevin Britland, 70cr Stephen Aaron Rees, 70br John Guard, 71 David Hughes, 72tl Stephen Aaron Rees, 72bl Tom Cunliffe, 72br Stephen Aaron Rees, 73 Stephen Aaron Rees, 74tl Sam Chadwick, 74cl Marina Cano Trueba, 74/75b David Hughes, 75tr Steve Beer, 76b tonyjburns, 76/77c Gail Johnson, 77tr Gail Johnson, 77br Gail Johnson, 78tr Corbis, 78cr Corbis, 78br Corbis, 79 Corbis, 80tr Richard Bowden, 80cr Richard Bowden, 80br Len Green, 81 Britainonview.com/RodEdwards, 82cr walshphotos, 82br L Kelly, 83 Marc C. Johnson, 84bl Kellie Diane Stewart, 85br Kevin H Knuth, 88tr David Woods, 88cr David Woods, 88br Jeff Banke, 90tr Gail Johnson, 90cr Joe Gough, 90br Joe Gough, 91 TTphoto, 92tr Bill McKelvie, 92bl Stephen Beaumont, 93t Bill McKelvie, 93br Stephen Finn, 94tr Allen Furmanski, 94cr Christian Noval, 94br Leksele, 96tr Tom Cunliffe, 96cr Marek Slusarczyk, 98tr Dhoxax, 99t Tom Cunliffe, 99br Marek Slusarczyk, 103tl Niels Quist, 103br Lukasphoto, 104tr Lena Lir, 104cr Igor Marx, 104br Jose Antonio Sanchez, 107b rubiphoto, 110tr Hugo de Wolf, 110cr Robert Soen, 110br Jason Pruden, 112tr David Hughes, 112br Sebastien Windal, 113 Elena Elisseeva, 116br Dmytro Fomin, 120/121b Irina Bort, 121tr Elena Elisseeva, 122/123 manuela szymaniak, 124tr Rui Vale de Sousa, 124br Four Oaks, 126tr Francisco Amaral Leitão, 126cr ultimathule, 126br Mikko Pitkänen, 127 José, 128tr Natalia Sinjushina & Evgeniy Meyke, 128cr Andrzej Gibasiewicz, 128br Alex James Bramwell, 130/131 Fernando Rodrigues, 132tr Johann Helgason, 132cl RJ Lerich, 132cr Ljupco Smokovski, 132/133 Andrea Haase, 133tl Paul Zizka, 133tr David Nielsam, 133cl Luís Louro, 133cr Kim Seidl, 134cr Dennis Sabo, 135 Ilja Masík, 136t 6696432756, 138cr Andrea Haase, 141t Andrea Haase, 141br Gary Blakeley, 142tr Cornel Achirei, 146tr Photoshot.com, 147 Photoshot.com, 150br fotoadamczyk, 152tr V. J. Matthew, 152cr RJ Lerich, 152br Robert Adrian Hillman, 153 Photoshot.com, 154tr Photoshot.com, 155t Dennis Sabo, 156cr RJ Lerich, 156br Sam Chadwick, 157 Photoshot.com, 158tr Getty Images, 158cr Andrew Bray, 158br Dennis Sabo, 159 Photoshot.com, 160br jaana piira, 162tr RJ Lerich, 162cr RJ Lerich, 162br Graham S. klotz, 163 Luis M. Seco, 164tr Byron W.Moore, 164cr Sharon K. Andrews, 166tr Travis Best, 167br Grigory Kubatyan, 168/169 William J. Mahnken, 170tl Rick S, 170tl Natalia Bratslavsky, 170tl Chee-Onn Leong, 170tl Adam Harner, 170/171 Carsten Reisinger, 171tr Mary Terriberry, 171tr Mary Terriberry, 171tr LouLouPhotos, 171tr felix casi, 172tr Anthony Ricci, 172br William J. Mahnken, 173 createsima1, 176tr Chee-Onn Leong, 176bl Christopher Penler, 177tl Anna Omeltchenko, 179tr Anna Omeltchenko, 180tr Ralph Roach, 180cr Steven Belanger, 181 Doug Lemke, 182tr Racheal Grazias, 182br Christopher Penler, 183 Lawrence Roberg, 184cr Carolyn M Carpenter, 190b Albert Barr, 192tr iofoto. 192cr iofoto, 194tr LightScribe, 194cr LightScribe, 194br kristian sekulic, 195 FloridaStock, 196tr UncleGenePhoto, 197t Gratien Jonxis, 214tr Natalia Bratslavsky, 214cr Lowe Llaguno, 214br Ocean Image Photography, 215 Anthony Berenyi, 220br Dennis Sabo, 221 carlos sanchez pereyra, 224br Alexey Stiop, 226tr vera bogaerts, 226br Eduardo Rivero, 228tr Armin Rose, 231 Jessica L Archibald, 232tr lfstewart, 236tl Andy Z, 236tl Jo Ann Snover, 236tl rebvt, 236tl Javarman, 236tr LouLouPhotos, 236tr James H. Boyum, 236tr Yuvis Studio, 236tr Stephan Kerkhofs, 236c Alfgar, 238tr Brent Wong, 238cr Feverpitched, 238br Bryan Michael Dirk, 239 Tiffany Chan, 240tr CarolineTolsma, 240cr Peter Sobolev, 240br foxie, 242tr David Thyberg, 242bl Javarman, 243tl Daniel Padavona, 243tr Foxie, 243b rebvt, 244tr Urosr, 244cr Urosr, 244br Robyn Mackenzie, 255 Sebastien Burel, 248tl Fernando Rodrigues, 250bl Marcus Tuerner, 251t Marie Lumiere, 264tr Matt Richards, 264cr Stephan Kerkhofs, 272/273 Brett Mulcahy, 274tr Thomas Hansson, 274tr Stuart Elflett, 274tr Markrhiggins, 274tr Oblong1, 274/275 Angela Hawkey, 275tl Micha Rosenwirth, 275tl Annetje, 275tl Anke van Wyk, 275tl Martinique, 276tr aliciahh, 276cr Sasha Davas, 276br Ingrid Petitjean, 278t AJE, 282 Tororo Reaction, 283t Holger Mette, 283b Ian Scott, 284tr Svolker, 284cr Ilya Genkin, 284br oksana.perkins, 285 Jenna Layne Voigt, 288tr BHE017, 288cr Xavier Marchant, 288br Harris Shiffman, 290t CJPhoto, 290b BHE017, 291 Alysta, 292t Thomas Nord, 292b Tororo Reaction, 300tr William Casey, 300cr Innocent, 302bl Bruce Amos, 303t Tbradford, 304cr Matsonashvili Mikhail, 304br Annetje, 308tr Sergey Khachatryan, 308br Alexey Stiop, 309 Mykhailo Kalinskyi, 310t Paul Cowan, 310 b Radovan, 311t Eugen W, 311b Alexey Stiop, 312tr Leksele, 312cr Gail Johnson, 312br Pozzo Di Borgo Thomas, 313 Lucinda Jane Bell